AGAINST CULTURE

D0066810

Fourth World Rising Series editors:

Gerald M. Sider
The College of Staten Island, CUNY

Kirk Dombrowski
John Jay College of Criminal Justice, CUNY

KIRK DOMBROWSKI

Against Culture

Development,
Politics, and Religion
in Indian Alaska

University of Nebraska Press

Lincoln and London

World Map: Peters Projection.
Copyright Akademische Verlags-
anstalt. Available from ODT, Inc.,
PO Box 134, Amherst MA 01004 USA;
800-736-1293 or www. petersmap.com.

Library of Congress Cataloging-in-Publication Data
Dombrowski, Kirk, 1967–
Against culture : development, politics, and
religion in Indian Alaska / Kirk Dombrowski.
p.cm. – (Fourth world rising)
Includes bibliographical references and index.
ISBN 0-8032-1719-6 (cloth: alk. paper –
ISBN 0-8032-6632-4 (paperback: alk. paper)
1. Tlingit Indians – Economic conditions.
2. Tlingit Indians – Ethnic identity. 3. Tlingit
Indians – Misisons. 4. Fundamentalist churches
– Alaska. 5. Haida Indians – Economic condi-
tions. 6. Haida Indians – Missions. 7. Alaska
Panhandle (Alaska) – Economic conditions.
8. Alaska Panhandle (Alaska) – Social condi-
tions. I. Title. II. Series.
E99.T6 D66 2001 305.897′2–dc21 2001027327

For Colleen, of course

CONTENTS

ILLUSTRATIONS

Map

Series Editors' Introduction

Against Culture is the first volume in Fourth World Rising, a new series of contemporary ethnographies from the University of Nebraska Press. The series focuses on contemporary issues, including class, gender, religion, and politics: in sum, it addresses social and cultural differentiation among and between native peoples as they confront those around them and each other in struggles for better lives, better futures, and better visions of their own pasts. This focus thus represents a departure from many of the monographs produced by anthropologists about native peoples, which often have sought to reproduce either visions of ways of life now long past or else pasts refracted through current idealization. In the process, traditional anthropology has helped enshrine a backward-looking focus to native culture that has, at times, been influential in the way laws are framed and even in how native peoples come to see their own identity.

Ideas, especially when enshrined in law and lent the authority of governments, have power. And the idea that native cultures and societies are historical artifacts rather than ongoing projects has served to narrow the politics of native identity or indigenism worldwide. One purpose of this series is to change this focus and broaden the conception of native struggle to match its current complexity.

This is especially important now, for the last two decades have provided prominent examples of native peoples seeking to recast the public—ultimately political—basis of their native identity in ways other than the reproduction of often fanciful, even fictional pasts. Our hope is that by offering a variety of texts focused on these and other contemporary issues, structured for classroom use and a general audience, we can help change the public perception of native struggle—allowing people to see that native cultures and societies are very much ongoing (and to a surprising extent on their own terms) and that the issues they confront carry important practical and theoretical implications for a more general understanding of cultural and political processes.

The primary geographical and topical emphasis of the Fourth World Rising series is the native peoples of the Americas, but the series will also include comparative cases from Australia, Africa, Asia, the circumpolar Arctic and sub-Arctic, and the Pacific Islands. Yet beyond its unique topical and contemporary focus, four critical theoretical and political features distinguish the series as well:

1. A focus on the struggles native peoples must fight, with the dominant society and with each other, whether they wish to or not, in order to survive as peoples, as communities, and as individuals, as well as the struggles they choose to fight.

2. A consideration of how the intensifying inequalities within and between native communities—emerging from social, cultural, and economic differences among native peoples—create unavoidable antagonisms, so that there cannot be any simple lines of cleavage between a dominant, oppressive, and exploitative state on the one side and its long-suffering victims on the other. Thus the series pays particular attention to gender, identity, religion, age, and class divisions among native peoples, along with differences in the goals and strategies that emerge from these struggles.

An emphasis on internal differences and tensions among native peoples is not at all intended to let the dominant states and societies off the hook for their policies and practices. Rather, this perspective calls to the foreground how internal complexities and divisions among native peoples and communities shape their struggles within and against the larger societies in which they find themselves. Indeed, it is precisely these internal differences among and between native peoples (and how these differences unfold over time and through native peoples' complex relations to one another) that give native people their own history and their own social processes that are, ultimately, partly separate from the history imposed upon them by the dominant society.

3. An emphasis on the praxis of native struggles: what works, and why, and with what intended and unintended effects; who benefits within native communities and who loses what, and why. The series monographs are thus not advocacy tracts in the conventional sense of that term, though they are undeniably political constructs. Rather, the emphasis on contemporary social processes and the political praxis of participants, advocates, and anthropologists serves as a stimulus for dialogue and debate about the changing pressures and possibilities for

particular native societies and the political situations confronting native peoples more generally.

4. An attempt to clarify the situation facing those whose concerns and fundamentally decent impulses lead them to want to help the victims of domination and exploitation. Such honorable commitments need to be developed in the midst of realizing that the radiant innocence of an earlier applied anthropology, and of many aid programs, along with the social world that sustained this innocence, has crumbled. It is no longer possible to say or to think "*we* will help *them.*" Now we must ask who is helped and who is hurt both by the success and by the frequent failure of aid programs, and why, and how.

The primary audience for this series is students in college courses in anthropology, political science, native and ethnic studies, economics, and sociology. Yet the series achieves its importance among a college and popular audience by being developed for a second audience as well. One of the major purposes of this series is to present case studies of native peoples' current struggles that have broader strategic relevance to those engaged in similar or complementary struggles, and to advocates whose concerns lie more directly along the lines of what has worked in the past or in other areas, what has not, and with what consequences.

Hence this volume becomes part of a new way of both doing and teaching anthropology and native studies. On one level, the case studies seek to bring together activists, native peoples, and academics, not simply by dramatizing the immediacy of native struggles, but also by dispelling the notion that native societies derive their nativeness from being internally homogeneous and externally timeless. On a second level, the series as a whole helps those currently teaching native studies to pursue an engaged, contemporary perspective and a broad geographic approach—allowing for and in fact encouraging a global, contemporary native studies that is deeply rooted both in a fundamental caring for native peoples' well-being and in the realities of internal differentiation among native peoples.

Gerald Sider Kirk Dombrowski

Preface

This study is based on work conducted between 1992 and 1997. My field research included three summers and one winter in Alaska, plus six months of archival research in New England, San Francisco, and Juneau. Much of this work was historical, little of which is reflected here, but it conditioned the way I later understood the events described here. In Alaska I lived primarily in three villages: Hydaburg, Kake, and Hoonah. Beyond this I spent time and attended church meetings in Juneau, Wrangell, and Ketchikan. I also conducted interviews with individuals from Craig, Klawock, and Sitka. My exposure, therefore, was to much of the region.

In the villages I conducted formal interviews and participant observation, meaning that I pulled the lead line and piled corks when fishing, ate Indian food at the several "doins" and "pay-off parties" to which I was invited, and attended church meetings and revivals whenever possible. I accomplished most of my research on Pentecostalism, however, during the four months of my last field season; up until that time I was more concerned with what might be called issues of political economy—including cannery labor, family politics, subsistence harvests and politics, and wage labor in the timber industry. I became interested in church membership and its importance when two friends invited me to attend a revival with them one long winter day. We had been hunting that entire day, and I felt as though I already had one foot in the grave. Winter hunting is, to say the least, very cold, and for someone who has done little of it, it is exhausting beyond measure. I wanted to say "no" to the invitation, but surprising myself, I agreed. I had never been to a Pentecostal service; and what I saw at the church came as a complete surprise, although I felt that I knew my hosts, and many other people in the church, quite well. To see them weeping and speaking in tongues—"gifts of the Spirit," I later learned—was, to be blunt, shocking. I knew then that my research was beginning anew.

In other places I found virtually the same thing. Many of the people

I knew well were members of Pentecostal churches, particularly those individuals on the margins of village and regional sociopolitical life among whom I had spent most of my time. Part of the reason this fact had escaped me was that I had spent time in Alaska mainly in the summer. Church is a winter event throughout the region. During the summer people travel and—more importantly for many of those who attended "radical" Christian churches—pursued subsistence foods. Had I never made a winter field trip, I might never have understood the role church membership played in the lives of many people.

Since that time I have tried to understand the importance of church membership—and thus also the rise of Pentecostal and other Fundamentalist churches in the region—in terms of the political-economic process I had studied up to that point. And vice versa, meaning that I have tried to better understand how people thought about and dealt with the political and economic processes in which they found themselves by asking why they found church membership so important.

This was my research. Throughout it was conducted entirely in English, as this is the first language of virtually every village resident under the age of seventy. Indeed, few younger than this speak the indigenous languages of the area, though at present classes in Tlingit or Haida are offered in the lower grades in village schools. These programs have met with mixed success due to a lack of commitment by most school boards, a lack of available teachers, and continued underfunding by the various federal, state, and local administrations. I do not speak either Tlingit or Haida beyond simple greetings and polite formalities.

One more issue should be made clear for the role it played in orienting my research. Beyond the actual topical interests I pursued—development, politics, Pentecostalism—I had come to Southeast Alaska with a specific tactical interest that never left me. It animates much of the discussion that follows, and no doubt underlies (in ways I am surely yet to realize fully) the types of questions I asked when I was in the field. Pursuing what seem to me the central unspoken and perhaps almost unspeakable issues of Native American studies, I went to Alaska seeking to understand how local, village-based inequalities were made, perpetuated, and tied into the larger process of resource extraction that dominates the politics of the region. Behind this lay a belief (still held) that local forms of inequality determine both how people—and peoples—at the margins are tied into a process of global production (a process seldom in their interest) and how they might resist this incorporation. This is, I believe, how and why people so often find themselves "within and against" the systems of domination that surround them, as Gerald Sider puts it (1993).

Because I did not go to the field to look at Pentecostal churches, the shift to looking at "radical" Christians required certain changes in my overall approach to local differentiation. Nonetheless, the focus on specific forms of village-level inequality remained at the center of my fieldwork and remains at the center of the anthropology I now propose. This is a risky undertaking, for local forms of inequality are apt to be understood in personal terms, especially when the people reading the stories and discussions that follow inevitably recognize themselves. This is an uncomfortable feeling, made more so by the fact that many of the people for whom this book is written—those on the margins of village life and politics—are unlikely to read it, some because they cannot read, many more because they have more important things to do. In part to protect those whose vulnerability might be further compromised by the work that follows, and to shield myself somewhat from the charges of those who see a discussion of village inequalities as a personal attack, some of the names of individuals whose stories follow have been changed, and where it seemed appropriate, place-names have been omitted as well. To those of my friends who might have hoped to see their names mentioned as a record of their time-consuming, difficult, and perhaps risky help, I apologize and try to discharge some debts in the acknowledgments that follow.

Acknowledgments

The debts accumulated in the seven years since I began this project are numerous. My hosts for several long stays were Joe and Anna Frisby and Owen and Betsy James, and to them I owe the deepest gratitude because they took a chance on me. Wise people that they are, they know that even now it is unclear whether or not it was worth it.

In Kake I would like to thank the entire Jackson clan, especially Mrs. Mona Jackson, Mike Jackson, and Larry Jackson. The people at the Organized Village of Kake tribal offices were always receptive and open, and their guidance was appreciated. Willis Jackson and Archie Cavanaugh gave me my first introduction to churches in Kake, and for their guidance and understanding I am indebted. Ruth Demmert and Gail Jackson introduced me to the Keek Kwan Dancers and helped me understand how and why people become part of village culture movements. In Hydaburg I offer special thanks to Lisa Lang and Pugie Sanderson, important and busy people who both found time to talk with me about how villages work, despite the fact that they had little reason to believe my reasons for wanting to know. Algie Frisby was a good friend who helped me get my feet wet and steered me clear of obvious trouble I still managed not to see even after three summers in the village. The late Sylvester Peele offered several open and sincere interviews for which I am very grateful. Adrian and Vicki LeCornu were more than helpful and consistently challenging on these same issues. In Hoonah I wish to thank Paul and Mary Rudolf and the crew of the *Inian Queen*, who put up with my questions and non-observations about fishing and native culture. Also in Hoonah, Carl Larson and Harold Dick accepted with patience and good humor my many questions, and Reverends Joe Thomas and Greg Howald were consistently patient and forthright.

Many of the church members to whom I spoke preferred not to be named, especially in villages where there has been conflict, and given the argument raised here, I have decided to use pseudonyms for all. To these individuals, who more than anyone else helped me understand the limits of my own perspective, I say thank you, and note that while the interests portrayed here are not necessarily your own, the representations that follow are made with the hope that they be seen as fair. If they are perceived otherwise, my hope is that the failure is attributed to ignorance or poor research, not a lack of concern. Special thanks are offered to the prayer groups at Juneau and Hoonah, who allowed me to attend their meetings and a joint revival, my very first one. Also to the members of the Assembly of God, Presbyterian, and Four Square churches in Kake, who also allowed me to attend both regular services and a revival. Of the several other ministers and prayer group leaders to whom I spoke I would especially like to thank Pastors Charles Bovee and Glen Wilson of the Southeast Alaska Presbytery and Lieutenant Trickle of the Salvation Army.

Most of the historical work included here is the result of archival work in Juneau carried out in or through the State Historical Library. Special thanks to Kay Shelton, the head of collections, and librarian India Spartz for their patience and guidance.

The majority of my fieldwork, including three separate trips in 1995 and 1996, was paid for by a grant from the Wenner-Gren Foundation for Anthropological Research (Grant no. 5876). Without this support, earlier and subsequent research would have lacked any foundation; so to Wenner-Gren, many thanks.

I would like to thank my dissertation committee for the carte blanche they gave me in deciding what sort of dissertation I would write, and with what goals. Their understanding and guidance in my attempt to chart my own path never flagged. Special thanks to Professors Jane Schneider, Shirley Lindenbaum, Abe Rosman, and Paula Rubel. The late Eric Wolf remained throughout a source of inspiration and personal encouragement, as is the work, guidance, and friendship of Joan Vincent. Leslie Gill read the entire manuscript with much care and provided several useful suggestions that have made this a better book. Barbara Price taught me much more than how to write, and later she read this book and offered many helpful suggestions; this book is, without exaggeration, a testament to her patience, help, and faith in me as an ethnologist. In an odd sort of way, some thanks are due the

Acknowledgments

Anthropology Department at Columbia University, many of whom are now departed, who, when I was a student there, encouraged me to seek out the Barnard Anthropology Department and later the CUNY Graduate School, without which I might never have had the opportunity to study with people I consider truly extraordinary for both their intellect and their humanity.

The people at the University of Nebraska Press encouraged us to begin this series, and their support has remained steadfast.

I am grateful to Colleen Syron for her input and ideas about the design of the series.

To all, many thanks.

Most special thanks go to Gerald Sider, mentor, adviser, and friend. Most of the good ideas in what follows were prompted by his teaching or drawn from his work. Although this is probably not the book he would have had me write, he always sought to help me make it better in ways that presumed it was my project, not his.

And finally to Colleen—who knows what sorts of things are caught up between these pages—praise, thanks, and love.

Hi Nate. Hi Elli.

AGAINST CULTURE

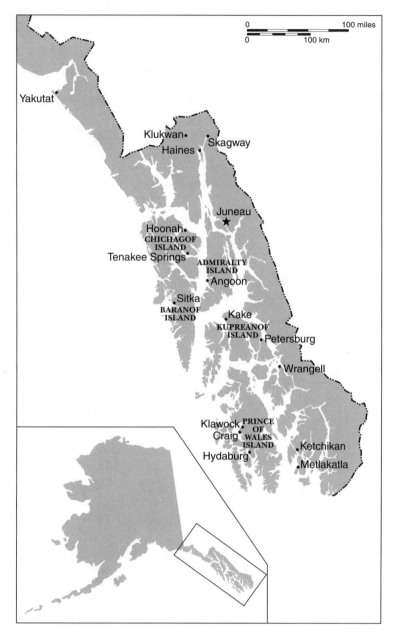

Southeast Alaska

Introduction

"You Won't Find Any Chilkat Dancers Dancing in Heaven"

In the autumn of 1992, in a village located along the Southeast Alaska panhandle, several converts of an all-native, native-led Pentecostal church started a bonfire of "non-Christian" items from their pasts as a way to demonstrate their new membership in the church and their "spiritual rebirth in Christ." Only those at the bonfire (who are still reluctant to speak about it) knew exactly what was burned, but rumors spread quickly that Indian dancing regalia had been thrown into the fire. Within a day or two, these rumors had reached every village and town in the region, and reporters were calling or visiting the host village in search of more details, and more drama. In the weeks that followed, people as far away as Seattle were listening to radio programs and reading newspaper stories about the demonstration, and almost all the coverage focused exclusively on the reports that native regalia had been burned. For months afterward, tensions between churches and native dance groups remained high throughout the region, and even today most native residents of Southeast Alaska are reluctant to speak about the burnings or their inspiration for fear of dredging up still sensitive issues and hurt feelings.

The revival was hosted by an independent Pentecostal church—one that had, at the time, an entirely native congregation and was led by a locally born native pastor. At the revival, the self-described "itinerant preacher" Flo Ellers raised the issue of native culture and, by her own account, challenged her audience to question the place of native religious and spiritual objects in their eternal salvation. Later, when asked to defend her stance against native culture, Ellers spoke of her own struggle with the role of culture in her beliefs. After much prayer and thought, she noted, she had come to understand that some elements

I

of native culture—especially those that had been used in past spiritualist ceremonies (from which at least some elements of today's native dancing are drawn)—were barriers on her path to salvation. When questioned further on this point, Ellers summed up her understanding by noting that, from what she understood of the book of Revelation, "You won't find any Chilkat dancers dancing in heaven."

Although Ellers was almost certainly not the only preacher to raise the issue of native culture at this revival or at others, her statement had reportedly set off the burnings that followed. At the completion of the service at which Ellers spoke, several out-of-town attendees supposedly told those around them that they had burned some of their own cultural items at a revival many years before as a way of cementing their own "rebirth in Christ," and had seen the image of a serpent rising out of the flames. The idea captivated several young people who had been "born again" at the revival, and they approached Ellers and the pastor of the host church and asked permission to burn some items from their past life. The ministers consented, saying, "Go ahead, whatever you want to get rid of, get rid of." Following this, a small crowd gathered in the church parking lot and started a fire in a metal oil drum. They threw many things into the fire, including rock-and-roll records and cassette tapes, "heavy metal" concert T-shirts, and liquor bottles.

Whether or not any older cultural or dancing regalia was actually burned remains a point of contention. Charred bits of cloth were found in the fire, as were coffee cups and windbreaker jackets bearing the logo of the local ANCSA (Alaska Native Claims Settlement Act) or "native" corporation—an intertwined raven and eagle in Northwest Coast style, representative of the two moieties found among most Southeast Native villages. It is unlikely that any older cultural heirlooms were burned, if only because in most villages such items are now so rare that few of the young people attending would have had access to them. Some who sifted through the ashes reported seeing burned buttons—the remains of the type of buttons used on contemporary button blankets—and bits of felt, possible from the same type of item. Button blankets are much more common than the older heirloom pieces. Virtually all are recently made by members of village dance groups, and some are made as part of native culture classes taught in village schools.

Despite the lack of clear evidence, the regalia issue dominated the reaction that followed, becoming the central focus of people's conversations on both sides. And while none of the revival preachers would say whether any cultural items were burned—and none, it seems, could have known firsthand as none attended the burning—all defended a firm stance against certain cultural practices. This included, especially, a condemnation of the kind of native dancing that had become very popular in recent years, and which included the making and wearing of costumes—primarily button blankets and headdresses—that featured stylized designs of old clan symbols, laid out as in classical Northwest Coast art.

On the other side, non–church members (especially those involved in the current village culture movement) found the events reminiscent of a past incident in the village.[1] For in this same village, early-twentieth-century converts to Christianity had convinced other residents to burn the nineteenth-century totem poles that stood in front of many of the village homes. The recent burnings, therefore, were eerily reminiscent of past attacks on native culture—and the people who supported it—by outsiders and their converts. Many culture-group members were led to ask, "Have we made no progress in the last ninety years?"

Ellers's dramatic stand and the faith and commitment of those in her audience place in bold relief the contemporary tensions surrounding "culture" in the everyday lives of village residents throughout the region, and for many they raise the memory of past tensions as well. Most people are ordinarily more circumspect, but very few people—perhaps none—are unaffected by the issues and emotions Ellers and her followers raised. Yet the sources of these tensions are not nearly as clear as they might seem.

The chapters that follow sketch out the complexity of the tensions surrounding the burnings, but not for the purpose of simply laying out the troubles of a single town—or even the problems of several towns, for these events might have taken place in any number of Southeast Alaska villages. Rather, as the title of this book is meant to reflect, no one, or at most very few people, anywhere, can live easily with his or her culture. This is true for Alaska Natives as well, as is dramatically apparent in the Flo Ellers incident (as the 1992 burnings have come to be called). But it is just as true for ordinary folks everywhere. Most people, in most places, have highly ambiguous relationships with what anthropologists and others have come to call "culture": the methods—ceremonies, customs, stories, manners, and resulting patterns of ideas—through which people attach meaning to their lives and to their relationships with one another, and through which they make sense of the world around them. Developed more fully below, this point is the main focus of the chapters that follow.

Before moving on to this discussion, it is worth noting that this is an unconventional stance for an ethnography and may catch many readers off guard. Ethnography usually involves an attempt to describe the way of life and worldview of a particular group of people. This book represents a change of focus—a change of analytical objects, if you will—that anthropologists have begun, but which we have yet to communicate very effectively outside our own circles. It follows the lead of ethnologists such as Eric Wolf, Joan Vincent, and Gerald Sider, among others, for its focus is not so much a particular place or group living in that place, but a particular situation. In short, it aims to be an ethnography of a problem, not a people.

This shift of focus has several goals here. I hope this change from the ethnography of people to the ethnography of problems will help us move away from the classical ethnographic stance that presumed collective identity rather than questioned it. Instead, we seek here to understand how ordinary people come to consider themselves a people—that is, the sort of social entity that conventional ethnography took for granted and sought to describe: the process through which distinctive, particular, and often superficially peculiar cultures come into being or, conversely, pass into history.

For historical anthropologists such as Wolf and Vincent, this approach involves placing the emergence of particular peoples and customary practices in an extended historical context. By drawing out the shifting political and economic contexts over time, historical anthropologists seek to show both the contingency of the conventional anthropological subject (i.e., how specific cultures emerged under specific historical conditions, at particular times, in particular places) and, consequently, how the stuff of culture (the ceremonies, customs, relations, and patterns of ideas) comes to be caught up with, and become part of, the political and social changes people faced at the time.

This ethnography is not so historical as Wolf's or Vincent's, but it is concerned with these same issues. It follows the lead of ethnographers such as Gerald Sider and Anna Tsing, who work backward from the present cultural situation to the context from which it emerged—and very frequently the context *against which* it emerged as well. The problem it takes up is the recent emergence of "radical" Christian churches in native villages in Southeast Alaska. These churches are Evangelical and frequently Pentecostal, and most are very recent arrivals to the region.[2] All practice adult baptism—the hallmark of "born again" Christianity—and all are active in recruiting new members from the region's poorest and most marginal households. And most importantly, all have, to some extent, taken a stance against native culture.

The title of this book is thus also a reference to these churches and their stance on native cultural practices. In fact, the phrase "against culture" was first related to me by a native member of a primarily native Pentecostal church. "I hate to have to make up my mind," he told me, "but if I had to say one way or the other, I'm against it"—the "it" being native culture as it is celebrated in the villages today. Many native Pentecostal and Evangelical church members feel the same way, though few are quite so open about it.

Not all native people in these villages are against native cultural practices—far from it. For very understandable reasons, reasons we will take up again in the conclusion, many are deeply committed to asserting, reshaping, and expressing a native culture they regard as both traditional and living. One aspect or side of this dispute cannot be understood without the other.

The situation is, in fact, more complicated than can be captured by the notion of having different sides of a dispute, for both sides agree on many things. Importantly, virtually all Southeast Alaska Natives use the phrase "our culture" to refer to some elements of their lives and not others. Most often the term "culture" refers to two types of activities: (1) subsistence projects—the processes involved in harvesting and preparing subsistence foods; and (2) the joint participation of members of the community in collective identity projects. It is also used to classify some very arcane abilities or knowledges, such as native languages or traditional speaking styles, though this is less and less frequently the case as such skills become increasingly rare.

No one, however—not even church members—would include Pentecostal church membership as part of native culture, even when referring to entirely native congregations or those led by native preachers like Ellers. In fact, most people—both church members and their critics—continue to view native culture and Pentecostal religion as hopelessly at odds.

This opposition has partly to do with history. The village in which the burnings took place had witnessed seemingly similar events before. In the early twentieth century, Christian converts assumed leadership of the village's main political institutions (primarily the school board) and convinced virtually all of the townspeople to take down and burn the totem poles located along the beach in front of most houses. Their reasons were partly practical and partly symbolic. In practical terms, totem poles had in the past been used to house the remains of post-cremation deceased kin, and some converts feared that these remains could still be used to invoke supernatural harm.

The other reason for burning the totem poles was to demonstrate to mission sponsors that the town had fully embraced modern ways. Much was at stake. Mission sponsors from the eastern United States had purchased industrial sawmills for Hydaburg and Metlakatla (two other villages in the region) and had also financed several local businesses. In the village where the totem poles were burned, church converts hoped that such an act would signal the sort of conversion that Hydaburg and Metlakatla had undergone, and consequently trigger the sort of support that might be used to gain financing and donations for their own salmon cannery. As will be discussed in part 1, salmon canneries had fully transformed the regional economy by the early twentieth century—changing the way people thought about kin relations, property relations, and political-economic organization in general.

In place of the totem poles, the town created a modern boardwalk along the beachfront, completing it with a silver spike forged from a U.S. silver dollar. Pronounced a holiday, the day of the completion is still celebrated in the village. Anthropologists have since helped label that which the missionaries and their converts attacked as "culture," a term contemporary residents have taken up as well. Few at the time of the earlier burning would have used this term, though certainly many village residents at the time felt that more was destroyed in the fires that day than simply the totem poles.

When, in 1992, revival attendees were rumored to have burned dancing blankets, many residents were instantly reminded of the totem-pole burnings, despite the fact that no more than one or two of today's residents were born when the first burnings took place. Still, the similarities between the two situations did much to galvanize after-the-fact resistance to the 1992 burnings and to Ellers—resistance that was used to mobilize support against Ellers and to cancel several future appearances she and others had planned for the revival.

Other church organizations were prompted into apologies as well. The Presbyterian Church, the moving force behind the original totem-pole burnings, issued an open apology to Southeast Alaska Natives for its past anticultural stance and proclaimed unambiguous support for the current regionwide culture movement. The Presbyterian church in the village in which Ellers made her remarks commissioned a traditional wood carving featuring an intertwined raven and eagle in classical Northwest Coast fashion, which is mounted at the rear of the church over the altar. The carving demonstrates ongoing support for, and creative integration of, native and Christian elements that the regional presbytery has endorsed. Russian Orthodox representatives went on local radio stations to proclaim their own regret for past intolerance and their strong support of contemporary cultural efforts.

Yet much about the two sets of burnings is not the same, and these differences can help us to understand why the mere suspicion of regalia burning became the central issue in the Flo Ellers incident. To begin, the culture movement of today is very much the public face of this and other villages. Supported by native corporations (discussed in chapter 3), village dance groups perform at most major village and regional social events. The work they do in teaching and performing contemporary versions of traditional cultural practices plays a large role in the symbolic representation of local identity—much as early-twentieth-century Christians had sought to do with the clothing, singing, and social groups associated with early Presbyterian and Salvation Army churches as well.

And just as the original totem-pole burnings had been quietly opposed by a group of non-Christians (primarily drawn from the community's more marginal segments), so too have today's born-again Christians quietly resisted the construction of a contemporary native identity by village culture groups and corporate elites. As mentioned above, these born-again Christians are themselves also drawn from among the more marginal segments of the community, as were the traditionals of the past.

If anything, the two situations mirror each other in the most literal sense, as seemingly identical events reversed in orientation. Today's culture movement may have much more in common with the past Christian identity movement than many people would normally suppose. The same is true for today's church members, whose closed ranks seem more like the traditionals of the past than they do the flamboyant Christians of the earlier era.

There are, however, ways in which these similarities and differences do not form such neat opposition. Clearly the two sets of burnings do not represent the same problem, and certainly not the same stakes. Much has changed in the villages, and today's divisions are very different from those of the past. Rather, in comparing the two I seek only to dismantle the easy explanations offered by many at the time—that the burnings were simply the result of long-standing, wrongheaded beliefs or bad theology on the part of the Christians who continue to fail to understand the nuances of native belief systems. There is much more to the recent burnings and confrontations than this.

If the burnings of 1992 can be usefully compared to those of the past, it is not because Christians automatically oppose native culture. Most culture-group members throughout the region are also members of Presbyterian, Salvation Army, or Russian Orthodox churches, and most attend church with at least as much regularity and sincerity as their suburban counterparts in the continental United States. Rather, the real purpose behind comparing the two situations is that the early burnings point us to what must be considered the central theoretical understanding on which the following book is based: the fact that, whatever the differences between the two events, *cultural divisions within this village* (and indeed in virtually every native village in the region) *continue to play a critical role in the relationship between all small communities and the larger political economy that surrounds them.* This is a crucial point, and I will spend much of part 1 explaining the current connections between local divisions (e.g., between the culture group and Pentecostal church members) and the ongoing political economy of Southeast Alaska.

In schematic terms, the guiding assumption of this book is the idea that, to understand Pentecostal church membership in Southeast Alaska today, one must examine it as part of the broader interrelation within and between village communities and their surroundings—particularly, as Gerald Sider points out, as differences *between* the local community and the larger political context are used by people in the local village to create differences *within* the local community; and conversely, as divisions within a local community are used to create and manage differences between the local and the larger as well. In short, what anthropologists and those around them have come to call "culture"—local meanings and the local ways used to produce and reproduce these meanings—is intimately caught up with the process of local/larger political-economic differentiation.

Yet if much of what we call "culture" (and equally, much of what we call "religion," a point we shall return to in chapter 7) is caught up in this process of local/larger differentiation, it is not because church membership or culture-group membership is simply a crude reflection of other, more primary social divisions. People in Alaska—and everywhere else I have been—join churches to save their souls, and they join traditional dance groups to discover their identity. Neither of these activities—or their accompanying hopes, desires, or cosmologies—is reducible to some calculus of political or economic gains and losses, and studies that have concluded this are generally misguided and wrong. Far more often, when marginal people join radical churches they simply add to the stigmatization and marginalization they already suffer.

Nor is church membership or religious conversion simply a quest for existential meaning—for some more rational, less contradictory system of beliefs—the sort of explanation that supposes that everyone will subscribe to some fixed ideology, that people will subscribe to the one that makes the most sense to them or makes them feel the most important. As Susan Harding (1987) points out, people join religious groups only *after* having learned the language and way of viewing the world practiced by the group. Once this language is learned, people are able to decide whether or not this new way of seeing the world makes more sense than the way they had seen it before. And once they decide to "believe," as we normally describe the term, it makes not joining the group or subscribing to a particular worldview seem foolish and nonsensical. Belief and affiliation come, it turns out, at the end of conversion, not at the beginning.

Rather, what makes the stuff of culture and religion intrinsic to the local and large divisions that we usually call political economy is that none of these things—belief, identity, cosmology—is ever something that can be had entirely individually. In contrast to the popular assumption

9

that issues of conscience are entirely personal, belief and cosmology are always social entities. They always involve acting with, upon, or against others.

In part this is because they are taught to and learned from others. But more than this, it is because each of these things is framed by signs and processes that do not operate according to the easy categories of individual and social. People culture the world around them—they assign it meanings that allow them to live with it and in it. So too do the people around them, who are both engaged in their own culturing of the world and caught up within the webs of meaning spun by others. For a long time anthropologists and psychologists have been content to call the meanings people come to agree upon or share "culture," and those a person does not share with those around them "personality." But this division has done little to clarify how people both make meanings, on the one hand, and come to be subject to meanings made by others, on the other hand. Nor does it tell us very much about how or when some people choose to throw off (or simply resist) some meanings and not others.

Instead of holding too closely, then, to notions of personality and culture—instead of asking what sort of personality or personal situation might lead one to convert to a radical church, or what sort of collective cultural signs might predispose one to a particular (perhaps Pentecostal) set of religious signs and meanings—this book will be concerned with religion and culture insofar as the elements that make them up come to be part of specific social strategies, strategies of making the world meaningful and thus livable: *strategies that necessarily involve and invoke action on, with, and against other people.* Thus this approach goes in the opposite direction from those studies that see cultural meanings as lasting and fixed. Instead, beginning with the extraordinary contingency of even our most meaningful and central beliefs, it seeks to ask how such meaning is created, continued, or constrained. As Eric Wolf points out, all of these processes involve power, and so it seems questions of culture come, necessarily, to involve questions of power as well.

Alaska Natives—or Native Americans in general—are not special in this regard. All people, everywhere, act against their culture, without ever ceasing to value it or live within its emotional and interpersonal grasp. Some anticultural feelings—feelings that express the failure of culture to provide a meaningful, livable life, even for those who accept it—are expressed in simple, individual, destructive ways, like alcohol abuse and other forms of substance abuse, or even in their most extreme form, suicide—both of which played a role in the events discussed above (as discussed in chapter 7). Such processes are prevalent in Alaska, but they are by no means limited to native villages.

Other anticultural stances are both more social and more aimed at reforming the parts of culture that are most difficult to bear. African American reactions to segregation in the South are perhaps the best examples. Barred from participation in many community institutions, black Americans rallied around the institutions they could control, and in so doing they transformed these institutions into something they were not. This was the basis for the creation of black Christian churches in the South during the era of Jim Crow segregation—institutions later able to strike out at segregation in a way and with a force that suburban churches in the North could not imagine. In so doing, African American churches simultaneously shifted the focus of Protestant Christian religious practice away from the smug self-assurance of Weber's Baptists to a redemptive theology of suffering and salvation, now seen in black Baptist churches everywhere.

Yet if there is no difference between the ambiguous relationship Native Americans or Alaska Natives have with their own culture and what ordinary people everywhere ordinarily feel—no real difference, for example, between what it *feels like* to be "Indian" versus what it feels like to be "black," or "Latino," or "poor," or "illegal," or "a welfare mother"—there is still a significant difference in how these feelings might be expressed, either to those in power, or to each other, or even to oneself. To understand just what this difference is, one must consider briefly the notion of subculture, which reveals critical hidden agendas within our ordinary popular and anthropological conceptions of culture.

The term "subculture" has become popular as a way to describe the dynamics of being within and against culture that we have discussed thus far. Subcultures (when the term is used as a noun referring to a group) are those groups that have found the culture they live within—the ways, that is, in which meanings are created and meaningful lives lived—to be unsatisfying, unfair, or most often, unattainable. Their response, however, has not been to overturn culture entirely, but rather to co-opt and redefine elements of the dominant culture and to make these elements into alternative systems of meaning, or alternative ways of living meaningful lives. The notion of subculture captures the fact that most people find ways to live differently within, and even against, a set of meanings and institutions they find impossible to live with—and that they do so without actually leaving entirely (or even mostly) those same meanings and institutions.

Thus African American subcultures have, for generations, made use of elements of the dominant culture to express resistance, autonomy, and, perhaps most importantly, ways to live meaningful lives otherwise denied to them. Notably, however, most of the elements of this subculture have been drawn, directly or indirectly, from the dominant culture. Christian churches are a very good example of this, but so are many contemporary elements as well—from hip-hop to all-black college fraternities. All of these are, to a certain extent, posed against mainstream American culture, but none are so radical as to make a complete break with that culture. Hip-hop fully embraces the commodified, market-driven dynamics of the recording industry, and of American business more generally. Black churches have continued an American tradition of gender bias and exclusion. Perhaps the best example of the inescapable ambiguity associated with the notion of subculture is the current casual use of the term "nigger" by young African Americans—a term that both alludes to and reverses a historical, cultural meaning, while at the same time, and intentionally, not entirely escaping the term's original derogatory meaning.

Issues of subculture work very differently for Native Americans and Alaska Natives, however. In fact, there are no Native American subcultures, at least according to most people's—and most natives'—understanding of the term. The reasons for this are complex and have much to do with the fact that Native Americans have historically been allowed to participate in the American political economy as "natives" (i.e., as people whose claim to participation is based on past ownership or claims to resources other than their own labor) only as long as they have maintained a clear and organized cultural distinctiveness (see Sider 1993; this point is addressed more specifically in chapter 4 and in the conclusion). Native Americans have been allowed to participate in the American economy as "natives"—as people with a hereditary, distinctive claim to disputed, important resources—only where they have maintained extraordinary sorts of distinctiveness. This special status has been the basis for both Indian gaming and mineral development—two cases where tribal autonomy has often allowed outside industry to operate within native communities and to skirt state laws prohibiting gambling in the first case, and environmental laws aimed at long-term public protection in the second. As discussed in chapter 3, under ANCSA, village-based timber corporations have since the 1970s been able to harvest timber in ways that would not be possible on federal lands, and they have received considerable support from the timber industry as a result.

Where that distinctiveness has become unclear or intermixed with other sorts of distinctiveness—like race or class—participation as natives has been denied, although, importantly, individuals within these groups have been free to participate *as individuals* in ways open to other minority groups and persons of color. Gerald Sider has discussed this issue specifically in the case of the Lumbees, as has James Clifford for the Mashpees. In both cases, native persons were denied participation as natives because they did not seem different enough—or, perhaps as importantly, because they lacked a significantly different social organization and culture that would have made them useful as natives. And tellingly, in both cases, while being denied status as natives, they were confirmed in their status as people of color.

In this way, Native Americans have been required to maintain a very different relationship with "their culture" than have other subordinated peoples in the United States. Native American groups, to remain such, must maintain clear barriers between their own culture and that of mainstream America. So while Protestant churches can become a mainstay of an African American subculture, these same churches have never been seen as part of Native American culture—even in congregations composed entirely of natives and led by a native preacher, as was the case above—*not even by the native members of these churches.*

This is the collective fate of Native Americans. Yet for individual natives, as well, there are differences between being part of an American subculture on the one hand and being part of Native American culture on the other. As has become clear in the history of race in America—and as my African American students are fond of pointing out—you cannot stop being "black," as ongoing issues of police profiling all over the United States make clear. But you can stop being "native"—meaning you can lose your right to participate as a "native" in America's political

13

economy (i.e., lose your right to special status participation based on prior claims to resources, rather than differences in race or ethnicity). This happens to most Native Americans who fail to maintain tribal membership with a federally recognized tribe. Like those groups who have failed to keep up the requisite cultural distinctiveness, individual natives without tribal affiliation are allowed to participate in the American political economy as persons of color, but not as people with special claims to contested resources.

All of this means that the ordinary ambiguity that virtually all people feel toward their culture—toward the sources and systems of meaning in their lives—must be lived differently by Native Americans than by others. For Native Americans to be against their culture, they must risk losing their claim to being "natives" in ways that matter immensely.

Pentecostal and Evangelical church membership, I will argue, is part of the process through which many Southeast Alaska Natives live against their culture. As will be discussed in part 2 of this book, Pentecostal church membership offers people an institution through which many of their own feelings about the failure of current identity projects can be expressed. It is worth recalling that whether or not contemporary dancing regalia was thrown into the fire that afternoon, it is quite certain that ANCSA corporation windbreakers and coffee cups were. This, it has been argued, is perhaps because these jackets and coffee cups bore a native design; it is also possible that individuals were expressing a sense of alienation or betrayal felt by many marginal individuals and families toward the original land settlement and the two classes of natives it has created. In either case, however, it is clear that in many people's eyes, the current identity movement is very much caught up in the ongoing issue of resource development and corporate ambition.

Beyond this, church membership allows natives to continue with those elements of their culture that many depend on for simple survival—subsistence hunting, fishing, and gathering, and the relations these activities entail. In fact, Pentecostalism's silence on these issues stands in strong contrast to that of the culture movement, for whom subsistence has become an icon of native culture. For while the culture movement's stance on subsistence has brought much attention to the issue, it has also turned subsistence into an identity issue, and thus not—or not necessarily—a survival issue (this is discussed in more detail in chapter

4). For many of those individuals and households most dependent on a subsistence livelihood, this change has proven costly.

Beyond this, Pentecostalism provides native church members the sort of dramatic break that the notion of subculture denies—and which is, ordinarily, denied Alaska Natives and Native Americans alike. In many ways, Pentecostal practice involves the adoption of an entirely new language and way of seeing the world—one in which being a Native American has no significance. Jesus, church members will tell you, became a living man for everyone, regardless of who they were before. All you have to do is put yourself in his hands and you will be saved, no matter who you are or what you have done. This dramatic denial of Culture per se—not just particular cultures—has special appeal to people whose particular culture has become an unbearable, unavoidable, undifferentiable burden, and for whom any alternative culture has proven just as unlivable. For this reason, many Pentecostal converts will tell you that they are not just against native culture, but against all Culture.

In the chapters that follow I will pursue two general strategies. Part 1 lays out the current political-economic landscape, the backdrop for the recent cultural revival in Southeast Alaska. In doing so, it will also show concretely why some Alaska Natives—individuals and families very much a part of these processes—come to find themselves in much the same position as working families everywhere: part of and simultaneously partly against a culture they consider very much their own. Part 2 takes up Pentecostal church practice and shows how this practice opens space for particular kinds of anti-native-culture practices and discourses, and thus some of the reasons why church membership makes a great deal of sense, and speaks powerfully, to the more marginal individuals and households in the region.

The order of the chapters should not be interpreted as an argument for or against any sort of causality. By placing the discussion of political economy first, I do not mean to imply that political economy is the cause of either Pentecostalism or the current cultural revival in Southeast Alaska. As mentioned above, people join churches primarily to save their souls, and join dance groups to discover their identities. What they find in either of these places depends a great deal on what they are looking for—and this depends a great deal on what is going on around them.

But to look for too close a connection between the logic of political economy and what people find in church membership would be to miss the historical contingency of the situation as a whole. Other issues and institutions might have answered just as well the resentments and troubles that bring many people to church. Pentecostalism is in Alaska because of the missionary efforts of some national organizations and because of the efforts of some uncommon individuals. Much the same could be said of the culture movement as well. None of what is presented here is intended to obscure the historical contingency of these and other events.

In this sort of situation, boundaries are inherently problematic, and all the more so if they are left unstated. Many of the boundaries used in this book are arbitrary. I have tried not to be too historical, which often requires a different sort of narrative strategy than I have chosen. I have also limited my discussion to villages in Southeast Alaska, though certainly there is much to indicate connections with other processes and regions. Each of the chapters in this book takes up a particular topic, but their order is not meant to indicate some hierarchy—that is, that beliefs are more important than material issues, or vice versa, because one appears in a chapter before or after another. The placement of topics is meant to provide provocation for what comes before and after. And no chapter attempts to make all or even most of the connections it might. Other boundaries are conventional, drawn from conventional categories of ethnography, largely for heuristic reasons—for they are written with several audiences in mind, including a non-anthropological audience seeking to understand more general issues of social life and living.

The conclusion is unique in that it does not restate the arguments and ideas raised in the preceding chapters but rather attempts to bring together the issues raised in parts 1 and 2 and to make sense of them in terms of the larger political history of the twentieth century. Here I take up the issue of (or language of) culture as it emerges from several quarters—from anthropology, from history, and as importantly, from the people who have, for the most part, come to be the subject of both history and anthropology. By placing this language in an extended historical trajectory, I hope to anticipate both the strengths and inevitable limits of the sorts of movements that continue to dominate the social lives of many Southeast Alaska Natives.

Part 1: Landscapes

I

Politics on the Other Side of the Mountain

Southeast Alaska has become a favored spot for cruise ship tours. The area is almost entirely an archipelago; the islands are actually a submerged mountain chain with deep waterways, rain forest, and glacial scenery on all sides. The mountains meet the water with steep faces, and between them are fjords and "canals" large enough that the glaciers or forests can be viewed up close, without leaving the ships, and often without even going outside. The area's artistic and mineral history fuels the accompanying tourist commodifications. The waterfronts of the main tourist towns—Ketchikan, Juneau, and Sitka—are dense with shops catering specifically to approximately half a million cruise ship passengers who visit each year. Most of the plastic totem poles they sell are actually mass-produced in Seattle or across the Pacific, and the dried smoked salmon is processed in smoker factories in Washington or Oregon. And little if any of the jewelry is produced either locally or from local materials. There are even a few shops that specialize in jade jewelry, capitalizing on the notions of precious materials and distant indigenousness, despite the South American origins of their products and design motifs.

The cruise ships tend to travel the larger north-south canals, and few visit the smaller, primarily native villages located further to the west and along the outer edges of many of the islands. Rather, the stock-in-trade of these tours are the stretches of scenic wilderness that line the fjord walls of the canals. When traveling by plane to and from any of the outside villages, or on the smaller ferries that service these villages, one sees clearly the paths of the cruise ships. Their routes are marked by long stretches of old-growth forest on the mountainsides that face the canals through which the cruise ships pass. These same mountains, however, like much of Southeast Alaska as a whole, are often clear-cut right up to their peaks on the sides opposite the scenic passages, leaving vast fields of stumps and the rotting remains of low-grade felled timber. The canal side is a camera-ready forest facade, the other side a virtual lunar landscape.

The forest facade is not extended to the ferry routes that service the twelve villages beyond the three large cities mentioned above. These ferries carry fewer tourists (especially on the slower outside routes), although some still feature guides from the U.S. Forest Service who give brief presentations on the villages they pass. The guides stick to the sensational and superlative whenever possible: "the oldest Russian settlement outside Sitka"; "the tallest totem pole in the world"; "the hiding place of Kaatlean." The stories seem radically out of touch with what appears outside the windows, though, and this quickly becomes clear to most of those listening. The performances have always struck me as parodies of the cruise ship tours, left to make do with the backside of the mountains and the lack of consumable items. Some listeners are sufficiently romantic to retain the nearly impossible illusion of tourism; others are not, though for them the parody does not dissolve, but rather seems to move to a higher level.

"Aren't any of the old houses left?" one asks. "No. There are in Juneau and Ketchikan," where the old houses are actually quite new, constructed for the cruise ship tourists. This the guide does not say, though most likely the listener, having just come from one of these cities, knows it already.

For many tourists, especially those who have never visited before, the villages no longer seem very accurate representations of themselves—sensibilities heightened by the newly built longhouses and totem poles mentioned by the guide, located along the waterfronts of the cruise ship towns. But the tourist traffic in the outside villages is too light and the villages too poor for this kind of investment; the ferries are seldom in village for more time than it takes to unload and load the cars and trucks. It is this disappointment, I think, that moves the performance from parody to ethnography. It is, in a sense, the Triste-Arctique of "off the beaten path" tourism in Alaska.[1]

Indeed, many of the ferry passengers leave feeling as though they have seen the "real" Alaska, for one indirect result of the facade—and it applies not just to the remaining trees, but also to the tourist longhouses and the entire physical landscape—is that it marks what lies behind it with the potential for exposure, the feeling of backyard clairvoyance.

Social Landscapes

All landscapes are social landscapes; all relations are social relations. Standing, for example, in Hoonah and looking across the bay at the long swath of clear-cut land, village residents see not only the place where trees once stood, but the means—the social means—by which the trees were removed. This can mean many things, because timber harvesting is a complex process in a complex business. For some, such means consist of their own labor, used for cutting or hauling or loading the timber; perhaps for building the road or for caring for children while a spouse or grown child did any of the above. Other means include the political relations whereby it became expedient—perhaps important—to cut timber, and to cut that patch of timber in particular. Others can look and see clearly the social and personal costs: the loss of former hunting, berrying, or fishing grounds.

All such issues raise questions about the relationships people have with other people. After all, ownership of a tree is never an agreement between a person or corporation and a tree. It is an agreement between people about who can and who cannot cut down and use that tree. Other relations may determine when the "owner" will choose to or be forced to cut it, while still other relations will determine to whom that owner will be able to sell the resulting timber, and at what price.

This chapter and the next are about the political landscapes of Southeast Alaska villages. The outline of this chapter is somewhat historical, but only because a historical narrative will help the reader understand how the present came to be the particular, peculiar way that it is. For people now living within that landscape, the relations discussed here are all present. By this I do not mean that people lack knowledge of the history discussed here, for many know it quite well; rather, I mean simply that for people living in the villages today, the relations discussed here are structured and interrelated in other, far more pressing ways than simply the order in which they came about.

This chapter explains the origins of political institutions and political-economic relations common to many villages. The next chapter concerns the predominant local political form to emerge in the twentieth century—"families." Unlike Indian Reorganization Act (IRA) tribal councils and tribes (which are federally, legally sanctioned bodies), Bureau of Indian Affairs (BIA) positions (which are positions within the

Above: Remains of cannery equipment in present-day Klawock
Below: Tourist exhibit of a precontact native dwelling

U.S. federal government), and city councils (which take a form mandated by the state of Alaska), "families" are the only locally developed political organization to emerge in the recent history of Southeast Alaska villages. All the rest have their origins in other places, other processes. "Family" organization, it will be important to remember, emerges in response to and often against all of these.

Seward's Folly

Known originally as "Seward's Folly" or "Seward's Icebox," Alaska was not purchased with the intention of colonization, though it was America's first overseas colony. Rather, government neglect aimed to discourage settlement. Seward and others intended the Russian purchase to be little more than a way station en route to the richer treasures of China and Japan (Paolino 1973). In Southeast Alaska this meant maintaining a commercial depot at Sitka (the former Russian capital of New Archangel) and searching for an accessible coal source somewhere nearby—later found near Killisnoo, not far from the present village of Angoon. Apart from these two areas, little concern was shown for the rest of the region, and even less for the territory outside the region.[2]

Native residents and their groups maintained a high degree of autonomy during this time, as they had under the Russians before. It was not until the late 1870s—when several salmon salteries were refitted to pack sockeye salmon in cans, a practice begun several decades before in northern California—that Alaska itself began to command the attention of politicians in the United States and the region's native peoples began to see hints of the colonialism that would follow. In the next six decades, cannery production and cannery politics would dominate the social landscape of Alaska, from the largest cities to the smallest villages.

By 1900 sixteen canneries were operating in Southeast Alaska (De-Loach 1939:17), and by the second decade of the twentieth century Alaska would outproduce both all of Canada and all of the mainland United States. This level of production quickly outstripped local labor, and canneries began to import from the West Coast large numbers of white and Asian workers to man the boats and packing lines of the area's many canneries. At its peak it was estimated that twenty thousand laborers spent the packing season in the territory, working in 116 canneries, and packing 7 million cases (over 300 million pounds) of canned salmon, mainly for export to the industrialized East Coast and England (DeLoach 1939; Gregory and Barnes 1939).

Throughout the cannery period the majority of Southeast Alaska's native population worked for the canneries, although, like the seasonal workers from San Francisco and Seattle, few worked year-round. Canning was limited to the summer months of July, August, and early September. During this time, however, the canning lines would run continuously from 6 A.M. to midnight. Women worked inside the cannery on the "slime line"—particularly after much of the rest of the processing had been mechanized—where fish were cleaned and arranged for processing. Others might have worked filling the lid machine or on the patching table, where cans imperfectly filled by the machines were finished off by hand to make the required one-pound weight. The remaining inside work—loading fish into and out of the various bins, maintaining and operating the machines, and heading and gutting the fish—was all done by the "China gang." After the Chinese Exclusion Acts of 1902, most of the Chinese laborers were replaced by Japanese, Mexicans, and later, primarily Filipinos (Masson and Guimary 1981:1–30). Throughout, the division of labor within the cannery remained the same.

Most of the native men fished for the canneries in company-owned boats. A few held jobs maintaining the physical plant, but most of the management and engineering jobs were held by whites. All of the shoreside crew worked the same hours: a twenty-hour day. Management justified this by saying that the fish would not keep if left in bins, so the plant had to operate as long as it had fish. Yet the demands made on fishermen for a continuous supply were just as great, ensuring that there would always be so much fish that there would be no choice but to operate around the clock.

The rule of thumb for cannery superintendents was that the total annual "pack" of a cannery had to exceed thirty thousand cases of salmon to create the acceptable profit margins for cannery owners. This was not always met, and canneries did frequently open and close, often reflecting insufficient packs in off years. Yet just as often, plant closings represented the efforts of one cannery to eliminate local competition for fish by purchasing a competitor and closing it down. What is more, once the goal of thirty thousand cases was met, virtually all of what was produced thereafter would go toward profit. This was because the greatest proportion of the costs involved in producing canned salmon was not the fish, cans, fuel, or even labor, but rather the mainly fixed costs of fish traps, canning machines, plant maintenance, and especially the transportation of all of these things to and from Alaska. These costs were fixed because they varied little with the size of the eventual pack. Once these costs were met, the profit on every case produced was nearly the sale price of that case. It was not uncommon for successful plants in areas with a good supply of fish to return two to three times their initial investment in a single season.

During the summer months, while working at the cannery, many native families would move out to the cannery location, even when canneries were built close to the villages in which these families spent the winter. In addition to building large houses for white managers and bunkhouses for the Asian workers, most canneries constructed a row of small houses—generally single-story houses measuring eight by twelve feet with mud floors—for use by native families working for the cannery (usually those families where both the husband fished on a company boat and his wife worked on the line). Whole families would move into these houses for the canning season, bringing along children and often an elderly relative who would care for the children and help prepare meals. The men working on the fishing boats would be gone for the entire season, alleviating some of the crowding.

Many of today's elders remember these houses, some of which still stand alongside now-collapsing canneries throughout the region. Surprisingly, memories of them are often fond, as these were frequently the first houses in the region to have electricity (supplied by the cannery generators). In addition, cannery camps were places where Western novelties—movies, new foods, music, and even alcohol, dancing, and gambling—were in good supply.

At the close of the cannery season, native families would purchase their entire winter supply of food and clothing staples from the cannery store. Very few stayed on at the cannery past the packing season. Most often entire families would load their summer possessions and newly purchased sacks of potatoes, sugar, coffee, pilot bread, and rice aboard smaller boats and head back to their permanent homes in the villages throughout the region.

For many families, however, autumn also meant another form of commercial fishing. This involved moving out to camps along the outer islands to collect subsistence foods and to troll for fall salmon (usually coho and king salmon) to sell to the remaining salmon salteries located in the region. In many areas, trolling required families to move into new areas to fish on a regular and evolving basis, and subsistence patterns changed to meet these new circumstances. By the 1910s, old clan property lines were giving way to the pragmatics of a short subsistence season and the opportunism of migrating families who were combining subsistence with commercial work.

Many of these families did not return to their winter homes until late October and early November. Because this caused many children to miss the entire fall school session, missionary teachers and some local leaders called for an end to the "camp" system. This early conflict between those families still dependent on subsistence resources and seasonal cash income (small-boat owners, crewmen, and generally anyone without year-round employment) and those able to remain in the village year-round (usually the large-boat owners with good cannery connections, store owners, or government employees) polarized many villages in ways that prefigure later and even current divisions.

New Villages, New Politics

In the late nineteenth century, canneries tended to be built near existing villages, especially early on when clan property forms were still understood by whites and natives to be at least potentially enforceable. This was particularly true in northern areas where several large native villages represented a desirable labor force and a potentially intractable obstacle to cannery owners and superintendents who would otherwise have invaded the area. In these areas, canneries remained particularly dependent on locally supplied fish for the first decade of their existence.

By the late 1880s, however, as canners became more assured that their own notions of property would be protected by an increasing U.S. military presence, they began to set up production near choice sockeye streams and to encourage nearby native groups to relocate. At times the summer subsistence territory of a single clan would become the site of a new village when other clans began to forgo their own subsistence territories for labor at the cannery. Several Southeast Alaska

Native villages—Kasaan, Hoonah, Kake, and Klawock—remain at or near these sites today.

Other permanent villages were formed when Presbyterian missionaries encouraged—and in some cases forced—migration and consolidation of one or more groups. Villages like Haines and Metlakatla were formed as "model villages," with missionary and government support. Hydaburg was created in 1912 from three Haida villages: Klinkwan, Sukkwan, and Howkan (Vaughan 1985). Here local dependence on missionary service for schools, financial support, and mail and steamer service was used to coerce families from these villages to take up residence at a single new location. When this was done, none of the old-style communal houses that had characterized villages throughout the regions were built. Rather, under missionary instruction, only single-family, European-style houses were constructed along a single boardwalk—at one end of which was the church and mission home, at the other, the cannery.

Along with these new villages and house styles came new forms of political organization. Continuing the example from Hydaburg: when the new village was built it was suggested that a city council be formed. Interclan cooperation had always been a concern among both Tlingit and Haida clans throughout the region, and Howkan and Klinkwan had both had village-governing bodies drawn from the leaders of the resident clans. In Hydaburg, however, the idea of a village-wide election for a village council was a relatively new idea. Missionary demands that the council business be carried on in English further alienated past clan heads. In the end, the elders from Klinkwan, Howkan, and Sukkwan decided to let the younger men lead the council. According to anthropologist Daniel Vaughan:

> When the annual election came up, the first group of [clan] leaders, sensitive to criticisms of their traditional meeting style, asked voters to elect younger men to office. The next group of councilmen were people of the age to have attended school in either Klinkwan or Howkan schools. The Haida lay-preacher [Sam Davis] was elected mayor. This council conducted town meetings in the "new way," bearing some semblance to parliamentary procedure. . . . This new council also requested that all business of the town be transacted in English. (1985:135–36)

In other villages, traditional clan elders continued to hold much sway in the selection and function of new councils. Yet in many of the cannery-dependent villages, outside influences and internal divisions made these councils relatively ineffective.

By the 1910s virtually all of the region's villages were company towns for almost half of each year, and individuals with close ties to the canneries were able to exercise informal power over others in the village. The cannery owners themselves also held considerable power over the fate of these villages. Decisions not to open a particular packinghouse in a particular year could cause families to move away, diminishing the impact of local leaders without any obvious change in formal organization.

This was the case in places like Ketchikan, where thorough immersion in the cash economy undercut the authority of local leadership without replacing it with any novel body or structure. In other areas, new sorts of entities such as school boards held great sway and gradually replaced other forms of organized politics. In Kake, the local school board was nearly able to eliminate the "camp" system of fall fishing and subsistence production by issuing fines of twenty-five dollars for each child taken out of school. Where households had once moved together from one remote area to the next, trolling fall salmon for the salteries and gathering subsistence foods along the way, the requirement that all children attend for the entire school year meant that whole patterns of life would have to be abandoned. The steep fines effectively confined most families to permanent residence in the village by the late 1920s. After this only men went away to the camps, and their time there became less frequent and less lengthy.[3] Smokehouses were built in Kake for the first time during this period as well, much to the dismay of many older villagers who found the practice of processing fish in the village, in the words of one resident, "unsanitary."

In areas where native-run village councils were able to win some power — usually through extremely careful and persistent use of legislation meant for white colonists in larger towns — canneries were often able to circumvent this authority by invoking jurisdictional conflicts between the state and federal governments. This was the case in Klawock in the early decades of the twentieth century. Here the village council had been able to win municipal incorporation under early territorial laws. This allowed them to tax the businesses within the municipality — the major one being a large salmon cannery owned by a California-based firm. In response, the cannery simply abandoned its current building and moved across the bay to an area outside the municipal boundaries but within rowing distance for the village laborers. Efforts to expand the municipal boundaries were blocked by the federal government, which had in the decade before claimed almost the entire Southeast Alaska archipelago as a national forest. In the end, the cannery paid no taxes and the village remained dependent on missionary support to keep a school open year-round (see Dombrowski 1995).

Permanent village locations and the creation of a regional native high school in the 1910s encouraged another novel sort of political body that did gain regionwide influence for natives. The Alaska Native Brotherhood (ANB), formed in Sitka early in the cannery period, was founded by several missionary-educated Tlingit and Tsimshian natives. Their original intentions are unclear, though fraternal organizations were popular throughout the United States at the time. Very soon after its founding, however, the ANB became active politically, mainly under the direction of William Paul, a native lawyer from Wrangell whose mother had been an early Christian convert and educator. With the ANB's financial backing, Paul litigated a number of important cases concerning native rights. One of them gained for Southeast Natives the right to vote several years before Native Americans in the lower forty-eight states were granted that right by Congress, and another gave natives the right to send their children to territorial public schools, putting an end to the "two school" system in Alaska. By the late 1930s the ANB was active in labor politics as well.

Paul's own leanings to the left had led him in this direction early on, and it is likely that the ANB was pulled along with him, rather than vice versa. By 1940 the ANB had won the right to be the collective bargaining representative for many of the cannery workers and most of the fishermen in Southeast Alaska. At this time they began to offer "associate status" to anyone who wished to join, and soon there were many more non-native associate members of the ANB than there were Alaska Natives. Throughout, however, William Paul and a central core of longtime members remained in control of the organization (Drucker 1958).

During this period, the ANB took as its main goal the outlawing of fish traps owned and operated by canneries. These traps were placed near stream mouths and convenient pinch points (e.g., where schools of fish must pass through a narrow area between islands) in the same locations year after year. By the 1930s, more fish were caught in traps than by boats. For native fishing labor, traps were a visible threat, for traps required few operators and fished continuously once set up. The ANB, under Paul, called for the outlawing of fish traps altogether. The cannery owners resisted, and despite the fact that the issue was taken up repeatedly by congressional committees over several decades, no injunction was ever issued. Eventually the fish-trap issue would tip the balance of local opinion in favor of statehood, and a fish-trap injunction was the first law passed by the newly formed Alaska State Senate. But this was not until 1959–60, after almost thirty years of steady advocacy.

Long before this, the declining importance of fishing to cannery operations was matched by the declining power of the ANB in labor arbitration. The ANB had never made advocacy for shoreside workers a priority in their negotiations, despite the role native women played in this work, and other Seattle-based unions had been organized among the Filipino crews, often affiliated with national and prominent West Coast unions. Thus when fishing declined as traps became more numerous and the price of fish continued to fall, the ANB was left without a role in the regional economy, and thus without a place in the region's politics. By the late 1940s, the ANB was out of the labor-organizing business, outmaneuvered by Seattle-based unions and compromised by internal disputes.

Fishing for the IRA

In 1936 Congress extended the Indian Reorganization Act to Alaska, attempting here, as elsewhere, to create more uniform means through which to monitor and transform native communities. The IRA offered several routes for political organization, and only a few Southeast Alaska communities chose to reform or re-create tribal councils along the lines laid out by the act. Most villages had by the 1940s already adopted village or city councils, and in many places the structural duplication of a tribal council was avoided. Instead, most communities favored the formation of economic or cooperative associations as vehicles to secure loans and coordinate BIA interaction.

By 1950, IRA cooperative associations in Hydaburg and Klawock and IRA councils in Kake and Angoon all owned canneries in their respective communities. None of these ventures was financially successful, however, and by 1960 they had together accumulated nearly $5 million in debt. The fishing industry in Southeast Alaska had suffered a considerable downturn throughout this period, with fish landings dropping and demand for canned salmon decreasing worldwide. Throughout, the BIA had encouraged these communities to continue to absorb debt—a policy that remained unchanged until an outside audit was performed in 1960.[4]

The BIA's Juneau Area Office had encouraged the purchase of canneries in an effort to complete the transformation of most villages to a full-scale wage economy. Its goals might have been lofty—to establish a modern economy where the electricity in most villages need not be turned off at the end of the cannery season, or where individuals need not leave villages seasonally for wage or subsistence work. Or they might have been more self-serving—as was probably the case for several well-placed natives in the BIA bureaucracy who stood to benefit from boat loans and the reopening of then-closed canneries. In either case, however, the Juneau Area Office went to great lengths to keep the canneries in operation, including the gradual assumption of total control of all four native-owned cannery operations.

In 1960, with the single largest economic asset in the villages fully under BIA control, local political power reached a nadir. Cooperative associations formed in the villages in the early 1940s under the IRA were largely defunct. The ANB was out of the labor-organizing business, and household economies were sliding as well, for as statehood approached many nonlocal cannery owners had closed up operations in anticipation of the coming fish-trap ban. Fishing had been declining for two decades, and despite the brief boom that followed statehood and the fish-trap ban, the market for canned salmon was shrinking—further lowering the price of fish. During this time many families left the villages, some for the larger towns in Southeast Alaska, like Sitka, Ketchikan, or Juneau, and others for faraway Anchorage or Seattle. Hoonah showed a decline by one-third in the late 1940s and 1950s. In Klawock it was just as large.

The exodus threatened the survival of many villages, jeopardizing such population-dependent programs as school lunch programs and trash and public utilities services, as well as the survival of those few small shops and suppliers found in every village. The housing shortage that characterizes most villages even at present began during this time as well. After World War II, few houses were built until the regional housing authority began construction in the mid-1970s. Although housing in the villages was easy to obtain in the early 1960s, it suffered from years of neglect.[5]

Unlike those in other areas of the state, Southeast Alaska Natives had been thoroughly immersed in a cash economy since the first decades of the century, and by the late 1950s this economy was collapsing.

Tlingit and Haida Central Council

Land claims had originally been advanced by the ANB at a regional convention in 1929 (Central Council of the Tlingit and Haida 1992:7). The issue was highly contentious, however, with some groups advocating a cash settlement and some others reservations (both in exchange for a cessation of claims throughout the region). Some local leaders, such as Paul, felt that the land claims should be advanced by clans and clan leaders—the aboriginal titleholders according to many historic sources—rather than villages. The BIA preferred the village approach, as did the majority of the post-Paul ANB leadership. As a result, no progress was made in advancing a single set of claims for several decades.

Hydaburg, partly as a result of its distinct tribal status—most Hydaburg residents are Haidas, while virtually the entire remainder of the region is Tlingit—followed a BIA initiative and opted for reservation status in the late 1930s. The land swap arranged by Secretary of the Interior Harold Ickes included the surrender of over 1 million acres on Southern Prince of Wales Island by the Haida for a 101,000-acre reservation in and around Hydaburg. Much of the logic of the swap rested on ownership rights of the water that bordered native lands, giving the Haida rights to three successful but privately owned fish traps to supply their own struggling cannery. But pressure from the fish-trap owners caused the reservation agreement to be overturned in a court decision less than a year after it was handed down.

Shortly after the issue was first introduced, land claims had created such dissension within the ANB leadership that it had nearly paralyzed the institution. At the time the ANB was at the height of its union power, and the paralysis threatened this success. As a result, in 1939 discussion of land claims was banned from the floor at ANB meetings and a separate body was formed to pursue the claims.[6] The new group was known as the Tlingit and Haida Central Council. When formed it was composed of many of the same individuals as the ANB Executive Council, although the groups diverged over the next several years.

The land suit was finally brought to court by the Central Council in 1957, and in 1959 it was decided in favor of Southeast Natives. The cash award, however, was postponed through a series of negotiations between the Justice Department and the BIA. The eventual award was quite small—$7.2 million for the entire Southeast Alaska panhandle—supposedly the value of the assets lost to the federal government through the creation of the Tongass National Forest in the first decade of the century. This was drastically undervalued by nearly all accounts, and despite the fact that the award was not made until 1968, it included no interest or adjustment for inflation.

Prior to the award's reception, there was little agreement on its disbursement. In the end the leaders of the Tlingit and Haida Central Council decided to retain the entire award amount and use the money to start a centralized tribal administration. This body would then act as a tribal representative to the federal government/BIA and apply for a self-governance relationship within the federal bureaucracy.[7] This was bitterly disputed by the ANB, which had always considered itself the central representative of the Southeast Alaska Natives. Eventually the ANB lost in its bid for tribal recognition, however, and the Central Council (or "T&H," as it has come to be called) emerged as the largest native political power in the region, particularly in relation to the federal government and federal Indian programs.

In the early 1970s, T&H created two separate branches of its own organization: the Tlingit and Haida Regional Housing Authority and the Tlingit and Haida Regional Power Authority. The former was designed to act as a subcontractor building low-cost, HUD-sponsored housing in native villages throughout the region; and T&H houses now make up perhaps half—and in smaller villages even more—of the total available village housing. The majority of the houses built remain owned by the Housing Authority, and residents pay rent based on their annual income. After making consistent rent payments for twenty years, residents are supposed to gain title to a house. This, however, seldom actually happens. Extensions on the payments are added each time the Housing

Authority comes in to renovate the houses, and most houses are so shoddily constructed that renovation is a near-constant need.

For families living in these houses, the added repairs mean additional years of payments before they receive title. Beyond this, an unbroken residency of twenty years is rare for families anywhere in Alaska (and perhaps anywhere in the United States), especially in areas with highly volatile economies. And each time a family leaves, the status of past payment lapses, so that if they move back to the village they must begin the twenty-year effort anew. More financially costly, perhaps, is the fact that for those who leave, past payments that might have gained equity in any other sort of ownership system revert back to rent and are, in effect, unrecoverable in any form.

The Power Authority produces the electrical power in most villages through diesel generator plants built in the late 1970s. Not surprisingly, most of the T&H houses are heated with "electric heat."

T&H's combined political, housing, and electrical control became an issue for villages seeking some independence from the regional body. In the early 1970s, when village economies had reached what must be considered the low point of the last fifty years, most village IRA councils had delegated what little tribal political authority they retained to the Central Council. When acting on behalf of most of the region, T&H's role in many federal programs was enhanced, and it was as such that the creation of the Housing and Power Authorities was possible.

By the mid- and late 1980s, however, a new generation of leaders had emerged in most villages, and an entirely new economic landscape had been created through the Alaska Native Claims Settlement Act, or ANCSA (discussed in chapter 3). These leaders sought some independence from T&H, which by then had grown into a largely settled and increasingly institutionalized bureaucracy. For T&H, the loss of delegated authority over local tribal communities meant a significant loss of clout in their relation with the federal government, and perhaps their dissolution as a centralized political body altogether. Movements in Hoonah, Yakutat, Hydaburg, Klawock, and Craig in the 1980s and 1990s, as well as the early exclusion of Kake, Ketchikan, and Sitka from T&H jurisdiction, made a gradual dissolution of the tribal administration a real possibility.

The result, many village residents suspect, has been a considerable amount of foot-dragging on T&H's part in promoting village self-

Above: Old houses at the center of a village

Below: New houses constructed by the Tlingit and Haida Housing Authority

government. Others have cited stronger (albeit entirely circumstantial) evidence of collusion between branches of T&H to punish those who seek some measure of village independence. More compliant tribal members seem to many village residents to receive faster repairs or modernizations on their houses; self-governance advocates, on the other hand, say that they wait far longer to get housing and to get repairs in the houses they eventually receive. Regardless of whether or not this is true, this perception is a basic political dynamic in many villages.

All in all, however, it is clear that the Central Council remains the paramount political entity in most tribal-federal relations for Southeast Alaska Natives. Its practical role in providing heat, power, and housing to many villages has underwritten its retention of this role. At present, most city or village administration budgets go primarily to supporting local public schools and minimal public services, such as water and trash pickup. Through its support of General Assistance Relief (the strictly Indian arm of the welfare system), through the Housing and Power Authorities, and through its role in seeking and receiving broader federal assistance for community development, T&H controls most of the money through which village economic and social transformation can and does take place.

Fishing after Statehood

When Alaska achieved statehood in 1959, its dominant industry—particularly in terms of employment and individual or family (rather than corporate) income—remained fishing. Although logging was an important source of jobs, it lacked fishing's broad political base in the region.

At the time, the fish-trap issue had come to be understood as local fishermen's opposition to "outside" cannery or fish-trap owners. In reality the sides were never quite so clear. Many of the boats that fished in Alaska, then as now, came seasonally from Seattle or Bellingham in Washington State. Likewise, by the 1960s many canneries were owned by people who lived in Alaska, and sometimes in the same villages in which their canneries were located.

As mentioned above, the first law passed by the newly elected state legislature was a total ban on fish traps. Within a year all of the traps were gone, and in effect so was the chance of the canning industry's surviving its ongoing decline. As canneries were forced to meet boat owners' demands for higher fish prices, the cost of canning salmon increased and its place on the dinner tables of European and East Coast working-class families quickly declined.

In addition, the trap ban did not stem the decline of salmon stocks. Instead, the brief boom for boats that followed the ban invited a renewed capitalization of the fishing fleet, with larger versions of the Alaskan "limit seiner" employing new equipment and catching even greater amounts of fish. Between 1960 and 1971, boat landings rose to three or four times their pre-ban level, then fell to well below half their peak (Rogers, Listowski, and Brakel 1974:175 [table 80]). By the mid-1970s, overcapitalization and decimated stocks were so apparent that the Alaska legislature was pressed to act to limit fisheries throughout the state.

The means adopted was a limited-entry system, enacted in Alaska in 1974–75. Under this system, a limited number of permits were issued to individuals for participation in a particular fishery—seiners had to have a seine permit, trollers a troll permit, and so forth. An individual could hold licenses in more than one fishery (trolling, gill netting, purse seining), but no more than one license in any single fishery. The principle behind the strategy was to fix the fishing effort by capping the number of individuals and boats pursuing fish stocks. Yet because the permits were limited in number, they had two critical economic impacts on fishing families and villages. The first was to depress the value of seine boats (still the most important element of the fleet in Southeast Alaska), especially those sold without a license, for without a license the boat was unusable. The second was to create a commodity market in licenses. And as a commodity, the right to fish and make a living in fishing became alienable—it could be lost through sale—something Southeast Alaska residents had never known before.

In the depressed value of seine boats, native fishermen suffered a setback in the single item of capital that most had accumulated. This, coupled with the alienability of the license, led to a rapid decline in the number of limited-entry permits held by village residents. Between 1975, the first year of the program, and 1979, the year of the first comprehensive study, Southeast Alaska residents lost one in four of their purse seine licenses, and nonresidents gained almost as many (Langdon 1980:20–29 [tables 6, 8, and 9]). Three-quarters of those that were lost were transferred through sale or purchase, and half of these acquisitions were financed by a bank, the original owner, a processor, or the state loan program (Langdon 1980:34). In short, most of those buying permits were doing so with borrowed capital. For purse seiners the level of "processor" financing was the highest, with fish buyers financing one of every five transfers.

In his report at the time, anthropologist Steve Langdon noted that the purse seine permits required the most financing because they remained the most expensive, averaging more than $50,000 in 1978. Yet financing was complicated by the fact that the limited-entry law was unclear as to whether permits themselves could be used as collateral for loans. Banks most often required collateral in the form of boats and nets or real estate, while fish processors often did not require collateral of any kind. On the other hand, those fishermen who became indebted to processors accepted radically limited marketing options, in effect becoming clients of the fish buyer who held the note on the license. In plain terms this meant lower prices and, with lower prices, a more tenuous place in the fishery.

In the villages, few native fishermen held the necessary non-fishing collateral to obtain a bank loan.[8] The cycle of outmigration in the villages further aggravated these trends. Throughout the 1960s property values had declined directly in proportion to the limited opportunities available to village residents, further depressing house values and thus the ability of those remaining in the villages to obtain financing for boats or permits. At the same time, the brief fishing boom and the statewide oil boom had the opposite effect in the larger, predominantly non-native towns. Here for most of the 1970s, property values rose and financing for corporate ventures increased. This meant that even for those licenses that were sold or transferred within the region, most moved from villages to the towns, and from natives to non-natives.

Indeed, in the first three years of the limited-entry permit system, rural residents statewide lost one out of five of those permits originally issued in 1975. Southeast Alaska was hit the hardest in this way, with well over half of the purse seine permits in non-village residents' hands within three years after the law was enacted.[9] The trend continues. In the late 1990s there are few purse seiners left in most villages. Those few that remain support the salmon and salmon roe (fish egg) export trade to Japan. Indeed, by the late 1980s about half of all U.S. salmon production was exported to Japan. And while Alaska continues to produce about

40 percent of the world's salmon, those species most available in the Southeast are favored mainly for their roe. It is not uncommon to see Southeast Alaska processors disposing of thousands of pounds of salmon carcasses that have been stripped of their roe, the actual meat of the fish no longer being sufficiently valuable to justify processing. The vulnerability of an industry with a single market has been felt recently by several sharp depressions in fish and fish product prices that have little to do with the Alaskan supply and are caused mainly by new competition from Chile and Russia (Knapp, Peyton, and Weise 1993).

The decline of commercial fishing in most villages marked a decline in two elements of local sociopolitical organization, one informal and the other formal. Family boats—those whose owners are captains and who employ members of their own families as crew—were once the predominant arrangement among native-owned purse seiners. The loss of a permit in such circumstances meant not just a loss of jobs, but the likely dissolution of a form of local corporateness that had been around since the early cannery days. At the formal level, village IRA councils, most of which had been set up in the 1940s as vehicles for obtaining boat loans for their members, found themselves bankrupt by their holdings of boats whose value diminished significantly without a permit—which remained the property of an individual and were non-foreclosable. Since that time, most councils have quietly arranged the sale of boats for which they hold the note, most often at a loss, always with the tacit agreement of the BIA's Juneau Area Office. Without boat loans, the raison d'être for most cooperative councils has diminished and even disappeared.

Politics in the Ebb and Flow of Capital

Many of the political entities discussed thus far still operate with limited authority or scope in most villages. ANB halls are found in most villages, though these have fallen into disrepair in many places because of a lack of dues-paying members. Young people no longer join the ANB or ANS (the women's equivalent) as a means to public recognition. Some local chapters have turned to bingo to help finance local activities and to maintain the hall itself. In some villages the ANB hall still serves as the site of most village-wide functions—wedding receptions, retirement parties, payoff parties, or dance group celebrations. At these events, however, ANB members seldom play a prominent role based on their

Above: Japanese workers grading and packing roe for shipment to Japan.

Below: Native workers in a fish-processing plant. The salmon are stripped of their eggs and, in most cases, discarded. The eggs (called "roe") are shipped to Japan. The fish themselves are not worth the cost of shipping to market in the United States.

status as such. In other villages, larger functions are held in the school gymnasium, marking a shift in the orientation of the village from the ANB to the state-financed school.

The IRA councils and related cooperative associations have, in all but four villages, turned over most of their relations with the federal government to the Tlingit and Haida Central Council. Some still meet, but their authority within the villages has attenuated. What relevance they retained after the failure of the canneries was lost through the limited-entry system. Very recently, some have tried to gain back some of the responsibilities (and subsequent authority) given over to T&H, which has in turn resisted these efforts; at present, no new village councils or associations have managed to achieve any formal recognition by the federal government.

The Tlingit and Haida Central Council continues to be the main regional native power. This has come through the associated Housing and Power Authorities, and through their role as intermediaries to the federal government. Grants and programs for economic development, general assistance, emergency relief, and a host of miscellaneous federal programs like Small Business Administration loans have allowed T&H to maintain a hold over dependent villages—which is, ironically, increased by the escalating dependency of most villages on federal programs. By taking a percentage of the monies gained through all of the programs, the Central Council pays for a fairly large administrative staff. These jobs are used to establish alliances with important families, the topic of chapter 2. As will be discussed there, village councils and administrations remain important as a source of employment in all villages. Here the wheels of patronage turn most predictably.

Administration budgets for most towns and villages, though, are relatively stable; and most income is earmarked for specific fixed costs (e.g., schools, past village debt, ongoing programs such as building roads or dumps, and, of course, village administration), the allocation of which is often overseen by the state. Little of any village's budget is left for discretionary spending, and what little there is is mostly reserved for capital outlays—garbage trucks and dock or town oil tank repair, for example, are frequent issues in most villages. Mayors and village administrators have few options and derive very little power through the control of local spending. Rather, most of their influence is gained through their ability to influence hirings in the administration—police or village public safety officers, garbage collection, local construction and maintenance—and in state- and federally sponsored programs such as public schools or Head Start. With full-time, benefit-guaranteed employment scarce in every village, these jobs are a priority for everyone. For this reason, mayoral races in some villages will be quite heated, despite the fact that the village administration has little real power to set policy or influence village life in any structurally significant way.

At different times each of these political entities—IRA councils and cooperative associations, village councils, the ANB and ANS, school boards, and even the Tlingit and Haida Central Council—has seen moments of considerable local influence. The gradual erosion of this influence has usually followed as the political economy once again shifted in a new direction. The ebb and flow of capital in what remains a resource-rich area has fostered and undermined several markedly different forms of political and social organization. Many of these still exist in a formal sense, though at present most of the power lies with the ANCSA boards of directors, as discussed in chapter 3.

Before moving on to ANCSA, however, we turn to a discussion of what is at present the de facto structural element of contemporary villages: "families." These groups remain the central players in every village I visited. They are the means through which patronage jobs and out-of-town money are turned into local influence and eventually votes. Family heads are courted by outside interests for their ability to influence local situations, and in return they are given the means for assembling or maintaining a "family"—primarily jobs. Within the village, other forms of patronage are used in similar ways, especially jobs with either the village ANCSA corporation or in the village governmental-administrative apparatus. Family form is, as a result, extremely fluid. And despite its allusion to biological notions of relatedness, kinship plays little actual role in composing or maintaining a family. It is to this institution, the foreground in most people's view of the village political landscape, that we turn in chapter 2.

The Ins and Outs of Village Social Organization

It's the summer of 1995, and I have returned to this village after two years to find that it now has two Indian Reorganization Act (IRA) councils. For the past decade, including during my first visit in the summer of 1993, there had been none. Actually, this isn't quite true. When there had been no IRA council here, the regional tribal government—the Tlingit and Haida Central Council—had been delegated as the village's official tribal representative. So in effect, even when there was no IRA council there was still a tribal governing body. And now, when there are two tribal councils in the village, that means there are, in effect, three.

The "radicals," as they half-jokingly called themselves, formed first. They consist of the former city administrator of the village; his wife; a Tlingit elder (and one of the few remaining Tlingit speakers in the village) who has lived most of his life in a nearby, predominantly non-native city; the president of the local ANB chapter; a logger who was born in the village and has lived

here occasionally but has moved around quite a bit as well; and finally, an out-of-work totem-pole carver who has lived all his life here and occasionally worked in logging. Altogether there are five men and one woman.

Their reason for forming, they say, is to take back control of the IRA council from T&H—the Tlingit and Haida Central Council—which is the regional tribal body, recognized as such by the federal government. In the late 1970s or early 1980s (no one from this group is quite sure) the village IRA council had turned over its management and representation responsibilities to T&H. It ceased to meet regularly, and eventually stopped meeting at all. The radicals have collected statements from several past council members acknowledging that they have not met in many years.

The radicals are largely self-appointed. For, as they immediately make clear, there are no up-to-date records of tribal enrollment, and thus it is impossible to have an election. At their first meeting they began collecting signatures for enrollment, and they now plan an election at midsummer. Until then, they refer to themselves as the "Tribal Council of the K—— Tribe."

This name has historical political significance. The original village delegates from here that attended the formation of the Tlingit and Haida Central Council in the late 1930s signed on behalf of the K—— Tribe—not the local IRA council. The IRA council was formed later, in the late 1930s or early 1940s, as part of the implementation of the Indian Reorganization Act in Southeast Alaska. By assuming the title "K—— Tribe," the radicals sought to impose alternative notions of legitimacy on themselves and, as importantly, on T&H and the federal government as well. Had they assumed the old title of the IRA council, they say, it would have signaled some acknowledgment of the federal government's right to dictate the political structure of the group. What they wanted to avoid, that is, was any acknowledgment of the IRA as a basis for tribal organization in the village. Likewise, by taking up the name K—— Tribe they assumed the mantle of the group that had originally lent its authority to T&H, and which could now take it back, presumably without regard to the wishes of that body.

The radicals met with instantaneous resistance from T&H. Soon after word reached Juneau, T&H sent representatives to the village to help organize a meeting of the current board of the IRA council. Yet because there was no currently elected board, the first priority of the T&H representatives was to appoint an elections committee that would enroll new members and update the membership list. They picked two women, which might have been a surprise to anyone not acquainted with the realities of village politics. Yet each of these women was at the center of a nexus of relatives and dependents—a "family," in local terms—and so each was in a position to bring to bear considerable local political weight. At the same time, neither had in the past been directly involved with the IRA council, so both could potentially seem like nonpolitical outsiders. The first is an older woman who was at the time the Tlingit teacher at the school (meaning that she gave weekly classes on local history, language, art, and lore). The second is a younger woman who has lived for a time outside the village, but who now lives here.

The enrollment lists—the one begun by the "Tribe" and the second collected by the re-formed election committee composed of these two women—functioned like a straw poll, with each side trying to enroll as many people as possible so as to appear the largest. After some initial resistance, however, the radicals realized that they are outmatched here and that their best bet was to try to win an election based on the combined list of enrollees. If they can muster enough town support, they now feel, and win a T&H-sponsored election, no one will be able to question their claim to represent the village. On the other hand, T&H had already made it clear that they supported a different set of candidates, and they would help decide the election by once again mobilizing the patronage system they had begun in the early 1970s.

It is now August, and it perhaps comes as no surprise to the Tlingit and Haida Central Council that it is the younger of the two women appointed to the election committee who turns the tide against the radicals. Her appointment made sense in two ways. She is bright, articulate, college-educated, and has served as the village representative to T&H in Juneau in the past. Even more importantly, she is on her way to becoming the central figure in the village's most important family.

Virtually single-handedly, she has enrolled well over half of the adult population of the village, including a number of people who had originally enrolled with the "Tribe." This adds further legitimacy to the T&H-sponsored election—at least in the eyes of the Central Council and the federal government—for it means that the radicals cannot claim that their supporters were barred from the election. Just as importantly, though, she has found a group to run against the radicals—all of whom favor a continued relationship with T&H.

Having lost the enrollment battle, the radicals opted to run as a slate, and most in town now view them not as a rival organization, but simply as the opposition in an election largely managed by T&H. The question of legitimacy has been dropped in favor of an election based on family connections, and the radicals are largely seen as marginal to the several important families in the village. In the end, the election is one-sided in favor of the slate of candidates favored by T&H. The radicals say they will continue to meet, but with no additional enrollment and continuing defection among those already enrolled, enthusiasm has dampened.

When I return again to the village in 1997, several members of the radicals have been "run off"—meaning they were forced to move away from the village, according to those who remain. Just as likely they left to find work, though this is itself often a political matter as well.

The new IRA council continues to request help from T&H for achieving independent status. This help has been slow in coming, though programs designed to promote self-governance have now become a regular part of the T&H patronage cycle. Council board members now attend regular self-governance workshops, sponsored and paid for by T&H, and are allocated money that can be spent locally, perhaps to hire someone to work as a coordinator for self-governance issues.

Family

The term "family" is actually used by Southeast Alaska village residents in two ways. It is used to refer to a household or nuclear family in much the same way that it is used elsewhere in the United States. But more commonly it is used as a political term to describe large, extended kin groups, of which there are usually between four and eight in any Southeast village.[1] These families—extended bilateral and affinally linked groups of three or more generations—have emerged intermittently over the past one hundred years. At certain times they have been the most important element in village social structures.

Not everyone in a village belongs to such a family. Some people—usually poor or displaced residents—may not be considered part of any family as such, even if they have relatives in a village. Other people can be considered part of a family, and even central members of a family, even if they share no actual kinship links with others in the group. Importantly, families have little to do with the types of blood or marriage links we normally associate with the term.

Part of the confusion comes from the fact that kinship has always been important in native villages in Alaska, and many still speak of "uncles" and "nephews" as special relationships, reminiscent of past matrilineal linkages and clan affiliations.[2] But today's local social organization is quite different from the clan and housegroup organization common in the past. Today's families do not resemble Tlingit or Haida clans or housegroups in organization, recruitment, or corporateness. Instead, families are shaped in large part by those same forces that have consistently destabilized other forms of social organization in the region and villages, including the historic clans and housegroups of the late nineteenth century.

Yet as will become apparent, families have emerged where other forms of social organization have disappeared precisely because families have as their basis no permanent or lasting foundation. They are ad hoc organizations, loosely structured by notions of kinship and extended kin ties. They can shrink and grow, and can emerge from nowhere as situations, opportunities, and problems arise. As a result, since the massive and continuous reorganization of the region began in the early twentieth century, families have become important, at times dominant, political units in every village in the region.

Their shifting nature should not be mistaken for a lack of political importance, however. Large families can dominate village politics. In fact, this seems to be the crucial factor for defining those groups that may be considered a family. This point is unusual, and it requires some clarification.

Briefly stated, families must exercise power to be considered real families. Indeed, the very nature of the linkages—general notions of bilaterality and inmarried relatives—means that an almost unlimited number of potential families could be assembled in any one village, for the necessary linkages are so loose that almost anyone can demonstrate some link to any number of such groups. Those families that are real (in the sense that they are recognized as corporate groups by themselves and others) act together to assert or dominate some aspect of village social life. Families, like Nuer clans of classical anthropology, are visible only when in pursuit of a goal.

Yet this structure causes tensions to arise between families, for in any village there are limits on the number and sale of political "goals" as such, as well as a constant need on the part of families to re-create themselves in pursuit of one goal after another. Thus "family politics" have the potential to wreak havoc on many local institutions: school superintendents and police chiefs are perhaps the best examples of this. I was once told that one could be a police officer in any of the larger native villages for as long as one wanted, but that no one will ever last more than one or two years as chief. This is because, in effect, families *realize* themselves (in the sense of becoming real or concrete) through political activity. And as such, political activity is important as much for its constitutive functions as for the goals pursued. Individuals in Hydaburg once described to me the removal of a school superintendent as simply a family "flexing its muscles." Yet to extend this metaphor, other families can in turn "flex their own muscles" by trying to block this same goal, all regardless of the performance of the individual or position at stake.

The repercussions are manifold, and they affect in important ways the political institutions introduced in the last chapter. Thus in one village, the present mayor (now in his third term) is a non-native from Texas. It is widely acknowledged that much of his election success stems from the fact that he is not affiliated with any one family. Were he to become a member of one of this village's four or five families, there is little doubt that the others would join together to prevent him from being elected to a further term. Knowing this, he maintains cordial but intentionally distant relationships with the leaders of all the families in the village.

What turns this broader social tension into tensions within families is the fact that the exercise of power in these circumstances (i.e., where power *must* be exercised for it to be held) inevitably means that crucial political economic issues will provoke, in most villages, a state of near constant struggle. This has a large effect on those who live their lives at the margins of these issues—that is, those whose fates are tied to the political basketballs that are bounced around between families. In these circumstances, some members of every family pay a higher price than others for the continuous constitution of family standing. For when a family secures a government job for one of its members, it secures a job for only that member, the benefits of which will never reach all of the members of the family that secured the job. In this way, no family is ever capable of meeting the needs of all of its members, and perhaps is incapable of meeting the needs of even most of its members.

Yet few families are in a position to free themselves from this situation by eliminating marginal members. The reason for this is quite simple: most families exercise power through voting. Numbers matter when electing village councils, mayors, IRA council members, ANCSA board members, ANB representatives, and so on. And even apart from formal elections, large numbers can also be important for the sheer magnitude of their collective participation in such things as churches or native dance groups, or even in town meetings, where numbers can add up to influence. For this reason, a family must be large to be powerful.

48

For family leaders, this means recruiting even those with marginal kin links to the family and unsure status within the village. For those on the margins, participation means at least the potential to gain some favor, and in the dire economic circumstances in which most families function, this potential is about all that many marginal households can hope for. As a result, less central members of families often remain members of these groups despite the lack of any immediate benefits.

One implication of this is that any family will be made up of people with very different needs, hopes, and expectations. And because past political and economic dynamics and contemporary systems of patronage combine to make all villages stratified, all families are highly stratified as well. The result is that all powerful families are also diverse, socially and economically. For to draw the lines sufficiently broadly to become a real family, it is necessary to include individuals and households with very different political and economic needs, needs that drive these marginal individuals to seek out powerful patrons or families that might meet these needs. This means that every family contains members with very different *but sometimes very immediate* political and economic expectations.

Thus, in an example drawn from the material covered in chapter 4, when a family is forced to choose—to throw what few resources even the most successful of them have—between subsistence rights on the one side and jobs in logging on the other, either choice will negatively affect some of their members. And either choice will probably cost the family some members, as those whose livelihoods are no longer possible will likely leave the village. Yet the family in question, to be a family, must choose. If individual members choose differently and for themselves, then the family ceases to be a real family and becomes just a group of relatives. When this happens, members are likely to leave and align themselves with other relatives or in-laws, hoping to gain thereby a better hearing for their needs or expectations. This is, in effect, how new families form and how all families try to grow in size, and thus in influence and power.

Movement in and out of the villages has always been a part of village life as well, and family dynamics reflect this. Family members who leave the village are still considered relatives and may be called on for help, as when college-age children board with relatives in Seattle or Anchorage.

But members who leave the village lose much of their influence in the family. Unless they are willing and perhaps even plan to move back to the village, they are unlikely to have any say in the use or sale of family resources, such as a family house or parcels of land. Likewise, those who leave are unlikely to have any say in family decisions regarding village or corporate politics, or the renegotiation of family alliances undertaken in their absence.

Yet families are seldom even remotely economically corporate. Some assets, such as old houses, tend to remain within families, but family-run businesses have a short life expectancy. In just about every village, one learns of a family store that went broke by extending too much credit to other members of its own family, who later could not or would not repay. In commercial fishing, once-common family boats are now very rare, partly because of the decline of the fisheries, but especially because of the inability of family boats to cut back on crew expenses quite so arbitrarily as non-family boats.

In the past, important families have been able to gain seats on tribal, village, or IRA councils, only to find that the demands made on the council members for jobs and patronage far outweigh the ability of the entire council, let alone a single councillor, to deliver. This has threatened the very existence of successful families, and some have disappeared as a result.

Note that this does not indicate a change in actual kinship relations, but rather reflects the many options open to any individual or household. For given the very general, loose means through which family affiliation is constructed, every individual has a number of options as to which family he or she will belong to. In this way, families can disappear without a single member actually passing away or leaving the village. Likewise, some families remain strong despite the near constant loss of individual members to outside jobs or other opportunities, usually through more strategic use of patronage and efforts aimed at recruiting marginal members.

In the following sections, continuing the vignette that began this chapter, I will provide examples of one powerful family (that of the election organizer) and one marginal household (aligned with the radicals).[3] Here it is apparent that differences between centrality and marginality in village political systems are necessarily incompletely tied to larger forms of differentiation, such as that between rich and poor in non-village Alaska. Yet (in an analytical point to which we will return at the end of the chapter) one must remember that all family politics turn on the ability of family leaders to simultaneously bridge the gap between rich and poor members and to selectively alienate members whose demands conflict with the potential of the family to sustain itself as a powerful entity. When operated well, families can assume long-term, corporate existence and considerable local power. When handled poorly, they can seem to disappear altogether, even without the passing or exit of a single member.

The Ins

The Jamisons are the current descendants of a former native school-teacher, Clara, who was born in Southeast Alaska in the late 1800s. The current Jamison family is among the most powerful families in its village, and until recently they had dominated village politics for more than three decades. Yet none of their power comes from any status in precolonial systems of clan or housegroup relations. The late Clara Jamison was an orphan and was raised, with her mother's brother's consent, by a family of missionaries. Later, as a young woman, she married a white man, one of the early colonists in the region. He had been a sawmill operator associated with a mission group in the village where she was born.

Her status, and the status of the family she started, came from her connections with the world beyond the village. Clara Jamison was one of the first individuals from the village to get a teacher's license, and she taught in the village where she was born for more than forty years. Her husband died long before she did—indeed, she passed away only recently, well into her nineties.

Beyond her connections to the world outside the village, Clara Jamison was also an authority on village matters. She spoke fluent Tlingit and had been instructed by her uncles (on her mother's side) in much tradition and folklore. Her place between the village and the larger political economy in which it was embedded allowed her to make critical political and social connections with the world beyond the village. The power of these connections was apparent at her memorial dinner, which attracted people from all over the region.

Together the couple had four children, three boys and one girl. Two of the boys remained in the village; the daughter and one son moved away to one of the larger cities in the state, where they still live. Evan, the elder of the sons who remained in the village, is a fisherman, one of the few commercial fishermen left in the village. He was and is a "highliner"—the owner of a commercially successful boat—and the status he gains from this allowed him to become mayor of the village several years ago. Today, to remain financially successful in the shrinking fishing industry, he has withdrawn from village politics and now fishes nonstop for eight months each year. He holds limited-entry permits in several fisheries outside the region and a purse seine license for local waters. He and his wife have no children. She remains in the village while he is away fishing, but she is not from there and remains apart from family politics.

The younger brother, Henry, works in the village as a maintenance man on village-owned buildings. He got this job when Evan was mayor of the village and has kept it ever since. Like his brother, he is well known in the community, though less commercially successful or politically prominent. He has never married, and has no children. Both brothers are known for their local knowledge and their use of subsistence resources. It is a common sentiment around the village that on any given day you will see one or the other heading out of the village at the crack of dawn to collect cockles or mussels, pull a crab pot or two, net some shrimp, gather wood for the stove, or go hunting on one of the nearby unlogged islands.

Evan was mayor for several terms. He was also involved in the IRA council when it gave over the majority of its responsibilities to T&H in the late 1980s. Many people in the village resent him for this. Even greater resentment concerns the IRA council's financial dealings during the time Evan was a central member. The village IRA council then owned a cannery and some facilities, which they had originally purchased in the 1940s. The cannery had functioned off and on into the 1970s, generally subcontracted to a processor who would then hire people from the village as laborers and buy fish from local boats.

The leasing system was always more of an employment scheme and a means for allowing local boats to "stay local" than it was a commercially aggressive business, and as a result the IRA council seldom received much financial compensation from the contractor. Membership on the IRA council at the time, however, allowed council members to have a say in which contractor ran the cannery, and thus they were in a position to assure their own and their family's continued role in the fishery—for like cannery owners in the past, IRA councils and cannery contractors in the 1970s often provided the financing for fishing boats and materials. After limited entry, when the number of boats fell and the canned salmon market, already depressed, was dealt its final blow, the cannery was refitted for several successive purposes: to process shrimp; as a cold storage for the fresh fish market; and as a fish-egg packinghouse that sent salmon roe to Japan. While times were troubled for many families, control of the IRA council at this time meant at least the possibility of having some family members hired on during the refitting or as workers at the plant when it did operate.

It is unclear to most people in the village where the funds for this refitting came from and what role individual council members had in choosing those contracted to run the operations. There has arisen some suspicion (though I emphasize that I have no knowledge of actual evidence) that several board members, including Evan Jamison, were compensated as a part of the deals that were struck.

The most recent contract holder, however, went bankrupt and sued the IRA council for money invested and opportunity lost as a result of breach of contract. The arbitrator found in favor of the contractor and awarded damages. The only asset of the IRA council, the revamped fish-processing house and cannery building, was awarded in lieu of damages. Many of those in the village blame the then-current board for the loss of the cannery, and some hold the two leaders of the board—one of whom was Evan Jamison—personally responsible. Since that time, Evan Jamison has gone out of politics, never again running for mayor or for the IRA council. His younger brother, Henry, had never been involved in formal politics. All of his influence is carried out informally, and this has diminished as the suspicions around his brother have grown. Thus, in effect, the older generation of Jamisons has been out of politics since the late 1980s.

In many villages, this might have meant the end of the Jamisons as a real family, especially because neither of these central members has any children. Yet despite past suspicions, a limited number of direct kin links, and a diminished role in the formal politics of the village, the Jamisons remain one of the most powerful families in the village.

Their influence comes from two places. First, two members of the most recent generation—a daughter and son of Clara Jamison's daughter (who had moved away from the village)—have been educated outside the village and now have returned. The daughter, Jean, has a college degree, and her brother, Tim, has a technical degree. Both have lived outside the village for extended periods of time, but they have used this time to forge important links with regional political entities: the BIA, non-native politicians, and T&H.

Jean was once the village representative to the Tlingit and Haida Central Council, and thus she knows and is well known to the administration of that body. Tim worked for several of the logging contractors hired to log the village's ANCSA corporation land. This experience, and his family name, have allowed him to play a central role in several of the village ANCSA corporation's board of director elections even when he was not a candidate. At present he holds a seat on that board. Jean has recently been part of an effort to revive the IRA council within the village, with the help of T&H, as discussed above.

Neither Jean nor Tim has a large household of his or her own, and neither is married to a member of another prominent family. In fact, both have married individuals from what might be called more marginal households within the village.

Yet the size of the Jamison family is not limited to these links, and in a sense it might be enhanced by the lack of relatives with strong ties to these two new, central figures. The lack of immediate family members has prompted a number of marginal families to emphasize links that go back to the original generation of Jamisons (the schoolteacher and her husband), such as: "My dad's grandmother was a cousin of Clara Jamison, and she told me before she died that we were the same family before that." These sorts of links, in a village where many people marry and have children with more than one partner during the course of a lifetime, allow just about anyone to claim family ties like these. What makes the Jamisons likely candidates for such connection is both their powerful positions in the past and present and the fact that a lack of immediate family members makes the central core of relatives more dependent on what might be seen as voluntary—and thus potentially reciprocal—links and kinships.

The result of this situation is that the patronage expectations of these marginal kin on the current generation of Jamisons (neither of whom actually has the last name Jamison, since they are the children of a married daughter) are very high. This pressure is felt by both, though neither has been in a position of power long enough to have felt the loss of disgruntled members.

What remains clear, though is that the actual decision-making and organizing responsibilities of the family now lie with the current generation. The two uncles who remain in the village can and do lend support and advice on some issues, particularly when it comes to dealing with the leaders of other families—most of whom are a generation senior to the current Jamisons. But by and large they remain above most of the current machinations, leaving Jean and Tim to deal with the family politics. The power they wield as a result was recently made clear when both were elected by a wide margin in a village-wide election for a new tribal council.

The Outs

An example of a more marginal household comes from the other side of the struggle. This household is composed of a native man, his wife, who is of Aleut descent, and their four children. Neither parent has close relatives in the village. His parents live in a nearby city, hers in the Aleutians. Siblings of both live in these places as well. Their two oldest children have left the village, the daughter to live with her maternal grandparents, a son to go fishing in a nearby, predominantly white town. The two younger boys still live at home. The older of these is in high school, the younger in grade school.

The father, Tom, is an occasional heavy-equipment operator, having been trained in the 1970s when he worked on the pipeline. The mother, Mary, was primarily a housewife for the first decade of their marriage, but she has recently gotten a job with the Head Start program and is now employed full-time. Tom now stays home with the younger son and is seldom employed full-time. When there is a log ship in the village he works as a longshorer, and he wishes he could get a job driving a crane for the loading and unloading of these ships. But he has no formal training in this, and only those people with family connections get the training, he says. Longshoreman work comes along about once every month or two in this village, though in the past it was more frequent. In a good day on the ship he can make one hundred dollars as a longshorer, and sometimes he will get three or four days in a row.

For the most part the household lives on Mary's salary and what government assistance they can get. They live in a T&H-built house that is in constant need of repair, but they have a relatively new truck and are up to date on their bills.

On the side Mary makes cakes for special occasions such as birthdays and retirement parties. These bring in a little cash, perhaps as often as once every two weeks. Tom pursues subsistence activities, though perhaps not as regularly as some. He has a skiff and a net, and often he will lend these out to a friend for a share of the catch. He has a partner in subsistence, a friend since childhood, with whom he fishes during the peak salmon runs, and they hunt deer together on occasion as well. He also receives fish from commercial boat crews and skippers who give him by-catch king salmon (for which they have no permit) for a share of the smoked fish he will make from it. Though Tom uses fewer of the alternative subsistence species (shellfish, crabs, seals, seaweed), and despite the fact that he takes a sometimes casual approach to fishing and hunting, their household is among the highest users of fish and deer in the village, and is known for its large smokehouse and carefully smoked fish.

Tom grew up in a commercial fishing family. His father and elder brother are both fishermen—his father now mostly retired. His brother inherited the family seine boat, and his father sold his seining permit years ago. Tom says that he does not feel excluded, though he wishes he had gotten some of the money from the sale of the license (based on the fact that he could have asked for it, he says, and they would probably have given it to him). But he does not like commercial fishing and is for the most part glad to be left out.

Jobs for heavy-equipment operators were available when ANCSA corporations first began road-building plans back in the 1980s (see chapter 3 on ANCSA), but Tom failed to act right away and was too late for anything but a second-tier job on one of the older machines. Rather than do this, he stays at home. He talks about going back to work at times, but knows that the situation has not changed and that he lacks the connections to get the type of job he wants. "It's all connections," he states plainly.

The lack of immediate kin connections with anyone in the village has caused Tom and his family to be loosely affiliated with several families in the past several years. Tom claims a distant link (great-grandparent

56

generation) to the most powerful family in the village, the Jamisons, and his middle son refers to a member of that family as his uncle. Most often in the past he has voted along with this family and been counted as a part of it by core members of the other families.

But these connections waned as that family gained considerable power in the village, including leadership of the tribal board and a seat on the village council. Tom had hoped that this might turn into a salaried job, but nothing came of it. Things came to a head when he was passed over for a village job about three years ago. The details are revealing of the expectations marginal households have of the families they join.

In this village, few families have paid their trash bill at any time in the recent past; some because they cannot afford to, others because the village government has shown little will to collect the money owed. In response the village decided to let those who wanted to, and who owed more than one year's bill, to work on the trash truck for a week. Rather than receiving pay, these volunteer laborers would substitute one week's work for one year's trash fees. Problems arose for Tom when most of the people in the village signed up to work on the truck rather than pay their bill—so many, in fact, that they had more weeklong volunteers than weeks in the year.

At the time there remained one permanent worker on the truck, the driver. The volunteers would replace the other permanent worker, who had quit. Tom wanted to be put on the list of volunteers in order to advertise himself for the full-time job, should the village decide to replace the second worker on a permanent basis. When the senior member of the family with which he was then affiliated—who held a seat on the village council—could not or would not place his name near the top of the list of volunteers, Tom became disillusioned with this family and more or less cut his ties to it.

A few years later, when the individuals who eventually became the radicals began to lobby for local tribal government to replace T&H, Tom backed the reformers, hoping to earn a place in one of the two families involved. When this movement failed and the radical tribal movement dissolved, Tom remained associated with one of these families. But this family, having lost its last struggle, is not in a position to help Tom or his family. The senior members of this family note that they have always considered Tom and his household members of their family, ever since he was a child eating dinner at their house.

Tom reconciles his marginal place in the new family by saying that he was not getting anywhere with the other family anyway. For the time being he is willing to be counted (as much as anyone is counted when there is little political activity) among this new group despite the absence of any obvious or immediate rewards. The situation is fluid, though, and my suspicion is that he is just as likely to return to the Jamisons as he is to stay away.

Jobs

Were it not for two related political-economic changes that coincided with the limited-entry program, most native villages might have been abandoned by the late 1970s, as many of the non-native villages were. Family power at this time reached a historic low, as the chief means for holding together large, extended family groups—family-owned and -crewed fishing boats—began to gradually disappear from most native villages. As is clear in the examples above, rather than depend on family-owned boats and the jobs these provided, most family power (beginning in the early 1970s) derived from the ability to deliver patronage jobs in any of the many political structures discussed in chapter 1. An increase in the number of non-fishing, primarily public-sector jobs available and a growing ability of individuals in the village to control who got these jobs coincided with fishing's regionwide downturn to transform native villages in ways that non-native villages were not transformed, and perhaps saved many of Southeast Alaska's native villages from abandonment as a result. In the process, the types of ties necessary to become or remain a family were redefined.

The ultimate source of both of these changes was the discovery of large reserves of crude oil under native lands on Alaska's North Slope. The discovery led to a statewide settlement of all native land claims in order to transfer title to most of the oil-containing land to state and federal governments and to facilitate the leasing of drilling rights on the remaining lands. This settlement led to the introduction of settlement-based native corporations and sparked a dramatic increase in the size of local government throughout the state. For native villages, the institutions that resulted brought with them a host of new jobs, virtually all of which were controlled locally (most especially, munic-ipal government and village corporations). Families that had revolved around fishing either disappeared or turned their attention to these new opportunities. In many villages, new families emerged that were better able—or perhaps simply more willing—to lay claim to the sorts of jobs and the machinations necessary to control them.

The settlement that followed the oil discoveries—ANCSA—is discussed in more detail in the following chapter. Here we are concerned mainly with the effects of the growth of village government bureaucracies and their effect on local social organization.

After the 1970s, revenues from drilling leases on lands eventually taken by the state and tax revenues from the exploitation of other reserves on native or federal lands rose dramatically. To this day, Alaska collects virtually no taxes beyond corporate taxes. There is no state income tax, and in fact the state pays out a yearly dividend to all state residents from an annual fund set up with money from the original oil leases. Since the 1970s, consistent budget surpluses have led to an expansion of public employment at all levels, including the local or village level, where state funding supports many village-based projects. In 1965, 5,920 people in Southeast Alaska worked for state, local, and federal governments, 3,160 of them for state and local governments (Rogers, Listowski, and Brakel 1974:174 [table 79]). In 1990 the overall total was 11,860, of which 9,263 were state and local workers.

The differences are telling. During the two and one-half decades of oil revenue, federal employment in the region has actually dropped, while state and local governments tripled in size. Yet the working population of the region as a whole went from 17,470 in the early 1970 to 32,670 in 1990, or an 87 percent increase in roughly twenty years. What is more, much of the growth of administration has been in rural areas, while the majority of the population growth in the region has been confined to the large cities. In fact, many of the villages have retained a near constant population throughout this same period, while their local governments have tripled in size.

The result has been a complete transformation of village employment patterns. Even in the most industrialized Southeast villages, such as Kake, close to one-third of all workers are employed by the state, federal, or local governments. If contrasted with the number of those employed full-time and year-round—which most government employees are, and many other village occupations are not—the percentage would be much higher. In poorer villages with little local industry, such as Hydaburg, the ratio is staggering: 55 percent of all jobs are now in the public sector.[4]

Yet beyond the statistical shift, other, more crucial changes have accompanied this trend. The most notable is that many of the new jobs—indeed most, in some areas—are held by women. Women make up the majority of the employees at any of the federal health care clinics, run by Southeast Regional Health Corporation (SEARHC). Likewise, most of the new Head Start workers are women.

Within village governments, men still hold many of the more "public" of the public administration positions (mayor, city or village council member, magistrate), but numerically women often outnumber the men, holding almost all of the secretarial and mid-level administrator jobs. And while the majority of the public school teachers in the villages continue to come from outside the villages (and often outside the state), the majority of the remaining school positions are filled by local women—the support staff, secretaries, monitors, cafeteria workers, and so on.

In small villages, like Kluckwan, women are twice as likely to be employed as men. In larger villages, like Klawock, men's unemployment rates are twice as high as women's. Perhaps the best example is Angoon, where the numbers of men and women seeking jobs are closer than in some other villages. Here, among natives especially, the differences are telling: of the 113 native men in the labor force, 49 are employed; for native women, 67 of the 87 are employed. Women hold 67 of the 116 jobs (58 percent), while comprising 44 percent of the labor force.

For village families, these changes have far-reaching implications. While past family forms—centered around family boats or family stores—depended on the ability of a core group to mobilize capital (through connections to outside sources, like the BIA, as well as through their own ability to gather it through savings and work), new systems depend on family leaders' ability to mobilize votes. Elected positions (e.g., mayor or city council member) are the key to patronage positions. These positions have become more valuable as alternative employment in most villages has diminished.

Likewise, gender relations seem to have shifted in families, with women now playing a more central role in the leadership of many families. While family boats had formerly been run and crewed by men only, the vast majority of the jobs available through the patronage networks are now held by women. This has raised the status of women, for quite often now the "spoils" of the family system must be realized through women. It is no surprise, then, that in the vignette that opened this chapter, T&H chose two women to head the election committee. Nor should it be a surprise that a well-educated, well-connected woman in a powerful family was able to turn an entire village.

Beyond the massive expansion of public-sector employment, the second change that grew out of the oil boom was the Alaska Native Claims Settlement Act of 1971. This act, described in the next chapter, brought an unprecedented inflow of money and jobs to most villages. Just as surely, it created an entirely new set of political entities and dynamics into which village families then moved.

3

The Alaska Native Claims
Settlement Act

Norman is a well-known carver from a Tlingit village about two hundred miles north of the Canadian border at the base of the panhandle. He carves silver work as well as wooden hats and masks, all in traditional styles. Most of his work is sold locally, mainly within his own village. He is a son in one of the largest families in a large village, and just about everyone in the village on speaking terms with his family wears some piece of jewelry he has made. He also goes to the biannual cultural gathering of Southeast Alaska Natives—called Celebration—that is held in the state capital, sponsored by the ANCSA regional corporation Sealaska. This year, once again, he has a table in the hall set aside for native craftsmen to display and sell their work.

Because of the unusual venue, Norman has brought with him a smattering of work to suit many audiences—white and Indian tourists, dance group members, and serious collectors. One mask is priced at seven hundred dollars, which would pay for his entire trip, though he doubts he will sell it.

Cruise ship tourists pour through the hall, but often the prices surprise them. They settle for a T-shirt or a machine-cut silver bracelet stamped out in a shop in Seattle, or maybe Korea: the kind they sell at the airport. Norman isn't jealous. "I'd rather they got what they were looking for, rather than buy something of mine just to buy it." Other people, mostly natives, pass through the hall. Many of them are dancers from one or another of the region's village-based dance groups. There is, in fact, at least one dance group in almost every village, and some villages have more than one. They sing traditional songs and perform traditional dances. They also make and buy dancing regalia, which consists of button blankets (blue and red felt blankets embroidered with pearl-colored buttons in the shapes of traditional animal motifs), carved and woven hats, armbands, carved knives, necklaces, and other jewelry.

The dancers tend to make some of their regalia, especially the blankets, and buy other items from vendors like Norman. On his table he has several spruce-root and carved cedar hats, and rattles inlaid with mother-of-pearl that are carved in traditional animal shapes. These he hopes will interest the dancers. All are made in the style of older pieces, which is something virtually all dancers consider a crucial element of all of their regalia.

As we stand talking, one hat has the attention of a passerby. Though native, he is not dressed in dancing regalia as many of the others are. He holds up a hat and looks at the design. It's a carved hat, cut entirely from a single piece of red cedar. The shape is simple—a "Chinaman's hat," Norman calls it—narrow and almost pointed at the peak, flaring out at the sides. On the front is painted a raven design in typical Northwest Coast fashion, in two dimensions with selected anatomical features reduced to broad, symmetrical lines and placed in semi-symmetrical fashion.

"You stole this design," the man charges, quite unexpectedly. "You can't use this. It's not yours. It's my clan's."

Norman sits quietly. He is much older than the visitor; already a large man, he swells somewhat. But he doesn't say anything.

The man continues to accuse: "This raven is ours, our rights." His companion, a woman in her mid-forties, looks excited but does not join in. The visitor looks at the price tag: $400. He puts it down. "You can't sell this. It's intellectual property of our clan."

The last term startles me, though not because it is unfamiliar. The cultural heritage wing of Sealaska has been pursuing intellectual property rights for native designs and design styles for the past two years. This is a new twist, however, for the main purpose in pursuing these laws has been to keep non-Indians from copying and mass-producing classical work for the "airport art" market favored by the cruise ship visitors. A dispute between natives is different, and not just because it will never be fought out in court.

After the man leaves, Norman takes the hat off the table. When I ask him where the design came from, he tells me he copied it from a book. "That's the way everybody does it," he explains. "All of the old pieces are in museums. It's the only way to see if you're doing it right."

New Traditions

In the program for the recent Celebration '96—a regionwide gathering of all of the native dance groups, held every second year in the state capital, Juneau, and sponsored by the ANCSA regional corporation Sealaska—the chair of the Sealaska Heritage Foundation used his opening letter to explain that Celebration is a "new tradition." His point was aimed at some segments of his audience more than others. For many younger Southeast Alaska Natives, and even some middle aged and older, Celebration is the only large-scale native cultural event they have ever participated in. Thus for those in the Heritage Foundation, and others concerned with keeping up more "authentic" traditions, some clarification seemed justified. He writes:

> Every other year we gather again, and Celebration '96 is the eighth such gathering. Celebration is strong, but we must remember that it is a new tradition. In the Old Way, a clan from one side was usually host to another clan from the opposite side. For example, an Eagle clan would host a Raven clan, or a Raven clan would host an Eagle clan. Those who danced together as hosts or guests were from one clan or one side. Since the old times, people from each clan have scattered far and wide in search of work. Some clanspeople now gather as single-clan dance groups, but most groups at Celebration '96 represent many clans. Some are Tlingit, Haida, or Tsimshian, but some are combinations. As times change, our people have adapted.[1]

New traditions are not specific to Alaska or to natives, of course; most of what passes for tradition in the twentieth century is little older. Yet more is at stake here than the "invention of tradition"—however useful this notion has been for other purposes.[2]

Given what most people say and think about tradition, the notion of a "new tradition" would seem an oxymoron. In ordinary language, traditions are traditions because they are thought to have been practiced the same way for a long time. Something that is new, therefore, cannot be a real tradition.

Yet the history of traditions is far more complicated than such simple chronology implies. To begin with, the notion of tradition is always linked to questions of domination and resistance, rather than, or in addition to, questions of age and continuity. Traditions can be (and

65

most often are) those things that allow a group to stand apart from and often against its larger social setting; the traditions of virtually all ethnic communities and of classes within these communities fall into this category. Many such traditions are not very old, or have taken on their current meaning only when placed in a new social arena. In this way, "tradition" invokes a second and perhaps more accurate etymological history: tradition as that which stands outside of and against the current political order—linked to "betrayal," Raymond Williams points out (1980:318–19), and "traitor."[3] Traditions are, in this sense, that which set their participants apart from the wider social context, and usually against it. "New" traditions are just new means for doing this.

Of course, the label "traditional" has often been used as a stigma—a way to identify something that is out of place in changing times. Historically, this stigmatizing label likely came first to Native Americans, and only later was it seized upon as a way of mobilizing and creating differences that could be used to counter those same stigmatizing forces.

Alaska Natives, like most other Native Americans, have at times been forced into such alterior status, defined for political purposes as "traditional" peoples and forced to take up this ambivalent stigma—which is both a romantic glorification and a condemnation by those around them—as an identity of resistance. Yet such tactics were never their only option. Nor was traditionalism uniformly accepted as the best strategy. The number of model villages in Alaska provides ample evidence of other strategies. Where traditionalism has become an important identity for resistance, it is at least partly the result of people's choosing it, and convincing others to do the same.

In doing so, natives have often—and knowingly—given credence to an "otherizing" strategy practiced continuously for centuries (Sider 1987). More than simply marginal, native peoples have come to be seen and come to see themselves as "outsiders" or "others." This has caused some of them much pain—from inferior schools and health care, to the forcible removal of native children from their communities, to the housing of hazardous wastes on native lands, to the relocation of whole communities.

Yet this alterity has also been the source of many native groups' ongoing resurgence. It is what gives some tribes the right to open gambling casinos in states whose laws otherwise forbid it, or to run tax-free stores catering mainly to non-natives. In Alaska, native corporations can harvest the timber on their ANCSA settlement allotments without regard to federal regulations for the environment or endangered species. For this reason, as will be discussed in more detail below, many timber-processing companies have favored the allotment of more land to Southeast Native corporations, for unregulated harvests usually mean cheaper prices for timber processors.

This alterior status was perhaps more easily justified—by both natives and government administrators—when Native Americans were more obviously "Indians"—that is, when their lives revolved around a set of social institutions, symbols, and mutual relations more obviously in contrast with the wider society into which they had been absorbed. Today, such differences are more costly and not available to all. The resources required to continue to be seen as "Indians" are often beyond the reach of many groups, like the Lumbees or the Mashpees, and certainly beyond the reach of those more marginal individuals and families among already-recognized Indian tribes—like the Haidas and Tlingits of Alaska.

The point here—and it is critical for understanding the remainder of the chapter—is that, where groups have succeeded in having their own claims to Indianness recognized, they have done so by emphasizing some members' claims at the expense of other members' claims. Often this has meant sacrificing those hopes and claims that were less obviously different. Where people are both poor and native, collective struggles have centered more on claims attributable to nativeness than on those that come from being poor. The implications of these processes have gone largely unrecognized (even by native advocates), for little attention has been given to the effects of these changes on the intra-community dynamics of native tribes, villages, or families.

Federal laws regarding the legal status of native differentness have been continuously intensified and broadened since the 1950s. The collective effects of this process—the ever-greater precision with which natives must demonstrate their differentness—have been recognized by anthropologists like Gerald Sider (1993, 1987) and James Clifford (1988), just as they were demonstrated to Norman, the carver in the vignette above. Often, these laws have required groups to define either their history or themselves in ever more exact, ever more special and particular ways.

Two features of the emerging legal context of native differentness

Above: Native dance group. Dancing regalia feature native designs sewn in buttons on felt blankets. Similar material was found in the ashes of the bonfire begun at the Flo Ellers revival.

Below: Pie-eating contest on the Fourth of July

in Southeast Alaska concern us here: (1) the effect this process has had on economic, personal, and cultural differentiation *within* native communities; and (2) the long-term processual consequences of the laws governing differentness for Alaska Natives as a whole. For both of these issues, the political context is composed almost entirely of the Alaska Native Claims Settlement Act, or ANCSA (pronounced ANK-sa).

ANCSA *Phase* 1

Since its inception in 1971, the Alaska Native Claim Settlement Act has been the axis around which virtually all Alaska Native politics have turned.[4] ANCSA is a law—not a treaty—enacted by the U.S. Congress to settle and extinguish all of the outstanding land claims of Alaska Natives. It involved a cash payment to Alaska Natives of over $980 million and the retention by them of 40 million acres of land, with all of the remaining land in the state of Alaska becoming the property of the federal government and the state itself.

Importantly, however, neither the cash payments nor the land award-ed under the act went directly to the native organizations, tribes, clans, or villages whose claims the act sought to settle and extinguish. Rather, ANCSA created a number of public corporations to which the land and payments were transferred. Alaska Natives throughout the state were made stockholders in these corporations, thereby gaining some control over the rewards of the claims process, but only indirectly through their participation in the development of natural resources by ANCSA corporations.

The initial expectation of the act was that the corporations would use the money and land awarded by the state to produce income for themselves and their stockholders, speeding development of Alaska's dispersed resources and relieving the federal and state governments of costly support programs for the many remote native villages.

Prior to the 1960s, the federal government had shown little initiative in examining or settling native claims in Alaska. This changed, however, when large reserves of crude oil were discovered in Prudhoe Bay on Alaska's North Slope. This discovery, coupled with rising oil prices on the world market, prompted intense corporate pressure for a clarifica-tion of claims—pressure heightened by a decision by Secretary of the

Interior Stewart Udall that held up development of these oil fields until claims were addressed statewide.

The corporate format for the settlement was unapologetically, though ineffectually, assimilationist (see Berger 1985). Its aim was to produce resources, business firms, and wage laborers/stockholders. All of the elements of the act were aimed at this three-part goal. Through ANCSA, a village corporation was formed in each predominantly native village, with the corporation's shareholders drawn from the current native residents of the village, former native residents, and descendants of past native residents (the latter two categories regardless of current residence). The only limit was that an individual could enlist in only one village corporation. Those with ties to more than one village were forced to choose just one.

Each village corporation in Southeast Alaska was allowed to choose 23,040 acres of land, in most cases contiguous to the village itself, for development. Those villages whose surroundings were off-limits or un-suitable for development—like Angoon and Kluckwan—were allowed to choose parcels from islands with no permanent native populations. This meant that these parcels were hundreds of miles from their own villages, and inevitably in areas used by natives from other villages for subsistence hunting and fishing.

Most village corporations in Southeast Alaska chose parcels with valuable stands of old-growth timber with the intention of using that timber for commercial development. Mineral resources were seldom considered during the initial selection in the Southeast, because the subsurface rights to the village corporation land were not held by the village corporation but rather by the regional corporation.

Regional corporations were the second tier of companies set up by ANCSA. Under the terms of the act, the state was divided into twelve regions, and twelve regional corporations were created, one for each region. Shareholders in village corporations located within a particular region were issued shares in the respective regional corporation as well. In addition, some who were not village shareholders (most often because they missed enrollment, or were residents of villages denied village corporations) were enrolled in regional corporations as at-large shareholders.

In addition to the twelve regional corporations formed throughout the state, a thirteenth corporation was set up for those natives not then residing in Alaska and unlikely to return. This corporation was given a share of the cash awards but no land. The remaining twelve regional corporations were awarded more or less the same amount of land as the combined total of their particular region's village corporation holdings. Thus for every 23,040 acres issued to a Southeast Alaska village corporation, the regional corporation Sealaska was issued 23,040 acres as well, usually contiguous to the area selected by the village.

In addition, throughout the state the regional corporations were awarded the subsurface rights for their own land and for the lands of the village corporations within their region. This was meant to facilitate the development of North Slope oil reserves by fixing the negotiating power for drilling rights with a single board of directors—that of the Arctic Slope Regional Corporation. In this way, the oil companies hoped not to have to negotiate with those people, families, and villages most affected by the search for oil beneath their homes. Instead, a single contract could be worked out with the regional corporation for development beneath all the villages, regardless of the individual villages' opinions about the arrangement.[5]

In the Southeast region, the distribution of settlement funds preceded the selection and conveyance of land. Half of the total cash award was paid out to the regional corporations immediately after the passage of the act, with the rest staggered over the next ten years. The regional corporations were expected to redistribute a portion of this award to the village corporations and to pay out a percentage in "dividends" to their shareholders. The funds received by the village corporations and those remaining funds held by Sealaska were to be used to set up the corporate infrastructure and begin the development process.

Resource development was made more difficult by the delays in the conveyance of the land to the corporations. Less than 1 percent of the 540,000 acres awarded to native corporations in Southeast Alaska was conveyed by 1979, eight years after the act. Oil drilling and development on state and federal land had begun right away, however, and most natives could see the "other side" of the agreement reaping the benefits of the settlement. This led to great pressure in the first years of the act for a show of results by the ANCSA corporations.

In most villages this meant a distribution of village corporation cash assets as "dividends." In every village some individuals ran for

Logging ship loading logs in Hydaburg. Longshorers—very small when compared with the large ship—can be seen loading logs toward the front of the ship.

corporation directorships on this promise and were made corporate board members on this basis alone. As a result, when the conveyance of land did begin after 1979, the vast majority of the village corporations were strapped for cash, and many had to pledge their timber holdings for loans necessary to begin the development process.

On the shareholder side, the desire for some show of results was understandable from a number of standpoints. As mentioned in chapter 1, during the 1970s commercial fishing in Southeast Alaska had reached a historic nadir. The cannery boom that had created many of the small villages in the early 1900s was completely defunct, with only a handful of the more than one hundred former canneries still in operation.

Beyond this, the limited-entry permit system was causing many formerly prosperous families to sell their homes and holdings and move out of the villages. Household incomes throughout the region dropped significantly, and many longtime fishing families lost their boats. Indeed, one of the reasons why some individual natives chose to enroll in the regional corporation Sealaska as at-large shareholders, rather than joining a village corporation, was that at-large shareholders were paid more in the initial distributions than were shareholders in the village corporations. Individuals who elected to take this route received double checks in the initial distribution, and still receive dividend checks from Sealaska that are half again or even twice the amount received by village corporation shareholders.

ANCSA Phase 2

Two aspects of the unfolding of ANCSA make plain how the act and its amendments both defined and limited the sort of differentness it simultaneously sought to create. The first of these is the Net Operating Loss/land swap issue. The second is the issue of the "new natives," a question that has bothered Alaska Natives throughout the state since the passage of the act.

In Southeast Alaska, both of these issues were greatly affected by what have been called the 1987 amendments to the original ANCSA legislation. These amendments are also sometimes called the 1991 amendments because they were originally intended to offset a number of changes in the original law that were scheduled to take place in 1991. First among these changes was the question of the sale of ANCSA corporation shares to non-natives. The original ANCSA legislation had called for exclusively native shareholdership for the first twenty years. After that, voting shares were supposed to become available to anyone who would be interested in purchasing them, regardless of ethnic or racial categories.

By 1987, the 1991 moratorium on the exclusion of non-natives was rapidly approaching. The potential alienation of corporation land frightened many village residents. The possibility that people outside the village could somehow gain control of what were still considered collective assets—as had happened repeatedly in Native American history when group resources were privatized and distributed—had caused much worry throughout the state. The original impetus for the 1987 legislation was to alleviate this possibility by turning over to the shareholders themselves the decision of whether to allow the sale of shares to non-natives. In this way, only by shareholder vote could the rules about the alienability of corporation stock be altered from all-native status.

Yet much changed once Congress reopened the can of worms that ANCSA had created. By 1987 it was clear to all natives and any outsiders who wished to look that the original assimilationist hopes of the 1971 act had faded significantly. Few, even in Congress, still believed that the act could turn rural residents into wage workers and stockholder capitalists.

73

Instead, by 1987 it was very clear to village residents throughout Alaska that the act had failed entirely in two of its three original goals. While allowing for the rapid harvest of many of Alaska's dispersed mineral and natural resources, it had produced neither successful firms nor wage-based rural economies and workers. Even many of the most successful examples—which included several Southeast Alaska village corporations—met only one or another of the early goals. Some village and regional corporations had provided jobs for shareholders, and some had even made a profit and distributed the dividends to their shareholders. Few, however, did both, and by far the majority of ANCSA corporations throughout the state had done neither.

As a result, there was by 1987 a well-formed fear in the villages that individuals who had grown discouraged by the act would sell their shares, losing what little hold natives still had on the claims of their ancestors. In response, many natives began to advocate for the "tribal option." The tribal option was, briefly, the turning over of ANCSA village corporation assets (especially land) to the tribes and organizations whose claims had been the basis of the original act. Most of these tribes had established standing under the original Indian Reorganization Act in the 1930s and 1940s. And even in areas where tribal governments had been inoperative or mere shell organizations since the passage of ANCSA, these organizations still had sufficient legal standing to hold assets as Indian tribes, that is, under a different set of laws of alterity than ANCSA. Congress's deliberations about the amendments to ANCSA—begun originally to relieve the fears caused by the alienability provisions of the original act—now had to contend with an entirely new possibility. For Congress, the tribal option meant more than just a rejection of the original assimilationist intentions of ANCSA; it also meant the reintroduction of Indian territory in Alaska.[6]

In areas where the village corporations had performed poorly, the tribal option had, by 1987, grown increasingly popular. Many people who then expected little financial reward from their shares saw the tribal option as an opportunity to ensure future collective, tribal ownership and simultaneously to frustrate those who still saw ANCSA as a potential means for furthering assimilation and control of rural groups.

Congress's solution was to try to split the solidarity of the native community in Alaska by exploiting a division between those profitable or potentially profitable corporations on the one hand, and those that were unlikely to ever create a profit, regardless of what Congress did or said, on the other. If a way could be found, it was thought, to make more corporations profitable, then the resulting rift within the native representation could be used to quash the tribal option.

Net Operating Losses

The problem with profitability did not stem from a lack of individual or collective familiarity with the for-profit nature of the corporations, as some have argued. Most Southeast Alaska families had been involved in commercial ventures—commercial fishing boats, cannery labor and wage work, general stores—for generations. Rather, it had to do with both historical and structural issues that confronted Southeast villages in the early years of ANCSA. Two issues in particular had a critical impact on the success of village corporations.

The first issue, mentioned above, is that the monies awarded the village corporations in the early years of the act were often spent or distributed before the land was officially conveyed, leaving many village corporations without the start-up capital needed to begin an efficient timber-harvesting operation. In fact, most villages in the Southeast region did not receive their ANCSA-allocated land until almost a decade after the act.

During the intervening years, shareholders put tremendous pressure on the directors of the newly formed village corporations to distribute some of the cash awarded under ANCSA as "dividends," mainly to allow people to remain in the village until the expected boom of ANCSA timber production began. When the land was finally conveyed, many village corporations lacked the funds to begin a harvesting operation. Some opted to subcontract their harvests to outside firms, but such firms were under no pressure to hire native labor from the village whose timber they were harvesting. These strategies were unpopular with shareholders living in the village who hoped that ANCSA would replace livelihoods lost when fishing declined.

Other village corporations went into debt in order to purchase the necessary equipment to begin their own harvesting operation, often borrowing money from Asian timber-marketing firms who would then have considerable control over the sale of the timber. In many villages, such as Hydaburg, these options were tried sequentially. First, a timber-harvesting project was begun, based on borrowed funds. When this failed to produce dividends, an outside contractor was brought in to run the harvest.

Taken together, debt burdens and limited marketing options ensured that few village-based timber operations ever made a profit, though for three or four years many did employ large numbers of village residents at relatively good wages.

While seemingly a boon to communities struggling from the collapse of fishing, the job programs formed through ANCSA actually led to considerable conflict between shareholders in many village corporations. This led to the second reason why many village corporation timber operations failed, though to understand the source of these tensions we need to step back to a discussion of how village corporation shares were issued initially.

In 1971, shares in village and regional corporations were allocated according to very loose notions of village or regional residency (Gorsuch et al. 1994). Individual natives had three options for ANCSA enrollment. They could enroll as a resident of either the village or city in which they were resident at the time, a village in which they had lived in the past, or a village in which their parents or ancestors had lived. All of these were acceptable, as long as an individual enrolled in only one village corporation and consequently only one regional corporation. Indeed, many village corporations encouraged nonresidents to enroll in their corporations, for the initial cash distributions from the regional corporation to the village corporations were determined largely on a per capita basis. Thus the more people who signed up with a village corporation, the larger that corporation's piece of the initial pie.

The result of this process was that even in the immediate aftermath of the act, many village corporation shareholders were *not* residents of the village in which they held shares. These nonresident shareholders were a minority in the first years following the act, but the decline of the salmon fisheries and the demographics of the shareholder system meant that each year the relative proportion of nonresident shareholders increased.

For some nonresident shareholders, especially those who had left only recently, having timber operations run by the village corporation meant the possibility of a job and a return to the village. Yet for those now established in a new area, and in a new life, such a relocation was not feasible. For them any village corporation investment in jobs-related programs was simply a squandering of funds that ought to be distributed as dividends.

The conflict of interest between resident and nonresident sharehold-ers grew more tense when village corporation timber operations proved unable to turn a profit while simultaneously depleting large amounts of village liquid and solid (i.e., timber) capital. At that point many nonresident shareholders voted for board members who would shut down the village corporation timber operations, sell the timber on the stump, and distribute any profits.

Resident shareholders regarded these attempts at dissolution as selfish and extreme, and more poignantly, as attempts to drive them from the village. Presently, nonresident shareholders own the majority of shares in most village corporations, and most villages have gotten out of the timber business (and the job-providing business) altogether.

In the end it was the power of the nonresident shareholders that allowed Congress to subdue the tribal option. To do so, Congress included in the 1986 tax code and the 1987 amendments to ANCSA a Net Operating Loss (NOL) provision. This complex provision involved two steps. First, it extended a timber industry tax loophole to the ANCSA corporations in Southeast Alaska. For many years, timber producers throughout the United States had been allowed to claim decreases in the value of standing timber between purchase and harvest as operating losses. These losses could then be deducted from gross proceeds in a before-tax manner, exactly like the costs of harvesting the timber itself (i.e., the cost of the machinery, labor, and administration of the harvest process).

For ANCSA village corporations in Southeast Alaska, the decreases in the value of their standing timber had been sharp, though the losses were in some sense an accounting gimmick, because native corporations had not paid anything—in an immediate sense, that is, though they paid and continue to pay a heavy price in the loss of hope that a large land settlement once seemed to promise—for the timber itself. This meant that Southeast village corporations could show huge "paper losses" in the value of their standing timber.

Second, however, these losses did little good for tax purposes to the village corporations themselves. Few had ever turned a profit, and hence few had reason to be concerned with the tax advantages produced through NOLs. But the second part in the NOL provision put in place in the 1987 amendments—the provision that turned the paper loss into an enormous gain—was the ability to sell the losses to more profitable corporations as tax shelters.

The math is actually relatively simple. At high-end corporate tax rates, every dollar of profit a company earns is taxed at close to 50 percent. Thus, every dollar of loss absorbed by a profitable company saves $.50 in taxes. In this situation, if the company is able to acquire losses at, for example, $.35 per dollar of loss, they actually make back the $.35 spent on the loss and turn an additional profit of $.15 in tax savings for every dollar spent. By lowering their tax rate by the difference between the original tax amount and what is paid for the loss, profitable corporations were able to retain tax-free a greater portion of their corporate profits. And the greater the size of the debt a profitable corporation was able to purchase, the greater would be its gain.

What made Southeast timber corporations so inviting to highly profitable companies—like the Disney Corporation, which played a large role in the purchase of one Southeast village corporation's NOLs—was that they could generate huge paper losses based on the fall in the price of timber since the early 1970s. Some village corporations who had yet to harvest much of their timber by the late 1980s could show losses of close to $100 million. This "loss" had a market value of somewhere around $30–35 million. And even paying this much, Disney or another profitable company could ensure its shareholders a legal, $15–20 million tax shelter beyond the $30–35 million purchase price.

The only drawback for the ANCSA village corporations was that the timber had either to be sold on the stump or actually harvested for the losses to be actualized, and thus salable. This meant either harvesting their entire ANCSA holdings at once or selling the total timber holdings of the village corporation "on the stump" to an outside buyer. Most village corporations in Southeast Alaska chose the latter.[7]

For some village corporations, the NOL provisions in the 1987 legislation meant sudden, vast windfalls of cash and an abrupt end to advocacy for the tribal option. Yet this has done little to quell the tensions between resident and nonresident shareholders in Southeast villages. In fact, it may have aggravated these tensions by raising the stakes.

Since the early 1990s, most nonresident shareholders have sought an immediate distribution of NOL money. Village residents have sought the use of some money for the creation of village-sustaining industries (mainly in the fish-processing industry). Yet, as mentioned above, nonresident shareholders now make up a majority of the voting stock in virtually every village corporation. As a result, in most villages the "NOL money," as it was called, has been distributed in monthly amounts of $500 to $1,000 for every holder of one hundred shares (the number of shares issued a single individual in the original 1971 distribution).

In those few villages where a portion of the money was used to develop industries, such as Kake, these operations have struggled (as have all fishing-based operations in Southeast Alaska), and most have yet to produce a profit. In these cases there are today renewed calls by nonresidents for a liquidation of corporate assets and a final distribution of corporate resources.

At present, many villages have cut or sold their entire original timber allocations and distributed virtually all of the capital proceeds from both the harvest of the timber and the sale of NOLs. And despite the seemingly vast sums distributed to shareholders, many village households now foresee a severely limited economic future. Hoped-for revivals in the region's fishing industry have all but passed by native villages, and the number of commercial fishing operations in the region's poorest towns is generally now fixed at zero (Langdon 1989; Dinneford and Cohen 1989). As mentioned in chapter 1, the "forest primeval" visible from the cruise ships is in some areas all that remains of once usable hunting and fishing grounds, leaving villages stranded in what has become, ironically, an economic desert amidst a rain forest.

Likewise, many of the region's younger individuals missed entirely the distributions of NOL money, having been born after 1971 or having failed to enroll in a village corporation (often because they were away working at the time of the enrollment). Some of these individuals, now in their mid-twenties, have families as well. We will return to this issue below.

In response to the very real possibility of renewed village abandonments, the federal government has begun to propose a series of land swaps—the trading of parcels of clear-cut land owned by village corporations for new land with still-standing timber. The fee simple nature of ANCSA ownership has always meant that such lots can be harvested without regard to the environmental requirements imposed on public lands, and there is great pressure from the timber industry to continue to allocate such new lands to ANCSA corporations for this reason, for it is considerably more efficient to cut timber when there are no restrictions on harvest techniques.

Inevitably, though, the new lots of land offered in the swaps are always smaller than those for which they are traded; one can easily envision a vast reduction in native holdings throughout the region after a series of such swaps. Likewise, as future lots come to border those lots already clear-cut at the edges of the villages, such a strategy will in the long run result in the complete denuding of forest resources for vast stretches in those areas formerly used most heavily by village residents for their subsistence.

A second way in which ANCSA has limited native differentness in Southeast Alaska—even as the act defined and empowered it—is through the shareholder system itself and the issuing of shares only to those born prior to the passage of the original act.

No accommodations were made in ANCSA for the issuing of new shares to natives born after 1971—the "new natives," as they are called in Alaska. Under ANCSA's original structure, these individuals would only receive shares if the shares were given to them by someone who had received them in the initial 1971 distribution. This has left these individuals—many of whom are now adults with families—without a share in the collective claims on the lands around the village and largely without claims on the central political entities for natives in Alaska, the village and regional ANCSA corporations themselves.

The 1987 amendments also made no provision for the issuing of shares to new natives. Instead, it left it up to each village and regional corporation to decide whether to dilute their own shares in order to provide some to the next generation. In Southeast Alaska, where only a few corporations have formally considered or voted on the issue, opinion has been primarily against issuing shares to new natives. In fact, few ANCSA corporations have taken up the issue at all. Juneau's urban corporation, Goldbelt Inc., was the first to bring the question of shares for new natives to a shareholder-wide proxy vote. And in 1996, nine years after the amendments allowed for it, Goldbelt shareholders voted overwhelmingly to deny shares to new natives.[8]

The Limits on Being Indian

Taken altogether, one could, without exaggeration, summarize the structural dynamics of ANCSA, its amendments, and the entire packet of NOL legislation as program to limit the possibility of being Indian in Alaska in both extent and duration. For by limiting special-status political-economic participation to those who are shareholders, ANCSA has ensured that, of all those who claim native status and identity, only a fixed number of individuals will be allowed to participate *as natives* in the ongoing negotiation of village life within the social system in which every village—and every individual in the village—is embedded. By not issuing shares to the new natives, ANCSA shareholders have participated in this exclusion, though notably, most would deny that they had limited anyone's ability to "be native."

Much the same can be said of the chronological limits imposed by a series of land swaps now under way. These land swaps have been initiated by the Forest Service, under pressure from both the timber-processing industry and advocates for native corporations. In areas where Southeast-region ANCSA corporations have cut all of their timber, or sold it entirely on the stump, and in turn distributed all of the NOL money gained, the Forest Service has begun to offer parcels of land with standing timber in exchange for those already cut. The new, uncut parcels are inevitably smaller than those they are exchanged for, though often they contain choice timberlands.

Timber-processing corporations have favored such swaps because it turns public land into private land where environmental restrictions do not apply. And they can be relatively assured, given the past history of the ANCSA corporations, that the timber will be harvested entirely and quickly—more entirely and more quickly than those parcels leased directly to timber processors by the federal government, for which these same restrictions provide costly, time-consuming hurdles. ANCSA corporations and most village residents also support the swaps, largely because they enable corporations to remain profitable and allow many residents to remain in the villages. Even the state of Alaska has stepped in to promote these swaps, for by making rural villages more viable, land swaps alleviate much of the financial burden now carried by the state for rural schools and services.

Throughout, however, one can see quite plainly that the long-term result of a series of such swaps is the gradual diminution of lands held by natives, and thus of people's ability to "be native" — at least in a way that shapes, rather than is simply shaped by, the surrounding society. As native corporation holdings in the area are reduced to insignificant levels, and as more and more people who consider themselves native find themselves left out of any say in the management of village and regional corporations, the long-term dynamics of ANCSA become clear. In each case, "being native" under ANCSA is increasingly limited, both in power and, more devastatingly, over time. And as a greater proportion of native residents in the region are excluded from shareholder status, and their holdings (and role in the regional political economy) diminish, people find that their claims for being native outside ANCSA depend on a host of identity issues, and not on the control of significant social and material resources. In the end ANCSA turns out not to have been an assimilationist vehicle, but one of gradual, increasing marginalization. And as both the new natives and land-swap issues show, it is a process of marginalization that natives themselves are encouraged to participate in.

In contrast, many Alaska Natives would object to any characterization that equates being native with participation in corporate development activities, and many have opposed ANCSA for this reason, an effort with which I am entirely sympathetic. Yet the alternatives available to those seeking another way of being native are increasingly circumscribed by the evident hopelessness of ANCSA. One side of this struggle, the struggle for native hunting and fishing rights, is taken up in the next chapter.

4

Subsistence and the Cost of Culture

It's winter 1996, and I am staying in Hoonah, a large village (by Alaska standards) of about twelve hundred people. Like most Southeast Alaska villages, it is built in a relatively sheltered area along the coast of one of the region's many large islands. The Alexander Archipelago, in which Hoonah is located, is actually a submerged mountain chain, and in most places the land rises abruptly from the ocean. In areas near productive resources, and somewhat out of the weather—areas where good winter hunting and forage were available, and good defensive positions against occasional raids from neighbors or more distant travelers—people have built villages along the steep shores for at least the last ten thousand years. When the salmon canning industry came to the area in the late nineteenth century, companies built their industrial canning plants near existing villages to take advantage of native labor. Other villages relocated to be near the canneries in order to take advantage

of opportunities for cash income and access to novel Western goods. Hoonah is something of both. Originally a camping and work area for one of the several clans that later came to be known as the Hunakwan, or "Hoonah people," the village itself was formed shortly after the building of a cannery in the late 1800s when the Hunakwan moved to the present location.

The village itself is rather compact, with houses built up the hill that rises behind the village rather than out too far from the town center. One can walk from one end of the village (by the airport and the school) to the other (by the grocery store and the road to the cannery) in about fifteen minutes. Yet despite Hoonah's compact size, most residents have automobiles and about half of the roads are paved. Outside Hoonah there is a logging camp at Whitehorse about twenty miles to the south, and a religious settlement referred to as "the camp" beyond that. But travel on the roads outside town is limited to vehicles that can withstand the rough surface built for logging trucks, and no roads lead off the island. People coming and going from Hoonah travel by ferry or, more recently, by one of the small airplanes that link many of the out-island villages throughout the region. The ferry and air service connect Hoonah to all of the ten or so native villages in the area and to the region's three large (again by Alaska standards) cities: Juneau, Ketchikan, and Sitka. The ferry arrives and departs several times each week, carrying most of the village's material needs.

On this trip to Hoonah I am staying with Owen, a friend I met when he was running a "culture camp" in Kake, the village he is originally from. He now lives in Hoonah with his wife and six children in a small, five-room house along the waterfront. Owen is a subsistence hunter and fishermen; subsistence is his "livelihood," as he puts it. He also works on logging ships—work that people call "longshoring"—when one is in town. This wage work allows him to earn the money he needs for hunting and fishing supplies, for staples like rice and coffee, for the "light bill," and for things for his family. Yet altogether his income seldom exceeds three or four hundred dollars per month during the summer, and less during the winter. Quite often his wife

goes to the store to buy on credit, a deal she renegotiates each and every time with the store manager. In the past, when everyone in the town was involved in some form or another with commercial fishing and cannery work, winter credit was a regular part of most people's lives. Now, with commercial fishing all but gone from Hoonah, credit is scarce for those like Owen who are known to lack regular employment.

The day after I arrive, Owen invites me to go seal hunting with him and Mike, his subsistence "partner." Owen and I fished together frequently during a summer visit, and he knows I'm interested in the sorts of daily activities he and other subsistence workers participate in. This is my first time seal hunting—here or anywhere—and both Owen and Mike tell me it is illegal for whites. "You're not even supposed to be in the boat if we're seal hunting," they tell me laughingly, though they take me along anyway. I try to reassure them by saying that if we get caught, I will tell them that this is anthropology research. Neither actually seems very concerned, nor are they any more relaxed by my assurances. Fish and Game wardens do not patrol the winter hunters. Southeast Alaska's winters are too cold and dangerous for any but those most dependent on hunting for their basic food needs, and the wardens are reluctant to halt this sort of harvest, legal or illegal.

Winter conditions in Alaska, even in the more mild Southeast panhandle, are difficult. Around Hoonah, the ice and water are particularly dangerous, for Hoonah is located in the northern end of the region, across an open and broad bay from Glacier Bay and the permanently frozen Saint Elias Mountains. We leave the village at about six in the morning. The sun won't be up for another four and a half hours, and then it will only stay up for three hours. By two-thirty in the afternoon it will be dark again. We will stay out hunting until six in the evening. The temperature is five degrees Fahrenheit when we leave, and it remains below five degrees for the rest of the day, dipping down into the negative numbers in the evening. The wind is worse in the morning, when it blows about twenty-five miles per hour from the northeast, the coldest direction. The wind chill is about thirty-five below zero; we picked what turns out to be perhaps the coldest day of the year.

We take Owen's boat—a sixteen-foot aluminum skiff with a twenty-horsepower outboard motor—to travel down into the bay south of Hoonah where the seals shelter themselves from the weather and lounge about on the patches of ice along the shore. Mike and I sit in the bow while Owen operates the motor from the stern. We face backward, he faces forward, taking the oncoming wind and freezing spray directly on his face. Altogether we say very little to each other. Mike and Owen seem to know implicitly where we are going before we set out, and there is no discussion of any plan once we are in the boat.

When we get to the head of the bay that morning—or at least as close as we can before the frozen ocean forbids the boat to go any further—it's about seven-thirty. Owen directs the skiff in to the beach. The first hunting we will do is on land, hoping to catch seals still resting on top of the ice, but the wind was at our backs as we approached in the skiff and the noise of the motor has scared all the seals off the ice. Mike explains that it is difficult to hit a seal in the water because they seldom surface and can travel great distances underwater, staying down for up to twenty minutes. With no prospects in the bay, we return to the boat and travel up another inlet. On the way Owen shoots at one seal bobbing in the water beyond the ice, but he misses and it disappears below the surface.

In the next inlet, however, there are two seals, both in the water. Owen fires at one and misses, and both disappear. But shortly after, one reappears closer to the boat. Owen and Mike both laugh, and Owen shoots the seal quickly and easily. We move up on it with haste, for a dead seal in the water will occasionally sink. Mike puts a gaff hook through the eye of the seal, and we tow it into the beach. At the beach, Owen and Mike leave the skiff to work on the seal while I stand and watch. They cut out the internal organs, saving most, which they clean in the salt water. They strip the remains from inside the intestines as well, and wash and save these. Mike removes the long bones from the seal, leaving the skin intact except for the first cut up the belly and neck. Even the skull is removed without cutting the outer skin covering the face. The organs are then placed back in the chest cavity and the seal is placed in the bow of the boat. In all the operation takes less than ten minutes.

We've brought no food along, only a thermos of black coffee that is, by ten in the morning, cold. By eleven it's frozen slush and we pour it out. I've done little work beyond simply holding the boat at the beach to be sure it doesn't drift away. Even my camera won't work in this weather. I watch what I can, thinking of what I will write in my journal when we return this evening, but just as much I think about how cold my feet are, and

wonder how Owen can strip off his jacket and gloves and work in knee-deep water while dressing the seals we catch.

Several times, Owen drops Mike and me off at a point near the entrance to one or another of the many inlets south of Hoonah. We wait while he runs the outboard around the bay, scaring the seals into the water. The hope is that they will try to escape the inlet (and the motor) underwater and resurface where the inlet opens into the bay. If they do, Mike will try to shoot them from the point where we are standing. When Owen hears a shot, he returns to see if we hit something. We try this in a few places, but the seals never surface within range of where we are standing. "It's a lot of luck," Mike explains.

While we are waiting, Mike tells me stories about hunting with Owen. Mike and Owen are about the same age—late forties—but Mike states plainly that Owen taught him how to hunt. "Owen's like an old-time Indian," he explains. His family is originally from a village south of here called Kake; he came to Hoonah when he was married, and his wife's family is still in Hoonah. Owen's father, who still lives in Kake, is among the last of the traditional Tlingit orators. He had many children, of which Owen was among the youngest.

By the end of the day we have taken three seals. Two of them are quite large—over two hundred pounds. Each was killed in the same way, by a long-distance rifle shot from a moving boat when the seal was momentarily at the surface. Though Owen killed all three, Mike will take one of the larger seals and Owen will take the other two. This distribution is made with no discussion. At the beach, Mike simply says, "I'll take this one?"—half question, half statement. Owen doesn't say anything, and like that, it is settled. In all the two partners speak very little at any point in the day, perhaps a dozen sentences over the twelve hours of hunting.

Owen and I carry his two seals up the beach and into his house, where we place them on a tarp on the floor in the kitchen. Owen's son Lyle then begins the work of carving up the seals and separating the skin from the meat and fat. Lyle is about fourteen and already a very good hunter—he would have gone today, but I was lent his Mustang suit and other gear. He begins by running a knife between the skin and the seal meat and then stripping the fat from inside the skin, all the while being careful not to puncture or thin the skin in any one place. Such a slip would reduce its value, and the money from the skin is counted on to offset the costs of hunting. Lyle puts the fat he scrapes from the inside of the skin into a large pot, and when the pot is full he gets another. From a two-hundred-pound seal, people will sometimes recover thirty or more pounds of fat. At the height of winter like this, perhaps fifty or more pounds.

The fat will be rendered to produce oil, which is considered a valuable specialty food. People dip dried salmon and halibut in seal oil (or "seal grease," as it is referred to when it is refrigerated and becomes a semi-solid), much as some people put butter on bread. It is also used in a number of homemade remedies. A tablespoon of seal oil is said to cure digestion troubles.

The organs of the seals are used more immediately. The heart and liver are sometimes used together to make a stew, as are deer heart and liver during the summer months. The remainder of the meat will be placed in a smokehouse—locked to keep the dogs from getting in—and used when necessary. People in Hoonah eat seal meat in stews, and they barbecue the ribs. They will deep-fry the intestines, cut into short pieces, which are little different from the deep-fried pig intestines eaten in the American South.

A large portion of the meat will be distributed to friends and to older people who like it. Owen talks about giving the entire smaller seal to the senior center in town. Around town, Owen is known as a good hunter and a generous man, and he is well liked as a result. The oil that is rendered from the fat will be distributed too, usually in pint mason jars, to people who like it or who "need it," as Owen says. When someone in town is planning an event, Owen can be counted on to donate "Indian foods," which raise the prestige of the occasion. When he does, he is acknowledged by the host.

While Lyle works on the seals, Owen and I sit and watch television. We drink black coffee and eat cake made from a boxed mix with sugar and lard frosting. There is rice mixed with seaweed on the stove, and when Lyle is finished working on the seals he will make a dinner of seal meat stew.

Owen and I talk a little about the day—mostly at my prompting—which he considered a successful hunt, though he had expected to get more than three seals. I ask about the danger, and whether he thinks the risk involved in winter hunting is worth it. On our return, as the temperature dropped and the wind died down, the entire southern section of the bay began to freeze, and at times our small boat had trouble breaking through the ice. In the end we went out further in the bay in order to

loop around and come in from a direction the remaining wind had kept clear, but there the waves were higher and more dangerous. To me, the chance of being overturned or trapped in the ice overnight seems a high price to pay for three seals.

To my surprise, Owen does not justify the risks with reasons drawn from the obvious economic necessity in which he is trying to raise a family, though he might well have, for he is very conscious of it in other ways and at other times. In fact, virtually all of the most regular subsistence hunters are among the poorest people in any of Southeast Alaska's villages. I knew there was nothing else to eat in Owen's house that day, and that—as was often the case during my summer visits—the fruits of our hunting or fishing were for immediate consumption. Instead, Owen justifies what he has done by saying that this is his life, his "culture."

Thomas Berger, in his survey of Alaska villages in the mid-1980s, found this to be a common sentiment throughout the state, and referred to it as the "subsistence way of life" (Berger 1985). By "way of life," Berger meant more than just livelihood in the sense we normally understand the term—more than simply a way of earning the necessities of life. He meant that it was a way of being in the world that created meaning—more than just survival. Had Owen read Berger's book, he would likely have agreed, and would just as likely have used the term "culture" to describe what Berger referred to as "way of life." Many of the Alaska Natives to whom Berger spoke did, in fact, use the term "culture" in this way.

Owen would add: "I like hunting." He would later tell me that he wouldn't know what to do if he didn't hunt or fish: it is what he does with most of his days. "It's who he is," Mike would explain.

Subsistence and Land Claims

For reasons that have as much to do with laws passed in the last three decades as they do with the long-term changes in village economies, subsistence—the fundamental place of hunting and gathering in native lives and families—has emerged as the key issue for village residents seeking to resist larger-than-local forces. In particular, native advocates have used subsistence to counter external political manipulation in two ways: first, and largely in the past, by demonstrating de facto possession of lands and resources sought for expropriation and development by outside interests; and second, by making use of the social relations and sentiments spawned by subsistence work that lie outside the relations of the current political economy, around which ties within and between communities can be mobilized.[1]

Much of the history of the former—the use of subsistence to demonstrate past occupation of disputed lands during the late 1950s and early 1960s—has been published recently by the Sealaska Cultural Heritage Foundation in Haa Aaní, Our Land: Tlingit and Haida Land Rights and Use (Goldschmidt and Haas 1998). In fact, the form of the final statewide land settlement—the Alaska Native Claims Settlement Act (ANCSA)—was in large part prompted by lawsuits fought and won in the U.S. Court of Claims on the basis of continuing de facto possession of subsistence areas. This and other small victories did much to demonstrate to natives throughout Alaska that their claims could be used to pose serious, time-consuming roadblocks to unsatisfactory land settlements, and hence could be used to delay government and industry access to Alaska's natural resources, most especially oil.

In these cases, and principally the land claims case brought by the

89

Tlingit and Haida Central Council in the 1950s and 1960s,[2] subsistence and traditional-use practices also played a large role in both mobilizing support among village residents—by counterposing development with people's continued reliance on certain areas—and establishing a historical record of land and resource use (Berry 1975; Thornton 1998).[3]

More recently, however, some natives have wanted to turn the issue of subsistence away from any direct historical connection to land claims, seeking instead to contrast subsistence practices with the sorts of relations that emerge through and from ANCSA. This change has been critical in reshaping the regional political landscape, but it has also, perhaps inadvertently, brought about deep changes in the place of subsistence hunting, fishing, and gathering in every Southeast Alaska community.

In one way, the opposition between subsistence and ANCSA was determined by ANCSA itself. One provision in the original act eliminated any special rights to subsistence use or harvest by natives on lands taken by the state of Alaska and the federal government (see Berger 1985:60–65). This meant no special access to roughly four-fifths of the territory within Alaska's borders, including virtually all of those areas that natives had previously considered crucial to subsistence and traditional-use practices. A host of litigation followed, and in 1980 the Alaska National Interest Land Conservation Act (ANILCA) was signed into law as a partial remedy to these problems. Even now, however, the implementation of ANILCA has remained partial, and the disputes generated by ANCSA's subsistence-ending provisions are far from over.[4]

Beyond this, however, subsistence has always been an issue with strong emotional resonance throughout Alaska. In his travels across the state, advocate and Canadian federal judge Thomas Berger noted the central place subsistence played in native reactions to the act. He was told: "Subsistence to us is . . . our spiritual way of life, our culture" and "This land is part of . . . our identity. The land is very important. It is part of the religion, it's part of the heritage, and to put a dollar value on it would be something that would [only] come from Congress." One Southeast Alaska Native noted: "Us Natives, we should have the right to live out our culture, something that cannot die . . . to take away our culture would be to take away our lives, everything we knew, everything our parents knew, everything our children should know. . . . What is that billion dollars? I'd rather have my fishing and hunting rights" (Berger 1985: photo captions).

The irony of this last statement, that culture is something that cannot—in the sense of must not—die if people are to live, and which the speaker clearly feels to be imperiled by ANCSA, seems to capture the central yet ambiguous place of subsistence and the culture that surrounds it in the post-ANCSA period. Over and over again, Berger was told (as was I) that subsistence and native culture are so closely knit that it is impossible to have one without the other.

The predicament most natives find themselves in, then, is that while ANCSA empowers some ways of being native, it simultaneously undermines what most natives consider the basis for a distinctive native culture—subsistence. For this reason, subsistence rights and traditional-use practices have emerged as key elements in native identity struggles in the post-ANCSA period.[5] This point is complex and surprising, not easily characterized by notions of insider versus outsider or white versus native. Understanding it begins, however, with recognizing that there is more to subsistence than simply traditional-use hunting and fishing. It is, for those most regularly involved, a livelihood. This point, which ought to accompany any discussion of subsistence, past or present, is conspicuously absent from the current discourse on subsistence as the basis for native identity and lifestyle. Recognizing it necessarily complicates the symbolic role of subsistence practice in contemporary debates, and muddies the water surrounding the sides that define this debate.[6]

The complexity of the situation is most apparent to those most dependent on subsistence foods for daily survival. Many of the more regular subsistence users I knew in Alaska—Owen or Joe, for example—would agree that subsistence means more to them than simply a way to make a living. They would agree with Berger's conclusions—that subsistence is a way of life that informs and shapes almost every part of their lives and the lives of those they are closest to. But they also insisted that subsistence is a livelihood, and that as such, it was something far beyond an identity. For most heavy subsistence users, subsistence is not something they felt they could choose to leave, or that they had chosen to take up. Even more importantly, for them, anything that limited or put an end to subsistence work meant not simply the loss of an identity, but far more immediately, the loss of family, home, and just about their entire lives.

Yet these same people—Owen, Joe, or the ten or so households like theirs in every village (out of, say, thirty to fifty)—are also among the more marginal individuals in their communities. And they are marginal for reasons that are closely related to their subsistence livelihood. For most, it is impossible to say whether they turned to subsistence because of their marginality or whether their marginality stems from their opting out of much of the local economy. Yet either way, the end result is the same: those who are most dependent on subsistence for their livelihood are also those least likely to have a say in how subsistence—as a political issue and central aspect of native identity—is manipulated, assessed, or even asserted.

The remainder of this chapter is devoted to fleshing out both sides of the subsistence issue: on the one hand, how it is that subsistence has come to be the central issue in assessing the failure of ANCSA in Southeast Alaska, and on the other hand, how this political centralization has turned attention away from the issue of subsistence livelihood—the perspective of the most regular, most dependent users of subsistence resources. The purpose of this discussion, however, is to rejoin the issues raised in the introduction—specifically, to examine how it is that people come to find themselves antagonistically opposed to a culture that is very much their own. For while subsistence identity has been a crucial element in resisting ANCSA, for those whose subsistence work remains first and foremost a livelihood, the cost of the symbolic role of subsistence in current cultural and political projects is very high.

Subsistence Relations

Beyond ANCSA's invocation of the subsistence issue, subsistence has become a rallying point in resisting the act for several reasons. The first is that the ecological decimation caused by ANCSA corporation harvests is the most visible, and most visibly disturbing, impact in the physical landscape that surrounds most Southeast Alaska villages. Around virtually every village, 25,000- to 50,000-acre patches of clear-cut forest constantly remind residents of the source and costs of their very limited political-economic success as natives. Most ecologists agree that it will take between one hundred and three hundred years to restore these areas to their pre-1980s condition.

The clear-cutting practices used by all ANCSA corporations create a host of problems beyond simple aesthetics, as well. Areas of ground without the normal, thick tree cover lose considerably more moisture to evaporation. As a result, streams normally fed by runoff tend to shallow up or dry up, both of which are disastrous to salmon that breed in these streams and to halibut that feed off the detritus where streams empty into the ocean. Likewise, streams left exposed to sunlight often rise in temperature, again making them unfit for salmon or trout spawning.

When clear-cut forests grow back, they raise another set of ecological problems. Normally, regrown areas sprout so many new saplings that they become, in effect, impassable, and not just for humans, but for deer as well. Without exaggeration, one can say that clear-cuts become impassable for even woodland creatures for at least the first one hundred years of their regrowth. Thinning the over-thick regrowth is possible, but it is also very expensive. Often ten or more trees must be cut for every tree left standing if the forest is to be returned to the density of growth it achieved in its old-growth phase.

Second, and just as important as the practical losses to subsistence caused by the act, subsistence practice seems a key element in resisting ANCSA because it provides people with a set of relations outside those imposed by the act itself—beyond the relations named in terms like "shareholder," "new native," or "resident" or "nonresident shareholder." Examples of this are apparent in the vignette that began this chapter and in the several stories that follow. Overall, subsistence practices in Southeast Alaska remain an important element in many local social relations, and more so in notions of community, kin ties, and people's aesthetic sense of the world around them. Indian foods are critical to many traditional social events, such as funerary services performed by the community (or one "side" of the community) for the family of the deceased.[7]

As importantly, subsistence practices provide the basis for critical patterns of cooperation among some segments of the village. Subsistence partners tend to maintain lifelong relations of sharing and cooperation in food-getting and food-processing practices. The total equipment necessary to any particular practice—beach seine fishing, for example—will be owned by individuals who fish together. One person will own the seine, another the boat and skiff. These individuals consider each other partners, and the relations so named tend to carry strong emotional ties, even if they are not always warm or close.[8]

Beyond partnering, aid in the production process allows many less physically able village residents to partake in subsistence products, and in the relations and prestige they provide. In villages where older people have less access to fish because they can no longer perform the labor of harvesting, elders will offer the use of their smokehouses and aid in processing fish caught by younger individuals in exchange for a share of the catch. The elders will wake frequently in the night to tend the smokehouse fire, curing all of the fish and keeping for themselves a portion. Such a system works especially well in areas like Hydaburg, where older individuals tend to own the prime fish-processing and fish-smoking locations along the beach.

A widespread notion of the historic importance of such patterns also plays a role in village-wide identities, even for those whose subsistence use is not prompted by economic necessity. People attach great value to Indian foods — to the extent that there is occasionally an informal cash market for rare products (e.g., *oolichan*, or "hooligan" oil). Likewise, beyond the actual relations of subsistence production developed between partners, many of the village's poorer families derive significant local prestige from their ability to provide traditional foods to those who spend little time hunting or fishing, but who nonetheless choose to demonstrate to the community their identity and native values. Thus a household known to take good care when processing fish will be given "by-catch" (i.e., fish that cannot be sold commercially because of out-of-season restrictions or lack of permits) by better-off commercial fishermen, which they will then process and keep a share of. When such foods are used for a party or social gathering, those who prepared them are always recognized.

The utility of the relations, sentiments, and identities produced in this way can be seen in one example from the village of Hydaburg. One summer in the early 1990s, an airplane used by Alaska Fish and Game enforcement officials spotted several subsistence fishermen fishing illegally. The fishermen knew that this meant an immediate visit from state enforcement officials. Knowing also that in addition to the illegal fishing, they already had an illegal number of fish, the crews returned quickly to Hydaburg, taking with them their entire catch, and radioing ahead to the village to tell of their predicament. When they arrived in

Hydaburg, shortly ahead of the game officers' boat, they were met at the dock by much of the town's adult population, altogether perhaps one hundred or more men and women. The boat's crew gave all of the fish to those gathered at the dock and then joined the crowd, waiting for the enforcement officials who would arrive by boat from the nearby non-native town of Craig.

When the officials did arrive, the gathered crowd prevented them from landing their own boat, taunting and mocking them. Eventually the officials gave up trying to land their boat or identify the individuals involved in the fishing. Later, when several state policemen arrived by automobile, the crowd reassembled to once again stand together for "native rights." In the end, no one was arrested and none of the fish taken. Many people, in speaking later of the incident, pointed out with pride: "We stood up for our culture."

Disputes between enforcement officials and subsistence users often mystify officials from the Department of Fish and Game. Most point out that the harvest levels are determined only after careful research on the levels of use common to particular villages and according to their best estimates of the ecological health of particular resources. As many natives are known to share these same concerns, Fish and Game administrators thus see the problem as deriving from a small group of overly stubborn individuals who flout the rules out of spite or ecological foolishness. Situations like that in Hydaburg—where entire villages seem to fall into the latter category—then seem strange and incomprehensible, feeding the stereotype that is common throughout the region: "Oh, that's just the Haidas. That's how they are."

Yet all of these issues point to a fact seldom discussed by advocates like Berger, and one that is especially absent among those who advocate subsistence as an alternative to ANCSA: subsistence use, and the time devoted to subsistence practices, tends to vary considerably within any community. Such a notion is similarly obscured by official statistics on subsistence harvests, which have been used to direct policy throughout the region.[9] Because these studies use only village-based aggregate figures, they seldom provide information on the variability of individual use. Thus native subsistence users are allowed six deer per year, based on the fact that most community-based studies show that the average household uses far less. Yet poor families—that is, those most likely to use subsistence resources for basic survival, who hunt and fish most frequently and are thus also most likely confront the enforcement personnel in charge of maintaining those limits—have told me that they need to harvest as many as forty deer per year, and to do so on a year-round basis. Their taking such a large harvest reflects a need for more than they themselves will eat. For while most of this harvest will be used within the household, some will be used to create and maintain social relations between subsistence partners and their kin and allies, and with the elite members of their own communities as well, or to forge links with a new family, or to intensify links with the family in which they are already members. All of these activities are critical in allowing more marginal households to remain in the village. This is what makes hunting more than simply hunting. It is also more than what Berger meant by "subsistence lifestyle." Importantly, the basis of this lifestyle, particularly for those who have no choice but to live within it, is more than simply the emotional attachment to particular practices and the sentiments these provoke. The sentiments aroused by practices that are as important and as fraught with the possibility of failure as subsistence hunting, fishing, and gathering—possibilities significantly heightened by laws against what many of the most regular users consider the minimum necessary harvest levels—are by no means clearly or unambiguously positive. I remember early on asking Owen if he liked to hunt. His expression was one of confusion and frustration. It was clear he had never considered it, and more clear that he was entirely unwilling to frame his work in such simplistic terms.

Similar issues of law and use apply to the harvest of salmon. Subsistence regulations in Southeast Alaska allow an individual to take six sockeye salmon on any given day. Issues of efficiency aside (for salmon are most easily caught when entire schools can be captured in a hand-pulled beach seine, and are otherwise seldom caught), many large households that are heavily dependent on subsistence require 450 to 500 fish annually. At six fish per day, this number would require more than seventy days of fishing. Given the fact that sockeye tend to school in places where they can be harvested for only two to three weeks, subsistence users dependent on a large number of fish must necessarily break the law and risk fine and imprisonment to do so. Likewise, the cost of fishing for six fish is not very different from the cost of fishing for one hundred or more, for one must still own and maintain a boat and seine and pay for the gasoline necessary to go to the fishing grounds. Likewise, the opportunity cost on seventy days of fishing as opposed to five or even ten—opportunity costs assessed in the loss of occasional, temporary cash employment or work on other, also briefly available subsistence resources like berries or other kinds of fish—is immense.

Throughout Alaska, those most dependent on subsistence as a livelihood are thus often forced to put themselves in serious legal jeopardy. Of those I knew in Southeast Alaska for whom subsistence was a livelihood, virtually all had been to court, and many had been to jail. Some had their boats or hunting equipment confiscated when they could not pay the cash fines levied for violations. Likewise, many of these same individuals live in houses that reflect the heavy toll that subsistence use extracts—houses that look more like workshops than like the other homes in the villages. Indeed, this has long been a necessity of large-scale subsistence production, and many older village residents point out that for this reason, most food processing in the distant past took place in camps built near resources, so the village could be kept "more sanitary."

In addition, all full-time subsistence users are dependent on the income of a spouse for the supplies necessary to hunt and fish: gasoline for boats, bullets for guns, heavy clothing for Alaska winters. Yet they also need their spouses to contribute labor to subsistence production—either through help in processing resources or in allowing them flexibility in other home responsibilities—to take advantage of briefly available resources or advantageous weather. Many relationships reflect this strain.

Changes in the village economy have further heightened these strains as well. Women are more likely to hold regular, year-round jobs than their husbands, meaning that they are better able to provide cash assistance to their husbands' hunting and fishing endeavors, but less able to provide the sorts of support that many women provided in the past—help in processing fish, for example, or in providing child care while a spouse goes hunting or fishing. Tensions like these tend to further marginalize those men who see their subsistence production as a livelihood, revealing a potentially hidden dimension of the dependence of subsistence work on the formal economy.

In fact, many women face the exceptional challenge of having to do both—having to provide the material support as well as the complementary labor for their husbands' subsistence work. At the same time,

Working on fish. Sockeye can be smoked or half-smoked in several different ways. Here, whole fish are hung up on stakes for about a day, then recut and rehung several times to ensure thorough drying.

their new role in the workplace further removes them, in the eyes of some, from the contemporary basis of traditional native culture and identity—that is, subsistence. Once thought of as particularly critical for their role in conserving native identity and tradition (see Drucker 1958), women now seem further removed from those roles. In response, perhaps, women now make up a majority of both dance group members and church members—activities that reflect how tensions surrounding culture and cultural production are intensified by gender lines.

Subsistence in the Larger Context

In general, households that take and consume more subsistence resources than others are those with the lowest or least-regular cash income. Underemployment contributes in two ways to increased subsistence use. First, families with lower cash income can save considerable money by using subsistence resources. A single deer frequently provides over fifty pounds of meat, enough to feed even a very large family for two weeks. Seal meat is similar in quantity (and usually greater), though because it is hunted by fewer individuals it is shared more widely. Fish provides constant summertime food, either fresh or half-smoked, cooked with potatoes or rice. Berries, seaweed, and grease or oil all provide vitamins and flavor. For poor families the importance of these resources is magnified by the high cost of groceries in most villages—due to the remoteness of most native villages, which increases transportation costs and, more commonly, allows a single supplier to set high prices.

A second way that unemployment and underemployment intersect with subsistence use is the time that most subsistence tasks require for any measure of efficiency. It makes little sense to drive all the way to the far end of the island (across, say, forty or fifty miles of gravel logging roads) to hunt one deer. Normally two or three men—"partners"—will make the trip together. If each takes a single deer, this cuts the expense of the trip (per person) by tripling the return. But this means waiting for all three men to take a deer, which frequently requires an entire, and often very long, day.

Seining salmon works similarly. Individuals who cannot commit to an entire day—and sometimes more than one, due to unforeseeable factors such as weather, mechanical factors such as boats or trucks

breaking down, or trouble with enforcement officials—cannot participate on the same level as someone whose time is largely his own.
Thus the households that make the greatest use of subsistence materials
are frequently *not* those employed in logging, or by the municipality,
schools, or health clinic, or in one of the few full-time occupations
in each village—checkout clerk at the grocery store, waitress or cook
at the coffee shop, or administrative employee for the village ANCSA
corporation.[10]

Commercial fishing might once have appeared on this list of full-
time occupations as well, though the nature of the enterprise has
always provided some resources for household consumption. More
recently, however, commercial fishing has been subject to rigid, frequently spread-out, official openings and closings such that commercial
fishermen now spend far more time tied up at the dock than they have
at any time in the past.[11] Altogether, it is not uncommon for seining
crews to spend three, four, or even five days at home between the end of
one fishing period and the beginning of another. Reduced commercial
fishing time has cut overall income for fishing families as well, further
contributing to the dependence of many on subsistence resources.

As a result, commercial fishermen of today participate much more
in day-to-day subsistence production than they did in the past. Yet
subsistence regulations require that no fishing equipment used in
commercial harvest be used for subsistence purposes. Commercial
fishermen who wish to participate in subsistence must thus maintain
two complete sets of fishing equipment. This means, of course, more
time and money spent in the purchase and upkeep of this equipment,
further adding to the cost of doing one or the other.

When ANCSA corporations elect to cut timber on land adjacent to
their own or to another village, they have a significant impact on the
"livelihood" side of subsistence use. Despite timber industry resistance
to the idea, logging greatly affects the ability of an ecosystem to support
and recover from human use. Timber harvests of 50,000 to 100,000 acres
around some villages mean, in effect, the elimination of vast stretches
of forest from subsistence production until the forest can return to the
ecologically sound old-growth status.

One result of the clearing of such large stretches of land immediately
around villages is that people dependent on fish and deer harvesting

must go further, at greater risk of accident and of encountering Fish and Game enforcement, to find foods that were formerly available locally. They also face greater competition in the areas to which they now must go, as other villages and an increasing number of tourists face similar problems of reduced habitat. Indeed, tourist competition has scarcely begun to affect the situation on the scale that it almost certainly will, and as more and more natives are now turning to "guiding" as a replacement for lost employment in the villages. In the near future, the number of tourists hunting and fishing in these areas is likely to increase considerably. Such problems are magnified by the possibility of further clear-cutting in areas made available through land swaps.

Yet there is seldom any open conflict between those who view subsistence as a key element of native identity and those for whom subsistence is foremost a livelihood. Individuals and households dependent on subsistence also view ANCSA as a threat to their ability to remain in the village or to remain together as a household.

One case where tensions did come to the surface, however, involved an attempt to establish in more formal political terms some elements of the identity argument that has been growing since the 1970s. The events took place in September 1994 and centered initially on a 1993 robbery by two young men, living in Seattle, of a pizza delivery person, during which they beat the delivery person badly. Both boys had kinship links to the village of Klawock, in Southeast Alaska, and it was at the urging of some of the boys' Alaska relatives that events unfolded the way they did.

Originally, charges in the case were brought by the state of Washington, though eventually an unusual plea bargain was reached. Both boys pleaded guilty to the robbery, but they were turned over to a "tribal judge" from Klawock for punishment. In addition, the judge and his panel assured the court that the "tribe" would absorb the responsibility for the $25,000 damages awarded by the court to the injured delivery person as a part of the settlement.

The main advocate for the plea bargain was Rudy James, of Klawock, who claimed to be a "tribal judge" of the "Kuiu Kwan" or Kuiu Tribe of Alaska. In August 1994 the boys were released by a Washington State Court into James's custody, and they returned to Klawock for a punishment hearing. During the hearing, James and eleven other "tribal judges" from around the region heard testimony from the boys, their

Hawaiian hard-smoked salmon. In this special recipe, the fish are soaked in soy sauce and pineapple juice before smoking.

victim, and the boys' families. After deliberations, the judges sentenced the two boys to banishment on one of the more remote islands in the region, separately, for one year. They would be provided with the equipment necessary to subsist for the year by the tribe, but they would have to survive without outside help or contact with family and friends. For this reason, the location of their banishment was kept secret. Following this sentencing, the boys were taken to the Klawock dock and from there by fishing boat to the punishment locations.

Reaction among other native leaders was predominantly outrage. The local IRA council president resigned, noting that the recognized tribal entity in Klawock, the Klawock Cooperative Association, did not recognize the court or any status claimed by James. Tlingit and Haida Central Council president Edward Thomas sent an affidavit to the Washington State Court noting that neither Rudy James nor any other member of the court was recognized as "tribal judge" by the Central Council; nor was James or anyone else empowered to pledge T&H tribal assets for the compensation awarded in the case. One native leader working for the Bureau of Indian Affairs agreed, saying, "This is theatrics. It has everything to do with Hollywood and nothing to do with truth and Tlingit culture."[12]

Indeed, the tribal judges seemed very sensitive to the numerous television cameras and magazine reporters that arrived to cover the trial. For the most part, the punishment had been decided before the hearing. The panel had spent the week prior deciding how long the banishment would be, what sort of supplies the boys would be allowed to take with them, and what would be forbidden. Finally, the panel made arrangements for the boys' removal to the island. Despite this, the hearing was held and testimony taken as though the decision was still pending. At the hearing itself, all of the judges wore ceremonial regalia. The boys also wore regalia, but it was worn inside out as "a sign of shame." The hearing was preceded by a cleansing ritual, in which a special plant was used to strike the walls of the local Alaska Native Brotherhood hall while invocations were made in Tlingit. The court panel entered in procession to the beat of a traditional drum, and rather than taking an oath, the boys were instructed to testify while holding sacred feathers—raven feathers for one boy, eagle for the other.

Even the gathering itself was given a native title, the "Kuye'di Kuiu Kwaan Tribal Court," although some pointed out that the Kuiu Kwan, or Kuiu people, were dispersed in the so-called Kake bombings by the U.S. Navy in the late nineteenth century. Indeed, the traditional tribal name for the village of Klawock is the Henya Kwan, and there is no current village whose residents are known as the Kuiu Kwan.

Many people in Klawock understood the events in local terms. By far the majority at the time (and more later) saw the trial as the effort of one family—that is, of James and his brothers—to move outside the traditional power politics of the village, controlled mainly by two families. Embert James acknowledged as much, saying, "This town is divided . . . there are some people here who are used to being the kingpins of this town, but this is not their show."[13]

Outside Klawock, where the particulars of family politics were less well known, the reaction was different. People pointed out that over the next year, the boys' families knew where they were and helped them out with supplies and visits. There were popular rumors that one of the boys had been seen around the nearby town of Craig prior to the end of his banishment. At one point, one of the boys was rumored to have been moved to another location after friends had found out where he was and the information became common knowledge.

For young people, the formation of the court was a welcome step toward tribal autonomy—one that the current bureaucracy had never undertaken. In addition, many appreciated the power of a "culture" that could cause a U.S. court to defer to its jurisdiction.

Among those most dependent on subsistence, the reaction was uniform and quite different. I was told: "If they're serious, it's a death sentence. And if they're not, there's no point in it." Others pointed out that none of the twelve court judges could possibly survive a year's banishment on an island. Still others noted that the boys, who were raised in the suburbs of Seattle, knew little of what it would take to survive alone in Alaska's forest.

The most dramatic comment came from Owen, who is perhaps among the most skilled hunters and outdoorsmen in all of Southeast Alaska. He said plainly: "I feel like they are making a mockery of my whole life."

Subsistence and Culture

In such stories it becomes immediately obvious that issues of subsistence are deeply caught up with cultural difference, as issues of culture are caught up with power, and issues of power are, at present, caught up with resource development. And resource development, especially in its current form, greatly affects subsistence. And in every instance, all of these struggles intensify, like waves in ever more shallow water, when they cross gender lines. As one of the judges in the Kuiu Kwan trial explained, no women served on the court because, "In our culture, we never let a woman tell the men folks what to do."[14] In each case, subsistence, gender, power, culture, and development nest inequality in overlapping, overdetermining ways.

This is, plainly, one of the reasons why subsistence issues have been so regular a part of the effort to halt development, and so sensitive to the shifting landscape of power that has emerged under ANCSA. It is also why the issue of native culture seems so quickly to become part of these same debates, even after direct ties to issues of land claims have been, in the eyes of perhaps most village residents, settled.

However, each of these connections—between subsistence, culture, power, gender, and development—rests on an assumption held by many, and introduced to us by Owen in the story that began this chapter: that by "culture," ordinary people like Owen mean something more than the sides that have evolved in the current political struggle, and also more than the plainly political notions of "tradition" (raised in chapter 3). In a way that Owen has never articulated to me, and which I can only estimate on the basis of our friendship, what he means by "culture" is a sort of connectedness to a particular set of meanings and practices, regardless of their political import, or even of their practicality, and probably regardless of their being shared by others around him (which, in increasing fashion, they are not). This, I think, is what he meant when he said, despite all the other reasons he might have given, that he went seal hunting that day because it was his culture. This point is taken up in more detail in the conclusion, but some introduction and justification of this interpretation are warranted here.

My own experience in working subsistence may lend some small credibility. During every field trip I made to Alaska, I participated in subsistence activities with my hosts. During the summer, this means salmon seining. Salmon seining requires three people and is most efficient with two powerboats and a skiff, though we almost always wound up fishing with one powerboat and a skiff, which means more sets, and thus more labor. On the day I describe, I am fishing with Joe and his son Algie, who normally fish with one of Joe's subsistence partners.

Most of the labor used in seining comes after the net has been set and the school of fish (hopefully) surrounded. Then Algie and I pull the net while Joe "plunges" near the boat—using a stick or long-handled plunger to splash, and frightening the fish from swimming through the opening that is left when the net is pulled aboard. The work is backbreaking and long—longer and more backbreaking if the participants are inexperienced, as I am, or shorthanded and unaccustomed to working together, as we are, or simply poor at fishing. Individuals who have worked together in the past tend to be much faster, and thus far more efficient, making fewer sets and avoiding "water hauls"—that is, sets that return no fish. For this reason, most people go subsistence fishing with the same people every year. Still, today is a good day for us. Though we are new together, we have only one water haul, and we net three hundred sockeye in under twelve hours.

Unlike commercial fishing, subsistence fishing is done near the creek mouths where the salmon school to ascend and breed. Different species of salmon (in the North Pacific there are five, and they are quite distinct)

Pulling a beach seine at sunset

use different types of streams for spawning, such that any particular stream is likely to have only one kind of salmon milling about its mouth at any given time. Sockeye breed in streams that feed freshwater lakes, and between July and August they can be found in schools at the mouths of creeks that empty from these lakes into the open ocean.

Fishermen will approach the creek mouth and wait, looking for "jumps" and trying to guess the location of a school. All salmon are fast swimmers, and contrary to many assertions, when near a creek mouth they will swim in any direction, with or against the tide. When a sufficiently large school is spotted and approached, an attempt is made to get ahead of it and to lay the seine in front of the fish (in the direction they are traveling at the time), and then to circle the school with the powerboat while laying out the seine from a skiff towed behind. It is the decision of the boat's driver, in this case Joe, when and how the seine will be set, and at least one person must stay in the seine skiff to cast over the end of the seine and make sure that the entire net feeds out smoothly. Today that is my job; Algie stays in the powerboat with his father.

The seine we use is not as long as commercial seines. It is only 100 to 120 fathoms (600 to 720 feet) long and 4 fathoms deep, but it is old and made of woven mesh that is heavy when wet. There is a row of floats across the top line, and leads (small, ring-shaped weights usually cast from lead) on the bottom or lead line, so that the seine will hang vertically in the water like a curtain. Because the net is pulled by hand, efforts are made to keep it light and fewer leads are used than are used on commercial seines. Still, the seine weighs several hundred pounds, much of which is lead. The use of this much lead is not uncommon because fishermen want the net to sink quickly and reliably. Seines that fish inefficiently—that let fish out under a net that too easily gets hung up on itself—cost more labor and time than they save by reduced weight.

When set well, the net encircles the fish, dropping to form a deep, circular curtain around the entire school. Once the loop is complete, Joe and Algie jump into the skiff with me. Algie and I begin pulling in the leaded line at the bottom of the net, hoping to close the only way out. Until this is done, Joe "plunges" beside the skiff, hoping to frighten the fish toward the back of the net and prevent them from escaping from the opening created where we are pulling the net aboard. If Joe can keep the fish from swimming under the boat, and if the leads can be brought aboard before the fish dive and swim under the net, then all of the fish caught in the circle will be trapped by the net.

Once the lead line is aboard and the fish more or less contained, we will pull the remaining web and "corks" (the floating line at the top of the net), freeing any gilled fish (those who have forced themselves partly through the net and gotten caught by the gills) as we go along. Those fish not caught by the gills continue to swim until there is no room left in the submerged portion of the web. These fish will then be pulled aboard with the bag formed by the remaining web or will be picked individually from the water. After the leads have been brought aboard, Joe stops plunging and returns to the powerboat to begin looking for the next place to set. Algie and I pull the seine from back to front—that is, beginning with the end attached to the skiff (which is also the last section laid out). This allows the seine to be pulled freely from the skiff when it is next set. If this is not done properly the seine will cross over or hang up, usually resulting in a water haul.

This entire process is referred to as a set and may net anywhere from zero to one hundred fish, depending on skill, season, and even time of day, for the fish tend to disperse into smaller schools as the day goes on. Much of the responsibility for the number of fish caught rests with the skipper of the powerboat, though obviously an inexperienced net man can ruin the very best set. Initially, success depends on the skipper's ability to guess correctly the size of a school and the direction in which it is heading. Once the net is set, though, the chance of success shifts to the group's ability to coordinate its work. Sockeye are exceptionally fast swimmers, and if the plunger misses his cue the entire school will swim out under the boat. Subsistence fishers may make as many as fifteen sets in a day, taking eight to ten total hours. Two powerboats (in place of one) can usually catch more fish—by towing the net in opposite directions they can close around a school more quickly—though inevitably it takes the same time to haul the net and clear the fish, and if anything more coordination between partners. If fishers save time this way it is because their efficiency allows for fewer sets, not quicker ones, and this is not always the case.

By the end of this day we have made more than a dozen sets. My arms are swollen with the stings of jellyfish that come aboard with webbing. We have two good-sized barrels of fish, about a third of which will go to Joe's partner, who was not here today but whose net and skiff we used. We will, I know, spend much of the remainder of the evening and go well into the night processing the fish we have caught—cutting them open and gutting them, removing the head and tail, cutting them into strips, and putting them on long, thin sticks to be hung in rows in the smokehouse. There is more work ahead, but it is made easier by the fact that most everyone we know is doing the same. The sockeye are at Hetta Creek for only two weeks, and everyone will take as many fish as possible while the supply lasts.

Beyond the sociality of the event, however, the process ensures that subsistence is seldom a solitary task. In fact, it is practically impossible when acting alone. Yet it is work that is done primarily in silence, as was the seal hunting of Owen and Mike. Beyond this, the fact that subsistence is, for many of those involved, an issue of survival, the silence is heightened by the fact that the issues, skills, and practices—in short, the meaning—of every element and stage of the process are deeply, personally, existentially important. And critically, it is this domain of meaning, and not (or not simply) the sorts of meanings assembled at Kuiu court, that Owen and others like him refer to when they speak of culture. It is this domain that allows culture to be mobilized with such suddenness and such gravity to some kinds of political processes, as it was in Hydaburg in confronting the state enforcement officials. It is also what makes these processes seem intensely risky to those whose culture is at stake, for meaning as such is not easily made—and thus the cost of its unmaking is very high. All of this points to culture as a domain of "feeling," as Raymond Williams (1977) proposed, but one whose stakes and vulnerabilities are not adequately captured by that term, or by the terms anthropologists usually use (like "meaning," used here). And it is the vulnerability of this domain that marks it as something people can never wholly embrace, and only ever accept with great caution, even while it is something they take great pride in making and continuing, and value immensely.

Within and Against Culture

In the introduction I raised the idea that culture is something people find themselves "within and against," in the words of anthropologist Gerald Sider. At this point it is possible to look at this proposition more closely in the concrete details of the case described thus far.

Without exaggeration, one can say that those subsistence users more dependent on subsistence for their livelihood potentially pay a disproportionate part of the cost of native participation in ANCSA, for they are most often the first to be forced to leave their villages when ANCSA corporations make subsistence livelihoods impossible. For them, the money from ANCSA—even during the heyday of the Net Operating Loss windfalls—can scarcely compensate for the gradual diminution of any chance of remaining in the village, and as such, of remaining part of the collective identity that these same individuals mean when they say "our culture." As one Southeast village resident explained to me, when speaking of moving out of the village: "Down south [meaning in the contiguous forty-eight states] we're just plain-old Indians."

Native identities that center on subsistence practices lend prestige to well-known hunters like Owen, or careful elders like Ester Nix of Hydaburg, who, at more than eighty years old, still tends a smokehouse fire for those who will give her fish to process. In this way, both Ester and Owen—and many others like them—feel as though they have a stake in the culture that surrounds this identity. But neither can be sure, regardless of how much their own this culture seems, that it can help them stay in the village. Along these lines, it is worth noting that all of the individuals involved in the Hydaburg confrontation with Alaska Fish and Game enforcement officials in 1992 have since had to move away from Hydaburg in search of jobs or new livelihoods. They were forced to move by circumstances that far outweighed the power of local law enforcement to accomplish this same end.

One result of this predicament—of being within and against culture— is that people often find themselves at odds with those around them over what will be included in culture and what will not: whether, for example, it is more "native" to conserve the environment or to use it to exist as a community; or whether it is better to spend some of the money recovering cultural heirlooms lost to theft or sale earlier in the century or, instead, to encourage better schooling. Outsiders, including members of Alaska's U.S. Senate delegation, and especially those who find themselves confronted by natives on issues like development, are fond of pointing out the contradictions in native culture—meaning opposing sides within the native communities on these and other issues. Such a predicament is not specific to natives, though. Many communities that are similarly within and against a set of meanings and values that are at least partly their own find the question of culture to be a *contest* of meanings, rather than a consensus.

Struggles such as these are capable of splitting communities. For some native communities—the Lumbees, Lakotas, Utes, and others— splits of this sort have formed lasting divides, sometimes so permanent that the resulting sides can come to see themselves as two different groups. More often, however, the issues are not lasting enough to render their sides so different. Instead, sides change and new sides form as the issues upon which the community is focused change and are changed—forming a community that appears to outsiders as one rife with factionalism and discord, yet which appears to insiders to be a single community in search of itself.

In part 2, I will argue that these sorts of divisions and conflicts—both community-forming and community-splitting divisions over issues of what is to be culture and what is not—have much to do with the struggles between Pentecostal church members and others in their communities. Yet were this simply the case and nothing more, were it simply that Pentecostalism's stand on native culture is but one more issue among an endless string of issues over which people must—yet cannot—come to an agreement, then there would be little value in understanding any more about the conflict than that. One would then only need to point out that churches tend to recruit most heavily among those most marginal in any community—that is, among those who, as we have already noted, pay a disproportionate share of the cost for an identity that does little to protect them, including, especially, women—to have "explained" church resistance to native culture. Little wonder, we might then conclude, that such individuals come to reject that identity, as many apparently did at the Flo Ellers revival discussed in the introduction.

But there is more to it—more to Pentecostalism and more to culture— than simply this. In part 2, then, we turn to examine just what "more" there is, with the aim of understanding why Pentecostalism is something of a culmination of the issues discussed here, and their undoing.

Part 2: Churches

5

The Spirit in Alaska

On the night the Juneau prayer group comes to town, I too have just arrived. Owen picks me up at the ferry, but rather than go immediately to his house, we gather eight or so others and arrange rides for them. Owen's brother-in-law is there in his Salvation Army uniform, and many of the prayer group visitors are staying with him. Other people—Hoonah residents I had not met before, many of them women—are talking, visiting, waiting, and helping as well. Indeed, I've never met most of the people gathered to meet the ferry tonight, though I have lived here for several months over the last two years. There is, it seems, a whole other Hoonah.

The pastor and his wife are staying at Owen's house as well. Owen knows them well, though the relationship is not exactly warm or close. Owen is polite. Betsy, Owen's wife, an active member of the Hoonah prayer group, is talking with the pastor, saying how glad she is that everyone made it in okay, by the grace of God. Travel in January in Alaska can be harrowing, and it's generally unreliable. The

prayer group is in town for just a weekend, to hold a prayer revival and services. Hoonah is near enough to Juneau that a weekend revival is possible, and the visit by the Juneau prayer group is a special occasion that is certain to liven up the village for quite a few days.

For most of the prayer group, and for those receiving them, like Betsy, the safe journey is a sign that the planned revival is blessed. Other signs will reinforce this conclusion. By the time services are held, there will be close to one hundred people in attendance, even though the largest congregation in Hoonah is only one-quarter this size.

From the ferry landing we drop off the bags of the pastor and his wife at Owen's house and go from there to the house of one of the leaders of the Hoonah prayer group, the official hosts for the revival. The house is brightly painted on the inside—one room in bright yellow, the other bright blue—with several wall hangings depicting romantic images of Native Americans on horseback, sometimes with a ghostly looking figure of Jesus in the background. Other hangings are more plainly religious — large tapestries with prayers and biblical images on them. There are "dream catchers" and elements of native religious decoration displayed: a carved silver cross, a crucified Jesus figure with accompanying American eagle carved from wood.

Before dinner, we pray. After this, the women vacate the table very quickly — so quickly, in fact, that I am uncertain whether they have eaten or not. They gather in the kitchen where a small TV broadcasts "Christian television." The dinner is deer meat, perhaps meant as a treat for the "city" guests from Juneau.

After dinner the group gathers for prayer, this time standing in the living room and holding hands. The preacher for the Juneau prayer group leads the prayer. He shakes as he speaks, modulating his tone for emphasis. Several in the group weep. Many speak aloud their own prayers while he prays, and several from the Juneau prayer group leave the circle to be seated or to kneel and continue their own prayers while the rest remain standing. Owen prays with the others, and knows the songs quite well. We sing several songs, in fact, though it is difficult for me to distinguish when one song ends and the next begins, or sometimes to distinguish singing from chanted prayers.

After this, Owen and I drive the members of the prayer group who are staying at his house back there and drop them off. It is well past midnight now, but we return to the car and drive around Hoonah, just the two of us. I have been given many tours of Hoonah in the past. This is the first tour during winter, though, and both the appearance of the town and the content of the tour change as a result.

The entire town is buried beneath perhaps three feet of snow, which quilts the town in silence and dims the lights while giving everything else an ethereal glow. As we drive, Owen points out the supernatural landmarks. There was a "witch" who lived here who used to jump from roof to roof across the town. Over there lived a "witch doctor" who could change his shape into a bear. One time, when pursued by people from Hoonah, he ran straight up that cliff over there. Actually, it took him two tries to run up it.

The New Churches

There are perhaps twenty or twenty-five Evangelical churches, Pentecostal churches, and affiliated prayer groups in the villages and larger towns of Southeast Alaska. Beyond this there are likely just as many mission churches without a significant following, but attended by one or two households nonetheless. There is usually more than one new church in each of the predominantly native villages. Some are affiliated with national or international organizations—Southern Baptist, Assembly of God, Church of God, United Pentecostal, and Four Square are all represented. Others are unaffiliated or marginally affiliated. Those with national affiliations tend to be run by pastors from outside the region. And some of these are missionary churches as well, meaning that they are not self-supporting, and as a result cannot choose their own pastors. Independent churches are not missions, of course, and these are the churches most likely to be led by a native preacher.

Few of these newer churches were established before the early 1970s, when the Assembly of God began a number of missions in Southeast Alaska. Some of these missions were more successful than others, but their general success led other church organizations to begin mission programs of their own. Part of the reason for their popularity was that the long-standing churches in the region—Presbyterian and Salvation Army—had difficulty maintaining regular church services in many villages. Despite their success in the early twentieth century, neither of these older organizations was able to achieve the sort of independent and self-sustaining congregations that early missionaries had hoped for, even after sixty or more years. By far the majority of these churches today are still missions. Beyond this, by the early 1970s both the Presbyterians and the Salvation Army were finding it increasingly difficult to fill vacating pastors' positions and maintain regular services for many Southeast congregations. It was in this vacuum that the Assembly of God began its mission program.

Contemporary members of the newly arrived churches explain their early interest in these same terms. Most were members of either the Salvation Army or Presbyterian churches when the new mission churches arrived. And many felt frustrated and abandoned when their Presbyterian or Salvation Army churches were closed for long periods of time or when pastors came and went quickly, displaying little commitment to the community. Many began attending Assembly of God services when they were the only services regularly available in the village. Once a few people began going, others—many of whom had been away from any church for a time—decided to attend out of curiosity.

Above: Presbyterian church. All five of the churches pictured in the following illustrations are located in the same small village.

Below: Salvation Army church

Above: Assembly of God church
Below: Baptist church

Surprisingly, especially to those long-standing mission programs in Alaska, many of the new churches quickly attained financial independence. Many lost their missionary status by the mid-1980s. In part this was aided by the original strength of the missionary programs—most operated out of new buildings, stocked with expensive amplification systems and well-decorated rooms, rather than churches built in the 1910s and 1920s. Another factor was the tithing practiced by some groups, where church members are expected to turn over a portion of their income (often 10 percent) to support the pastor and the facilities—a practice not employed by either the Presbyterian or Salvation Army organizations.

For this reason, some of the most financially successful churches today are the newest ones, despite the fact that these churches most often draw their membership from the more marginal portions of the community. This rapid financial success has caused them to be viewed with even greater suspicion by nonmembers, and with some envy by other pastors.

The success of the Evangelical churches of the early 1970s brought three consequences. The first was the arrival of a number of even newer, and sometimes even more dramatic or dynamic, Evangelical and Pentecostal groups. The second was the increased participation of Alaska Natives in pastoral training programs, and from this the creation of a number of village prayer groups and Bible study groups, run by church members rather than formally trained church pastors. The third result was that many of the older Presbyterian and Salvation Army churches have since taken on a more Pentecostal air—so much so that one Presbyterian pastor in a popular village church now has a reputation of being "more Pentecostal than the Pentecostal preacher" in the same village. This tactic, he explained, was to help draw people to the message, though the message itself, he maintained, remained in keeping with traditional Presbyterian ideals. Indeed, almost all churches have been pulled toward the more dramatic type of service and practice that marks the new arrivals.

In most villages there tends to be considerable movement between Pentecostal churches by church attendees. Some go to other churches only for special events—guest preachers or revivals that tend to break the monotony of regular services. Others will go to one church for a year or so and then change congregations, perhaps at some future

Evangelical/Pentecostal church

time ending up back at their original starting point. In all churches, revivals—special services, usually during the fall or winter, that may involve guest preachers from out of town—attract members of all of the Pentecostal and Evangelical congregations in a village, and from nearby villages as well if the host village is accessible to its neighbors. They also, increasingly, attract regular members of the Presbyterian and Salvation Army congregations who live in these same villages. These meetings can be quite large, with seventy or more people in attendance. They are, however, not held very often—maybe once per year, maybe less.

All congregations in the native villages are characterized by seasonal fluctuations as well. During the summer months church attendance is low, since many people are more concerned with summer activities like subsistence food harvests, travel, and seasonal employment. Participation begins again during the fall, and winter is the high point of attendance in every church. In addition, in many villages there is a prayer group that meets most often during the winter. In the summer, when there is seldom enough interest to support a regular meeting of a prayer group in any but the largest towns, most groups fade, only to be rejoined with enthusiasm in October or November.

Altogether, village congregations are not large by suburban standards. A popular church will have twenty to thirty attendees—six to eight households, or one or more "families" (in the sense developed in chapter 2). A few congregations are larger, of course, but just as many are smaller. Much of this has to do with the isolation of the villages and the competition from other churches. Kake, for example, has six active churches in a village of less than a thousand people. Two of these are quite small (one or two households), and each of the others is attended by fifteen to thirty people weekly.

Church and Culture

Four issues run through the chapters of part 2. As discussed in the previous chapters, Pentecostal churches are the main focus of the second portion of this text because of their strong anticultural stance, both in general and on specific occasions—such as the Flo Ellers incident discussed in the introduction. Church members stand outside and against their culture as Southeast Alaska Natives in four particular ways.

First, church membership offers ordinary people an entirely different and largely independent arena for making and adjusting local social relations. Through testimony, attendance, prayer, and prayer group leadership (all discussed below), church members act with and upon each other according to a set of rules and understandings that stands largely outside the political economy of the region and village. Through testimony and witnessing (the Evangelical aspects of church practice), church members also seek out nonmembers for inclusion in this circle of belief and social relations, in effect changing the basis for local social organization from families to churches for these individuals.

Second, church membership offers people a language through which they can criticize ongoing native identity projects, including the corporate sponsorship often associated directly or indirectly with these projects. By drawing upon a language of sin, demonic possession, and contagion (the Fundamentalist aspects of church practice), church members can make these criticisms in ways that stand outside the language of political economy and culture through which most identity projects are constructed. In this way, members of the culture group find these sorts of accusations and criticisms particularly frustrating—"It's like they won't listen to reason," I was told.

Third, church membership allows people the opportunity to stand outside mainstream American cultural practice as well, taking up the oppositional stances of Fundamentalist church members elsewhere in the American margins. Particularly around issues of economy, jobs, and work, such a stance allows those involved a way of criticizing and expressing the high personal price people pay for being both ordinary people *and* Indians within the larger American political economy. These stances are seen most clearly in the testimonies offered by people when they first become members of a church—that is, when they first begin to understand and explore the power of having an independent discourse of causality and accountability beyond that offered by non-church social language and life.

Finally, as mentioned briefly in the introduction, Pentecostal church practice allows people to not only stand outside of and against any particular culture, but against Culture more generally. Put another way, it allows people to stand outside the idea that local, tight-knit, and logically closed systems of meaning are primary in people's visions of themselves as people—which has become, for reasons discussed in the conclusion, the critical definition of culture for many identity projects. This anti-Cultural stance is clear in two aspects of Pentecostal practice—in speaking in tongues and other "gifts of faith," and in the absolute insistence on a transcendent notion of divinity (i.e., a God who stands before and above the universe, and before and above any person's conception of God).

This last point will be taken up in more detail in chapter 7. The others are discussed throughout this chapter and the next—this chapter on the nature of church practice, and the following on the testimonials and witness accounts given by church members.

Church Practice

Regular Sunday service at most Pentecostal churches follows a similar pattern. It begins with a song service—songs sung from a hymnal, or from sheets handed around if the songs are new. Some are old Protestant hymns, others are quite new, and it is not uncommon to sing songs written by the preacher or his or her spouse. Christian television also has had an impact on the content of services, for many church members watch one of the several national Christian channels that are broadcast in most villages. Songs from these programs are very popular even for regular Sunday services.

Quite often members of the congregation will play instruments to accompany the singing. Indeed, successful churches often have expensive amplification systems that support electric guitars and microphones, even though the church buildings do not seem so large that they would require them.

During the song service there is usually no preset number of songs to be sung. The pastor will have picked out several that support or introduce the subject of the day's sermon. In addition, members of the congregation are invited to—and often do—propose songs. These can come out of the hymn book, or might be "specials." In the latter case the church member proposing the song will go to the dais or front of the congregation and sing, perhaps accompanied by instruments. This is more common at a revival, but it also happens occasionally during regular Sunday services. When it does, it marks these services with a special air.

Most of those at the service participate in the singing enthusiastically. Some have instruments of their own, tambourines or shakers that they bring along. Many people in the village point out that this sort of participation was common for early church membership throughout the region, and that early-twentieth-century Salvation Army bands in various villages were always well supported and very popular, though this is not the case today. Indeed, many older Southeast Natives, even those who do not now attend church, can sing traditional hymns from memory.

Song service usually takes up about thirty minutes, or half of the regular service, and is followed by prayer, readings, and a sermon. The prayer is usually begun with a request for prayers by the pastor, who begins by announcing his or her own prayers, generally pertaining to issues that affect the congregation as a whole, or for ill relatives of members who are away and cannot request the prayers themselves, or, in those churches with a national affiliation, for national church issues such as mission work. The pastor will then solicit prayers from the congregation. These are generally volunteered in large numbers—prayers for sick or troubled relatives, home lives, absent friends—and some are left unspoken when a topic might seem too personal or controversial to mention. The preacher will generally make a list of these prayers, and this list will be repeated when he or she and the group pray. Overall, prayers for help are more common than prayers for guidance, and prayers for success are the least common.

When a congregation in any of the more Pentecostal churches prays, the members stand, bow their heads, close their eyes, and either join hands with a neighbor or raise their own hands over their head. The prayer leader, usually the pastor, will recite all of the requested prayers, including those with which he or she began. When given by the preacher, the prayer is usually done in a dramatic voice, with the volume modulated to accent certain words or phrases in a way that can be described as penetrating. While the congregation members' heads are bowed, the prayer leader's head begins bowed but normally rises, like the volume of the voice used in prayer, and at times he or she speaks directly at the roof of the church.

While the pastor is praying, the members of Pentecostal and many Evangelical congregations will say aloud their own prayers, though their heads normally remain bowed and their voices lower. The modulation in people's voices draws attention to their own emphases in their prayers as they follow along with the prayer leader. Thus it might sound like this:

Prayer leader: [gaining volume and pitch, until the final syllables] . . . and we ASK you Lord, praise Jesus, to remember the Dear FRIEND of Anita, as she enters the hospital, this coming Tuesday . . . Church member: [quietly, timed to coincide with "as she enters"] . . . yes Lord, for Anita's friend . . .

The style of prayer practiced by most non-pastor prayer leaders is similar—and drawn, one might guess based simply on cadence, word choice, and even assumed accents—on the Southern Baptist style of prayer of the mid-twentieth century that has become the emblem of the evangelizing preachers on Christian television.

Not all prayer leaders assume this style, of course, and some preachers do come to Alaska from the southern United States, and as such their accents are clearly not affectation. Yet by far this style pervades most prayer and prayer leaders, even those born and raised in Alaska who do not otherwise speak in that fashion.

Prayer is generally followed by readings from one or another Protestant Bible. Annotated Bibles are especially popular among church members (for reasons discussed below), but the King James Version is usually preferred by pastors and used for readings in church services. The latter may reflect a preference for the archaism of the language used in the King

James Version, which sometimes reappear in the wording of prayers or sermons. Among some groups, the King James Version is given special status as a "divine" translation. For these groups, the language of the King James Version is itself inspired, with a status equal to that of the original texts from which it and the other translations are drawn. For these groups especially—though to some extent it is true of all the radical Christian churches I attended—the words do not just represent power; they themselves have power. This is most apparent when used in healing and casting out demons, but a sense of this power pervades most services.

Quite often, in regularly attended churches where things can be arranged beforehand, the readings will be done by members of the audience, at times standing where they are, and at other times going up to the altar. Most people bring their own Bibles to church, and some bring more than one version. In most Pentecostal churches time is usually taken to allow the congregation to find the passage and read along. The readings and sermon are sometimes done together, with the pastor or the day's speaker reading the passages and then giving the accompanying sermon. In virtually all cases the readings are selected to introduce or underline certain elements of the sermon that will follow. This helps establish a clear emphasis on Bible reading and interpretation in all of these churches.

The function of the sermon is generally to interpret the read passages—yet by "interpret" I do not mean "explain." Stories or passages are seldom contextualized either historically or in terms of their place in the Bible. Rather, interpretation consists of the recognition of patterns of signs within stories—that is, interpretation is foremost the isolation or recognition of significant elements and the attempt to link them to other significant elements within the story and—beyond this—events and concerns of a church member's daily life.

For example, the following passage was read at a revival service at the Assembly of God church in Kake in 1995: "And I saw when the Lamb opened one of the seals, and I heard, as it were the noise of thunder, one of the four beasts saying, Come and see. And I saw, and behold a white horse; and he that sat on him had a bow; and a crown was given unto him; and he went forth conquering, and to conquer" (Revelation 6:1–2). Following this reading, the interpretation focused on the significance of the crown, and what it would mean to be a conqueror should Christ arrive (again) today. "Who of you will receive a crown?" the preacher asked several times.

This sort of interpretation allows Evangelical and Pentecostal church pastors to use biblical language as a verbal texture that will be evoked in the sermon. Readings become, in a sense, sources of potent, usually unfamiliar signs that can be manipulated and applied in ways that lend significance to current events — or at the very least, lend contemporary events an alternative, often emotionally charged significance.

This may be why church members prefer the annotated version of the Bible for their own use as well. Annotated versions are often valued because they provide expanded versions of the biblical text itself, rather than for adding historical background. Church members spend considerable time in Bible study and interpretation, and the textuality of the Bible is a significant factor in their relationship with church practice and membership. And while it is common for many Pentecostal churches to insist on a literal translation for points of doctrine, much of the emphasis that church members place on biblical understanding is based on seeing the significance of elements of the Bible in their daily lives. This explains the preference for annotated versions, for in expanding the text they multiply the potential number of signs contained in any particular biblical passage.

During normal services, sermons usually follow immediately after Bible readings. Their topics vary, and they are generally held to less than twenty minutes. In contrast to church members' prayers and testimonials (discussed below), sermon topics seldom address village happenings. Nor, in general, are topics concerning business or economics ever broached by the preacher from the pulpit. Rather, by far the majority of sermon topics remain quite clearly pointed at traditional sorts of theology — notions of salvation, judgment, and sin — rather than at local happenings, and in this way they contrast strongly with the prayers that precede them and the interpretation and discussion of Bible reading that takes place outside church services.

People react to the sermons in much the same way they react to their own Bible study, however. That is, they weigh the images and interpretations they hear against the events and issues of their everyday lives, such that sermons on traditional theological issues tend to be treated as multiplications of the text as well. As with archaisms and annotations, particularly poignant sermons are "heard" as though they contained the same sacredness as the more formally sacred (in theological terms) text. In this way, devout church members ordinarily deal with a greatly expanded "text"—one that includes actual text, annotations, and powerful interpretations of the text. Nor do they necessarily differentiate or hierarchize this expanded text. Instead, *all are treated as capable of revealing divine activity in people's ordinary lives.*

There is, however, a definite sense among church members that this practice is something they engage in personally and one that others—including church pastors—ought not to undertake for anyone but themselves. Thus many find it crucially important that sermon topics avoid any reference to the personal lives of the individuals in the congregation. People will, in fact, react negatively to any overt reference or obvious connection between the sermon topic and the life of one or another person in the congregation—any hint of being singled out. Such incidents have split some churches and caused longtime members to leave for other congregations. This fact has led many non-churchgoers to assert that church members do not really go to church to live a better life, but rather to be told glowing stories of an afterlife. Critics note: "Anytime anyone says anything to them they change churches."

Revivals

Revivals are infrequent occurrences, happening once per year or once every few years in most villages. Quite often they are associated with a sponsoring local church, although the visiting preachers as well as much of the audience will be drawn from many separate churches and denominations. Crowds for a revival can be large, and some people will travel several days by ferry to attend revivals held in more distant villages. Quite often as much as half of the audience at a revival will be from outside the host village.

Many revivals are themselves traveling groups, going from village to village throughout the Southeast region and into other regions, holding revivals in many towns and villages along the way. In such cases they are organized by the revival preachers with the support of the host churches at each stop. In these cases, some of the participants will travel with the revival as well, at times spending several weeks traveling and attending services in many different towns. Such services can take place during the day or at night, but the most active revival sessions usually happen in the evening and continue past midnight and into the early hours of the morning. In some villages the meetings go on for several days as well, with one or two services each day.

Revival services follow a pattern similar to regular Sunday services. They begin with the song service, although the production is generally larger and more rehearsed. As many as six or seven musicians and singers will take a place by the altar and perform songs. The audience generally knows these songs, as some are taken from a hymnal. Many are the more popular songs from Christian television or radio, or even from Christian music tapes and CDs that have wide popularity in many villages.

Local musicians of the host church may be asked to join in, but the lead is generally taken by the revival preacher. The preacher selects the songs and singles out audience members for song requests, calling those he or she knows by their first name, preceded by "Brother" or "Sister"—"Sister Mary" or "Brother Tim." Those making requests are often invited to the altar to lead in the singing, and they usually do so. Likewise, several "specials" are usually performed, which are carefully rehearsed as well. People singing specials that are not standard hymns will sometimes bring portable stereos up to the altar with them and play accompanying music.

Song service is the first of several opportunities for individual expression at a revival. People will frequently preface a selected hymn or special with some words about why they chose it or what its particular significance is to them. In such cases, unlike in the sermons discussed above, singling out other audience members is quite common, as are expressions of personal feelings or happenings. Many will bring someone with them to the altar to support them and help lead in the singing—a friend, sibling, parent, or (less often) spouse—sometimes holding hands or joking together. If the sound system has more than one microphone, the preacher retains one and the other is left for those who come up to the altar. In these cases, and even sometimes when there is only one microphone, the revival preacher will usually stay on the dais and offer support or humor.

Throughout, the song service is lively, not least because the musicians will break into an up-tempo, tambourine-shaking song if things appear to be slowing down. It is also during the song service that the first interaction with the supernatural may take place. Like Pentecostals in other areas, those in Southeast Alaska practice "gifts of faith" (also called "gifts of the Spirit") and acknowledge two forms of spirit possession—possession by the Holy Spirit or, conversely, by demons that seek to undo the work of the Holy Spirit. It should be noted that both of these are far less common during the song service than later in the service. Thus some may speak in tongues momentarily when discussing the choice of a song, or may get carried away by the Holy Spirit in the passion of dancing and begin to jump or move much more vigorously and uncontrollably around the aisles. These are generally brief incidents, however, and do not generally affect the musicians or the preacher. The preacher will often use these opportunities to interject between songs that the Holy Spirit has seemingly entered the congregation and is "with us tonight."

Song service at a revival can last anywhere from one to two or more hours, and it usually ends with the preacher taking back control of the proceedings. The musicians will acknowledge this by putting down their instruments, though they most often remain on the dais along with the preacher. As in regular service, song service is followed by prayer and by the request for prayers from the congregation. When given from the congregation, these prayers are generally very similar to those offered on most Sundays, though they are more impassioned. Prayers are given for those in the community who have left the church—that they may return—and for those who have returned only recently or are attending a revival for the first time—that they be "born again" in Christ, and thus become a regular member of this or another congregation. The request for prayers can also be joined with or take the form of altar testimonies. Here people take the dais to address the audience, make a confession, announce their intention to be reborn in Jesus, or tell the story of their rebirth.

Testimonies are always to some extent stories about the village, the people in it, and the speaker's relation to them. In ways that reemphasize much that was noted above, testimonies are opportunities for people to discuss their own conclusions about the significance and signification of local events, happenings, and relations—most often in relation to specific Bible passages. But sometimes testimony topics are limited to the sort of "general order" theological symbology of Pentecostalism. Throughout it is a process of drawing the lessons of salvation from daily life and from other individuals (most of whom, if they have had an impact on a person's salvation, are likely themselves to have been reborn and so are just as likely to be in the audience) — in all, a matching process between the signs of biblical salvation and the events of ordinary life.

These are always very personal statements, revealing of both the speaker and many of those who hear them. Old personal feuds or antagonisms are revisited, sometimes to announce forgiveness, sometimes as testimony to forgiveness already made and now kept— "Two years ago I stood up here and said that I would never again . . . and since that time I have not. And I have Sister —— to thank, especially for the times when I wanted to . . . and she said . . ."

And while testimonies are ostensibly about a person's own faith and discoveries, almost every speaker raises issues of contemporary social relations and processes. Divisions and relations between important families are frequent topics, as are divisions within families. Indeed, very few personal and interpersonal issues seem inappropriate when the speakers are members of the community. People will speak of former marriages or affairs that they or their spouses and ex-spouses have had, fallings-out with siblings or children, or bad blood between neighbors.

Perhaps the most common theme, though, is alcohol. Drinking problems are common in many villages, as are problems with drugs. Few villages have bars or even liquor stores, and many are ostensibly dry. But all have bootleggers who buy alcohol outside the village and resell it locally at greatly inflated prices. Most testimonies involve a confession of being a former hard drinker and of having hurt spouses, children, friends, and neighbors as a result. Altar testimonies seldom involve announcing the intention to stop drinking; more often they take place after the drinking has stopped, and are thus used to announce that it has been some number of months or years since the speaker last had a drink.

People exhibit a great deal of emotion when giving testimonies, but very few are overcome by their emotions while speaking. This is surprising in that such topics are not common in conversations outside church, and the emotional pitch of a revival is very high. Some have practiced by giving multiple testimonies over the years, but others, giving their testimony for the first time, seem surprisingly calm even when discussing very difficult subjects. At times the stories and examples are as long as five or more minutes. Most end with a request for prayer (which is the ostensible purpose for an open microphone).

When the preacher does eventually take back control of the service and pray, he or she replicates the cadence and intonation for prayer discussed above, though the level and volume of audience participation is much greater at a revival than at a normal Sunday service. People yell and shriek during prayer at a revival, and in a spontaneous fashion, that is, less in time with the prayer leader. Gifts of faith become more common at this time. The preacher will frequently speak in tongues while praying, and audience members will weep, speak in tongues, or move erratically, sometimes shaking or falling down.

Most people pray aloud—often loudly—while the prayer leader is praying, such that the collective volume is constant and rising gradually throughout the prayer to a crescendo after several minutes. The body movements of those in prayer are initially quite similar to what occurs in regular service. Most begin to pray with their eyes lowered and hands held with those nearby. But often at a revival people will raise one or both hands when praying and look directly at the ceiling while saying their prayer aloud. Many of those experiencing the Holy Spirit will sway, and most seem to punctuate their prayer with jerking body movements. Yet even those who do not move so dramatically seem still "moved" by prayer. They flinch and bob and sometimes shake softly while speaking their own prayer more softly but still audibly.

During and following the prayer, many in the audience will exhibit gifts of faith or manifestations of spiritual struggle. This can include the preacher. On one occasion a preacher was overcome by a "demon" upon finishing his prayer and prior to the start of his sermon. The manifestation of the possession was a loss of strength and pain in the side. One of his regular congregation members—this was a traveling revival, but part of the preacher's own congregation had joined him at this particular meeting—called out to the others, "Come on, prayer group, your minister needs your help." All of the members of his own congregation who were present then went up to the dais, gathered around the preacher, and laid hands upon him, and the leader of the assembled group prayed aloud several times: "Lord, cast the demon out of this man" and "And he cast out the spirits with his words" (Matthew 8:16). The group gathered around and prayed in a loud murmur, with very little else said that was understandable.

The preacher recovered after a minute or two. During the time he was lying on the floor, most of the rest of the revival audience actually stayed seated. They did not pray, or at least not uniformly, and only a few seemed to have any idea what else they might do. It was my impression that this was not necessarily a normal part of even a revival service in this village, though immediately afterward few seemed distracted by it, nor did anyone comment that it seemed out of place or suspicious when I questioned them about it later. It was, perhaps, unusual but not unordinary.

All revival preachers in Pentecostal churches will speak in tongues while praying. This will come quite suddenly, interrupting the prayer briefly, and can be spaced sporadically throughout it. This is a sign of possession by the Holy Spirit, and it is demonstrated by congregation members at this time as well. Generally, the "words" spoken during these times are strings of monosyllables that contain no recognizable words. Church members believe that these acts represent the recitation of extinct biblical languages. As discussed in chapter 7, many treat speaking in tongues as proof of the authenticity of their beliefs.

As with normal Sunday service, readings and sermons tend to follow prayer. Sermon topics at revivals tend to focus on salvation. Many speakers draw on apocalyptic imagery—joined to a discussion of rewards and salvation—to impress upon their audience the importance of immediate conversion. Thus at the revival discussed above, the sermon topic that followed the passage from Revelation joined these two themes—crowns and conquering—to implore listeners to prepare for the immediate return of Christ. For those not already a member of a "born again" church, this preparation meant conversion.

Many of those not attending Pentecostal services tend to see this theme as emblematic of church strategies as a whole—the somewhat frenzied atmosphere joined with apocalyptic imagery and promises of salvation and reward. However, as will be seen in the next chapter, there is much more to conversion than this. Most of those "reborn" at a revival have been actively involved with other church members for a time. Indeed, anyone who attends a revival is viewed as a prospect and will be contacted by church members. Their hope is to prepare the prospect to receive Christ at a later revival. In all, "instantaneous" conversion is often a long process.

Along these same lines, audience members at many revivals seem to exhibit as much patience as enthusiasm when listening to revival sermons. Thus many village residents are likely to sit and nod and say "Amen" when asked to respond by the preacher, but few among those I have spoken with worried deeply about either the pressure exerted in such speeches or their internal consistency or sense.

After the sermon, the preacher or another of the guest preachers may have an altar call, this one for special, individual prayers made by the preacher—often involving requests for healing, loosely defined. Here the revival preacher will normally exhibit speaking in tongues, the band will begin again their songs, and people in the audience will pray, dance, or move to the front to be healed. Most often a line forms of those who seek healing or special prayer, and people will approach the altar one at a time. The preacher will mark the petitioner's forehead with holy oil or water, lay hands on the petitioner's head (unless some specific body part is to be healed), and pray quietly, seldom understandably. After such prayers, the petitioners return to their seats and continue to pray, or if in the course of prayer they are overcome by the Holy Spirit, they will faint and be caught by two of the preacher's helpers. Those "lying with the Spirit" are carried to the back of the church and laid in aisles or in empty pews. Those whose unconscious actions are more erratic and dramatic may be watched over to make sure they do not harm themselves.

Other gifts of the spirit are common at this time. Among the healed are some who are overcome by tears, wailing, joy, and fits of hysterical laughter. Many dance and sing erratically as the musicians play continuously and the remaining congregation sings, dances, and sways rhythmically in their seats. Virtually all of the conscious audience stays standing and praying in one way or another for the entire altar call. The scene can become very chaotic, and most of the responsibility for maintaining a working situation falls on the close associates of the preacher, who are more accustomed to these circumstances. They help clear the aisles of those "lying with the Spirit" and aid those whom the Holy Spirit has overcome.

Note that not everyone at a revival practices the gifts of faith. In a revival of one hundred people, perhaps thirty or forty will respond to an altar call for prayer and healing, and of these perhaps twenty or twenty-five will be overcome by the Holy Spirit and lose consciousness or become affected in some dramatic way. Many simply stay in place and remain standing, praying and singing. The preacher may also call out to some in the audience who do not volunteer to come up to the altar for prayer and healing. These might be individuals who have given testimony previously or who the preacher feels are close to being born again. Here the preacher must exercise careful judgment. I have not seen anyone called up who did not go, but those I spoke with uniformly expressed the idea that untimely, unwanted attention would likely result in the loss of the person singled out as a potential new member.

When the altar call is finished and the preacher has called out all of those he or she intends to, the music is slowed and the congregation is allowed to settle. Those who had been moved to the rear of the church have usually regained consciousness by this time and have retaken their seats. All of the dancing has subsided as well, and the weeping and laughing are either finished or muted. Then the preacher will ask the whole congregation to join him or her in prayer. All stand at this point and once again join hands. Like the opening prayer, this one tends to be loud and performed with the same cadence and intonation.

Often this prayer will reiterate themes from testimonies and from the previous prayer, and it will be one of the few times the preacher is able to single out individuals in the audience. This is often heavily coded so as to be less obvious, and prayer of this sort always lacks the personal issues and references of testimonies, song requests, or prayer requests. This prayer, often closing the revival, is generally lengthy, sometimes between five and ten minutes. During it, gifts of faith will be exhibited, including speaking in tongues by the audience and the preacher. Few here will wail or laugh as they did during the altar call, but many sway and sometimes move spasmodically while in prayer. As before, the prayer of the audience is loud and less synchronized to the patterns of prayer used by the pastor than at a regular church service.

A revival normally involves more than one service. If it takes place over a weekend, two or three services may be held. Interspersed between the services are other social functions, such as group meals and visits. Often after the service a reception will be held with coffee and cake. Here people have a chance to visit with those who are from out of town or to speak with the preacher about the service.

Prayer Groups

Beyond the regular services and revivals, some Pentecostal church members will form prayer groups or Bible study groups. Usually specific to a particular village, these gatherings may draw individuals from several different congregations. Both kinds of groups practice prayer of the sort common to revivals and Sunday service alike, with a single individual or leader taking the role normally assumed by the pastor—collecting and noting the prayers, introducing one or more themes for prayer, and so on. Likewise, both types of groups tend to spend time discussing biblical passages, forming and discussing their own interpretations. Unlike in formal services, discussions of this sort will often involve taking direct examples from village happenings or from the daily life of the speaker. In this way individual members allow themselves considerably more liberty in introducing personal issues than is allowed the preachers during either normal or revival services. Like testimonies, these sorts of discussions often raise very personal issues involving others in the group.

Prayer groups tend to be more heavily attended by women than by men. On the other hand, prayer group leaders are usually men. This does not necessarily mean that the topics tend to be dominated by men, however, for quite often women take the lead in introducing and maintaining discussions.

In this way, churches in Alaska parallel both the culture movements in their own villages, which are often weighted toward women in the number of participants, and radical churches outside Alaska, in which women frequently represent a majority of church membership (see contributors to Hall and Stack 1982, and Garrard-Burnett and Stoll 1993; also Burdick 1993 and Chesnut 1997). Yet there are important differences in how gender differences are integrated into each group's ideology. In contrast to the example of the Kuiu Court discussed in chapter 4, the larger number of women participating in Bible study and prayer groups seldom receives comment, even when it is questioned directly. When addressing participation, people tend to point to issues in their personal lives and to their personal relationship with Christ rather than to any ideology of difference (gender or otherwise). All people note that female church members tend to try to get their husbands more involved in church, while the husbands seldom face the same sorts of struggles in recruiting their wives. But this difference within the church stems from differences in the ideology of gender in the society at large—one that affects church dynamics and is thus reproduced there, but one that is not intrinsic to church practice or organization.

The members of prayer and Bible study groups are well known to one another, and the groups are usually small, drawing between five and ten people. Most meet weekly in the home of one of the members. They are at once insular (in that their activities are not usually discussed outside the meetings) and expansive (in that they will actively seek new members and make a considerable effort to see that current members continue to attend).

This inward-looking/expansive pattern is perhaps true of the more radical churches as a whole, and it is even replicated at times in church architecture. By way of example, one church, the host of the Flo Ellers revival, reflects church insularity in dramatic form. From the outside there is very little to indicate that the building is a church—no sign, no steeple, no list of times for Sunday services. Made of corrugated aluminum, the building resembles a large storage barn for a public works department. There are no windows, and no panes or openings in the doors. Indeed, from the outside there is no indication of what might be going on inside. For someone wishing to attend services, the only option is to be invited—for otherwise one could not even know when a service was in progress. At the same time, it is among the larger church buildings in the village, large enough to hold most of the village's churchgoing population. And for a while it was the most popular church in the village, with fifty or more regular attendees.

This inward-looking orientation is both individual (in the sense of spiritual introspection) and collective (meaning that there are clearly defined boundaries between members and nonmembers, and little concern shown to those outside the group). Service schedules at many churches are arranged in advance but changed with little notice other than word of mouth, and thus those who are not already part of the church will have little luck in gaining access—unless, that is, they are actively sought out by the group itself. At the same time, virtually all of these churches are known for their tendency to constantly recruit new members, mainly through inviting individuals to church functions.

These two features arouse much suspicion among nonmembers.

Many have commented on the insular nature of church groups, and of prayer groups in particular. Nonmembers voice resentment at the active recruiting, noting that once someone expresses an interest in a church or prayer group, there will be someone from that congregation at that person's house all the time until he or she actually joins (at which point the newcomer is expected to help do the same for other prospective members). Most of these accusations are true to an extent, although the suspicion they arouse is, I suspect, less a sign of concern for those targeted—who are often among any village's most marginal individuals or households—than a realization of a social dynamic quite apart from that of the non-church community.

Members of prayer and Bible study groups occasionally encourage this perception by marking themselves off from the remainder of the village. Black T-shirts similar to the popular black rock concert T-shirts or Harley-Davidson motorcycle T-shirts, but emblazoned with religious and often radical statements, are popular among a few members. At one revival I saw a shirt with a picture of a crucified Christ figure on the front along with a mock Harley-Davidson logo with the slogan "Jesus Christ Lord of Heaven." On the back it had more iconography and symbols on a cartoon-like landscape with a slogan underneath: "Worship the best or burn with the rest." Of course, not all—and probably not even most—church members would feel comfortable with such a statement, but the evocation of the insularity of the church groups was very visible.

Church Praxis

Several themes emerge from this discussion. As mentioned above, church services provide both an opportunity and a language for a very different set of social relations from those discussed in part 1. There is no notion of shareholder versus nonshareholder status, or even questions of native versus non-native status. If such thoughts are still present among church members, they hold no special place (or even *any* place) in the language of church services. Yet services do present many opportunities for the making and remaking of local social relations—through prayers offered and asked and through altar testimonies. Here people can and do single out others in ways that nonmembers and the preacher are forbidden to. This will become more apparent in the next chapter, where several testimonies and witness statements are discussed.

In addition, the overall otherworldly focus also keeps references to ordinary issues of local political economy to a minimum. One seldom hears prayers for financial help, job help, or related issues. I never heard discussions of village or regional politics at church or after-church functions.

Perhaps the biggest way church membership affects local relations, though, is that people are able to become members of just about any Evangelical church and be assured of an intimate and warm welcome. Because all of these churches are constantly seeking new members and are immediate in their use of members to evangelize nonmembers, people who join a church find themselves part of a group quite different from "families" or other local social forms. Drawn mainly from the more marginal members of the village, churches often provide for their new members their first sense of "community"—that is, a group of people engaged in a common life task. In this new community, people are encouraged to speak about their past lives—in order both to reinterpret them in the language of church practice and to move beyond them, to make new friends and relations out of people they may have known their entire lives.

Prayer group leaders are particularly aware of this issue. They frequently express their position or role as involving the creation of a community—meaning both a sense of group bondedness and a common purpose. Perhaps even more than preachers (who tend to come from outside the village), prayer group leaders take up the task of reinventing individuals, of helping people change their relations to others in the group and thus their image of themselves. This sort of reinvention is common for church members, though it is always highly emotionally charged. Altar testimonies (discussed in chapter 6) are perhaps the best examples of the subjective elements of this process.

6

"Jesus Loves You"

She began by telling me that her life with alcohol had begun after she got married. Her husband had been a drinker, even before she married him. But he was drunk more and more as the fishing got worse, and she used to drink to defend herself—or so she thought at the time—because she was a lot braver when she was drunk. She was often drunk in order to live with her kids as well, she said. There were a lot of them, and they always seemed to be asking more from her than she could give. So she would drink to be brave enough to tell them no. Usually when she drank she became so scary, she said, that she didn't have to say no. They would just leave her alone. Her husband as well, even when he was drunk, knew better than to start in on her.

When she was living in Wrangell, she came to know Jesus through a friend who explained to her that there was more to her drinking than this. She knew she had lost control, and that was what the drinking was all about, but she didn't know how she had lost control. Her friend explained that drinking, like all sin, was a demon that got inside of you

and didn't leave. Even when you weren't drinking, the demon was still there, and it would take over again at some other time.

As we speak, she is sitting in a soft chair that makes her look small. Her hair is white and short, and she is probably sixty-five or more, though admittedly I am guessing. There are pictures of family and friends on the wall. There is a set of freestanding shelves with other items accumulated over time. Little of it is religious, but the house is very neat. The chair she sits in has lace covers over the armrests that she made herself. Her demeanor is entirely passive on the outside, but she appears amazingly steadfast. As I sit I think, "Should a terrible wind strike the house, she would not have the power to run and seek shelter. But if she did not move, no wind could dislodge her."

She doesn't know how the demon came to take control over her. Probably through jealousy or anger with her husband . . . some sin that let it in and it stayed. Without Jesus, no one is strong enough to get a demon out of his or her body. So people who drink continue to drink, and those who sin in other ways—"like abuse," she says—will continue. They don't have the power to "evict" those demons. Only by praying to Jesus and accepting him as your savior, she says, can demons be banished from a person's life. And even then, you have to have great faith, because by trusting Jesus you are giving up on trying to do anything about it yourself. You put yourself in his hands.

Part of the reason she had such trouble, she says, is that demons have always been around this area. Ever since the old days, when the Devil had his hand on this land, demons have been in and out of people. What people don't

realize, she says as she sits up, is that by bringing demons into the village, even from their own greed, they make it dangerous for everyone.

We eat lunch. Home-cured and canned salmon on pilot bread, and black coffee. It is summer, so she has plenty of fish around. "How do you like our Alaska salmon?" she asks me. "When people get old like me," she says smiling, "its all that we eat. White people say it's good for you, and I think we've known this all along. But I eat it because it's all I really like to eat. If I could just have fish, I could be happy all the time." I smile when I catch the allusion, and she smiles back, laughing a little at the test she gives me.

Testifying

Much of the description of services in the previous chapter might easily represent Pentecostal worship in other parts of the United States, or even in other areas of the world where Pentecostal missions have grown popular. Yet here, and I suspect elsewhere as well, the movement itself and the practices associated with it are far more revealing of the immediate social and personal dynamics of the particular churches and church members than of the theological appeal of the mission message.

By way of example, most individuals in Alaskan Pentecostal churches, like most Pentecostal churches "down south," practice a form of expression of faith called a "testimony." A testimony is simply the story of how one came to be saved. When given at the altar, the act is referred to as "testifying." When addressed to a non–church member, outside of church, it is called "witnessing." For most Evangelical Christians, witnessing is considered a quasi-sacramental act, one through which people deepen their relationship with Christ. For while testimonies are usually formal and often rehearsed, they are never finished. As people come to be conscious of the day-to-day manifestations of their salvation, their testimony grows and is multiplied, and hence so is their relationship with Christ. At each step, a person's consciousness of the supernatural significance of his or her life grows and new understandings are added. In this way, people come to "know Christ." When individuals sit down and formalize their testimony, and then relate it to a listener, they mark and manifest that deepening relationship with Jesus.

Testimony stories often involve supernatural interventions in the life of the speaker—hence the idea that following these encounters the individual then acts as a witness for Christ, relating supernatural events he or she saw and experienced firsthand. When encouraging others to speak of their salvation, people will say, "Go ahead, give him [i.e., the person listening, in this case the author] your testimony."

Testimony stories often appear as a paradox. They are highly personal, even intimate stories, yet they follow predictable sorts of patterned, narrative development. On the personal side they involve elements that can only be described as local, and often these elements are critical to the conversion/salvation process. In the accounts that follow, several elements—the Bureau of Indian Affairs (BIA), the local tribal council, and even particular (and for most of those listening, identifiable) neighbors—are named and arranged or rearranged vis-à-vis the narrative.

Yet for most testimonies, this narrative draws its form from an even deeper structure, the simple understanding that "Jesus loves you."

Tom's Testimony

The first testimony is from Tom, a retired fisherman (partly disabled as the result of a stroke) in his late sixties who has been a member of the local Assembly of God church since the mid-1970s. In fact, he was among the first important converts after the Assembly opened this church several years prior. Up to that time the church had served mainly itinerant white workers (working on Sealaska's first logging projects) and children from the village in an after-school program. Tom was among the first natives to join, beginning a process that eventually led to the development of the Assembly of God church as a self-supporting congregation of primarily native membership. His wife, Kate, is also a member, and she joined after he did. Most often she defers to his testimony, saying that her inspiration came mainly from seeing the changes that salvation had brought to her husband.

Both were saved, however, as members of the Salvation Army, moving over to the Assembly of God church only later. Both said that they moved because they had felt there was "something missing" at the Salvation Army church. Kate noted that she had never seen people at the Salvation Army church pray with a hand above their head, something she interpreted—I think—to mean a different approach to communion with the Holy Spirit.

Underlying this, however, is the different level of participation offered by the Assembly of God church, for both described their enthusiasm for their salvation by describing church (and often meeting- or service-based) practices. Both were led to the Assembly of God church by a native-led revival featuring a visiting Makah pastor from Washington State. At that revival, they noted, many people from the village's other congregations attended, and perhaps thirty or forty people were saved. This was, in effect, the start of the Assembly of God church as a congregation and was perhaps the turning point for Pentecostalism in all of Southeast Alaska.

One other point is worth noting before moving on to the testimony itself. Though Tom and his wife are native and both would once have been considered central figures in their "family," the family itself is now relatively small and somewhat torn by his and his wife's salvation. Several of their children still drink heavily, and this has caused some tension. One son lost a seine boat in an accident, which his father blames on the son's drinking and the Devil (who is ultimately responsible for his son's drinking). In addition, their public affiliation with several of the more radical Christians seems to have limited the number of extended family members who might otherwise have made this family a larger and more important group.

Altogether this makes their family one of the more dispersed and least politically powerful in the village, though Kate's role in one of the village government positions counters this a little. In all, the family holds no power on the village corporation board or in any of the corporation hirings. All this is true at the present time despite the fact that Tom and

Kate have what might be considered among the larger kin networks in
the village.

My field notes summary of Tom's testimony follows:

When Tom graduated from High School at Sheldon Jackson [the all-
native boarding school in Sitka] he came back to the village to go fishing.
His father had been a fisherman, and Tom had grown up on the boats,
along with his father and brothers. This was in 1948. His brothers were
all still in the service, and his father had died in a shooting in the village
while they were away. His mother had died when he was young, and so
the loss of his father left Tom relatively alone at twenty years old. At the
time he drank liquor, he notes, but not so much as he did later. He had
plans to avenge his father's death, but he was waiting for the return of
his brothers and looking for a fishing job.

Shortly after returning to the village he was approached by several
members of the Juneau Area Office of the BIA and the village tribal
council. The BIA had initiated a series of loans through the Indian
Reorganization Act of 1936/38 [which did not really reach Alaska until
after World War II]. The tribal council was going to use money loaned
through the BIA to buy the cannery in the village, and to loan some of
the money to individuals who could then buy seine boats and go fishing
for the cannery. They wanted Tom to take on a loan and to become a
seine-boat skipper. He was nervous at the time but felt like he couldn't
say no to the council, and he had always wanted his own boat. The BIA
representative were all whites: "Caucasians, like you," he says to me.

By the time he got his boat it was the mid-1950s. They had a few good
seasons, especially after the fish traps were outlawed. But by the early
1960s the cannery was closed and they were sent by the BIA to fish all
over. Fishing was bad at this time, and lots of canneries were closing.
This was when he began to drink more heavily. With no family, he had to
settle for what crew he could find, and these were usually hard drinkers
as well. The more people that left the village, the less choice he had in
who he could take on. His own drinking got so heavy that he had trouble
even keeping a crew, and his wife began to drink as well.[1]

By the late 1960s Tom could not afford to keep fishing. The boat
had deteriorated, and he could not keep a good crew. Technology was
improving the seining fleet across the region, and especially the new
boats from Seattle and Washington State, but for those who could not

afford improvements things got worse. At the time he blamed God for his troubles, he says, and for the loss of both parents, and he was very bitter.

One day Tom was sitting in his living room considering suicide, and he asked God for a sign or some miracle to give him faith and spare his life. Just as he was asking, someone knocked at his door. It was one of the local ministers who said that he was just walking by but had a feeling that he should go in and pray with Tom. As he stood at the door he just kept saying, "Jesus loves you, Jesus loves you." This Tom took to be the sign he was looking for, and he started to feel better. The next day was Sunday, and the pastor asked Tom and his wife to come to church that day.

They went to church together for the first time that Sunday. During services the preacher asked Tom to come up and pray. He said that he didn't know how, but the preacher said that he would lead him through it. When they had first come into the church, a man had come in behind them—a "Caucasian" who had sat in the pew at the back. When Tom did go up to the altar to pray, the Caucasian followed and kneeled behind him and prayed: "He was talking to God while I prayed." After the service the preacher invited everyone to stay for cake and coffee, but the Caucasian left. When they sent someone to look for him, he was gone. No one knew who he was, nor had anyone seen him before. After much conversation over the next couple of days, people decided that he was an angel. Tom said that he knew it to be so because after that day he never had the desire for another drink. Since that day, he has been a "good witness" for Christ in the village.[2]

Irene's Testimony

Pentecostal churches have been most successful in those villages hardest hit by the economic collapse of the 1960s and 1970s. Within these villages and wherever these churches have proved successful, they have drawn new members from those most marginalized by the vast economic changes of the past fifty years. Sometimes this might include half or more of the native population. In villages with high unemployment and consequent poverty, two or more radical churches have sometimes found success.

This has not always been at the expense of the other established churches. Indeed, doctrinal differences and even differences in practice are not always the cause of an individual choice of church, at least not at first. Rather, both the Salvation Army and Presbyterian churches have often become the province of one or two powerful families in each village. These families dominate church orientation (often to the open dismay of resident preachers), and the salvationist mission of the church is subordinated to other causes or other dynamics. One active Salvation Army pastor told me that his initial successes in bringing people into the church (especially those who, like Tom, had never been to church) are frequently countered by his inability to retain them. The new prospects are easily dismayed by family politics within the church—which recent converts perhaps more than old members see as a contradiction of church purpose. As a result, new members often leave to seek out the more radical, and more institutionally independent, Pentecostal churches.

The marginality that drives membership in Pentecostal churches also plays a role in determining the content of many testimonies. Drinking and abuse (sexual, physical, emotional) are consistent themes in church testimonies, and are topics used to hook new members or to relate to new members the signification of church practice. "I used to be a real hard drinker, but Jesus turned me away from all that," a new prospect will be told. Irene, a more recent convert to a well-established Pentecostal church, notes this as a crucial part of her own conversion (from a recorded testimony; I added explanations and comments at the time of transcription from my notes and recollections):

[Irene takes the podium. She is wearing a green sequined jacket and blue stretch pants and her hair is dyed red. She wears glasses with thick frames and speaks with a sort of graveled voice. She is about thirty-five, I think, though at first glance she looks considerably older. She knows the pastor from their youth, even though he now lives in another village and preaches to a congregation there. He has said throughout the evening that he had once been a hard drinker, and it is apparent that she knew him as such, and that he knew her as one also. When she speaks, he remains behind her on the dais, and she speaks into the microphone facing the congregation. But her testimony, at least at first, is directed to him. Later she names several in the room in particular incidents, but not before her younger sister joins her at the podium in a show of support.]

Every time you [to the preacher] would come to town you would see me but I would try not to see you. Sometimes I'd go down to [the bar in the village, one of the few villages to have a bar] just because I knew you wouldn't come in there. And then if I saw you you'd say, "Irene, I'm prayin' for you." And that used to make me so mad, because I would think, what's he got to pray for me about? I do what I want and if I want someone to pray for me then I would do it. And there was one time when I was just standing by the store when you come in and then you were waiting for me outside when I come out and you said, "Lets pray together," but the whole time we were standing there prayin' I was just wishing that you would stop and go away. Now it's been about two years since I've had a drink, but I still think about it every day but I know that's not me talking, it's the Devil.

[Here she pauses because she is near tears, but surprisingly her voice is unwavering. Her sister joins her on the dais. They look nothing alike at the podium. Her sister is younger and heavier, and she is a regular church member in the congregation hosting this meeting. After she comes up, Irene starts again.]

Now I never thought I was a very good person and I still don't know how Jesus could find it in his heart to love someone like me. I been known around this town for the things I've done. And I know that I have said some terrible things about some of the people here in this room. And I know some of you have said some bad things about me. But it was always because I was real hateful towards people who thought I was no good. And I knew that some people, like when Sister M., a few years ago said what she said about me to the whole town, that made me real mad, and so I would get drunk and then cuss and holler and make myself look real sorry. But I know that that was the booze, and that the Devil, once he gets ahold of you, he will do things that make you want to keep on drinking and being hateful towards your fellow man. And like I said, I ain't a good person, but Jesus loves me and he is stronger than any demon that could come around here. And I know that all I got to do is stay by him and he will help me. But like I say, there ain't a day that goes by that I don't want another drink and so I know I'm still fightin' but that Jesus is right there fighting for me too.

[Later, in the same revival, Sister M. goes to the podium and makes a speech in the form of a testimony about how hard it was to forgive Irene for something she had said to a member of her family prior (apparently) to the incident referred to in Irene's testimony. It is obvious she feels wounded and wrongfully accused, and she cries while at the podium. By the time she is speaking, the emotional pitch of the revival is at full swing and many people's emotions are right at the surface. The pastor gets her to move on by suggesting that she lead in a song, apparently knowing that she prides herself on her singing. Irene continues speaking, now again to the preacher.]

When you came to town a couple of years ago and you saw me I had been off booze for about two weeks and I was trying to quit but I was having withdrawal and not knowing if I was gonna be able to make it or if I was gonna die or what [she laughs, as do many of those in the church]. And then you said, if you are gonna die, you should accept Jesus as your savior and pray to him so when you die he can find it in his heart to stand up for you when sins are counted. And so that was when I started thinking about Jesus and how he could love someone like me and I still don't know how he could, but I'm countin' on it. And I didn't die [laughs, congregation laughs as well], and it's been two years since I had a drink and I just wanted to say thanks 'cause otherwise I don't know where I'd be right now.

Re-Signing

The two testimonies together, Irene's and Tom's, present examples of several important issues raised thus far. The local elements of the story—the BIA and tribal council; the collapsing fishing economy; the death of Tom's parents and his family's participation in World War II; Irene's reference to local talk and a shared history with the preacher—are all resignified by their respective positions in narratives that, like many other conversion narratives, follow a pattern. Thus there is often a progression where life prior to being "born again" follows a general spiral of loss and self-destruction coupled with the denial of one's own involvement in the problem. Following rebirth, both of these factors reverse themselves: life is made good again and is seen as getting progressively better, and the denial of responsibility is overturned, though at the same time control is relinquished yet again. In the latter instance, control is seen to rest with Jesus and not with worldly circumstances, and those things that had formerly been blamed on others are taken to be one's own fault.

The patterning of the story helps resignify its elements for other church members, who can see the significance of any particular element by its placement in the narrative. Thus when someone begins a testimony, "When I was younger I used to like to go to Juneau on the weekend and go to the movies," those hearing the testimony know right away what sort of role "Juneau" and "the movies" will take in the story that follows, and in the path to rebirth.

The elements of religious resignification include many different kinds of relations and institutions: Alaska Native Claims Settlement Act (ANCSA) corporations, local family politics, even very personal relationships. Some will testify that they are up there to ask that the congregation help their spouse (often husband) find Jesus and join the church so that he or she can find the strength to stop drinking and be a better person. Indeed, the extent to which the spouse is not already a "better person" (and just what this term is meant to relate) is likely known already by most of the audience. What becomes important, then, is that testimony signifies such things according to its own ties and meanings. Narrative relations rewrite personal relations, at least for the extent of the service. This is what theorists of religion mean when they say that religion *rationalizes* people's experiences. But it must be remembered that many forces outside religion do this as well, often in equally cosmo-historical terms. Thus it might be better to speak of this as a resignifying practice, and more importantly, to note that all such practices have as their implicit backdrop another system of signifying practice which they stand against or in contrast to.

This signification is captured for many people in the phrase "Jesus loves you." Most Pentecostal church members will state plainly that understanding the significance of this phrase is the first step in living "a new life" or, which means largely the same thing, of being "reborn." The phrase itself hints at two understandings, both of which are central to the process of resignification. First is that to understand who Jesus is and what this love means, one must read Scripture, which is itself the source of the majority of the signification involved. This is the new reality that church membership promotes. Thus, in addition to referring to local events in a new narrative form, the testimonies also invoke a host of supernatural entities that become tied to these events in almost seamless fashion.

The second critical observation that follows from the importance of the statement "Jesus loves you" is that it comes as a revelation to a majority of those who discover it. This is significant because it reveals the marked contrast between the reality proposed by Pentecostal practice and people's prior notions of signification, in which they obviously feel unvalued and insignificant. This is Irene's point in stating and repeating her own disbelief at the prospect of salvation, for the nature of her experience prior to being reborn was entirely the opposite. She reiterates several times that still does not know how Jesus could love someone like her, but she has accepted that he does. The power of such a statement, then, is its implicit contrast to the present—the present reality of family and regional political economy that results in poverty and desperation, abuse and alcoholism. To say to oneself that "Jesus loves me," as both of the above testimonies make plain, is to undertake both of these two processes—to invoke a host of new significations and to note these in contrast to those of one's current conceptions.

Angel, Demon, and Holy Spirit

Testimonies like these make plain the involvement of supernatural entities (for lack of a better term) in ordinary people's daily lives. This is very clear in the testimonies above. When people say that drinking is a demon or caused by the Devil, they do not speak metaphorically. Though invisible, such spirits are real, with an objectlike-ness unhindered by the fact that they are, most of the time, invisible. The same holds true for those spirits whose work is to help in the process of salvation. These include the Holy Spirit, who is the most important of these entities, and who is God himself in the form of an active presence in "this world." Alongside the Holy Spirit there are also angels, and guardian angels in particular.[3]

Guardian angels are like devils and demons insofar as they are active in the world regardless of human knowledge. Indeed, an individual need not be saved to have a guardian angel. One church member noted: "When I get to heaven I'll know my guardian angel by the way he's beaten up and full of holes. He saved my life several times that I'm sure of. I was checking a saw when I worked at the mill when the blade caught a spike that somebody missed.⁴ When I looked up, there was holes in the walls on both sides of me and all around in the ceiling and sticking out of the log, but I didn't even have a scratch. So I'll know my guardian angel by all the holes he took for me that day." Stories of guardian angels frequently invoke work circumstances. Quite often, in fact, they center around industrial accidents, whether in logging or fishing or mill work or even mining, mainly because many Pentecostal church members have held jobs in these industries.⁵

Like guardian angels, demons are also active without people's direct understanding or acknowledgment. And they are considered potentially active in anyone's life, believer or nonbeliever, saved or unsaved. Yet unlike guardian angels, who are ever present but whose ways are unknown, demons and the Devil are not always present (though they are always potentially present); instead they must be invoked. Once invoked, however, their manifestation is not limited to any individual. Made present by even just one person, they will affect an entire village. And, again unlike guardian angels, their ways are known. They work through "sin," and frequent and unremorseful sin is both an invocation and evidence of their manifestation. Such sins are often discussed in church meetings, where they are frequently and directly associated with demons:

> There was a time when the Devil had me in his hand. I would drink and cuss and swear and be a real embarrassment to my parents. Those were my hard-livin' days and before I found Jesus and that was when I didn't have no knowledge of the Devil, but he had me. And every time I would be drinking I'd get this feeling like I wanted to fight or holler at people, and I had a real foul mouth. And now I know that this was the Devil talkin' through me, and that I had brought the Devil down on my family cause my parents had been real God-fearin' people when I grew up, and it really pained them to see me like I was. And I sometimes think that it was his [the Devil's] way of getting back at them. 'Cause when I was drinking I was a miserable person, and I made them all miserable and caused them a lot of pain and hurt.

Another stated: "People who [practice "Indian dancing"] don't know that by bringing spirits into the town like they do that it affects the whole town and that even good people will get caught up with it and lose their way. Once the Devil gets ahold of a town, then it's very difficult to get him to let go, 'cause he holds on tight to what he's got."

The Holy Spirit, however, is unlike either angels or demons and the Devil. The Holy Spirit is seen to be the active presence of God (creator) and Jesus (God in human form) in the world. During worship he comes into the bodies of Pentecostal church members, and gifts of faith are seen as evidence of his presence. While anthropologists might see this as a form of spirit possession, church members do not view this as in any way an equivalent to the type of spirit possession that they accuse native dance group members of practicing, or the type of demonic possession that is manifest in drinking or sin more generally. The two—visits by the Holy Spirit versus spirit or demonic possession—are said to be entirely different states, accomplished in different ways and with unrelated manifestations.

Gifts of faith were discussed in the previous chapter, and little need be added here except to note that unlike stories about guardian angels, which are often told only to other church members, stories about demons or the Devil and visits by the Holy Spirit have as their implicit backdrop relations with non–church members in the community. That is, while both of these notions engage people outside the church—for people will occasionally share with others their stories about guardian angels—gifts of faith are emblematic of Pentecostal church membership and are thus much more tightly guarded.

Indeed, relations between church members and others in their communities are frequently mediated by notions of the supernatural. While those on the outside identify church membership with speaking in tongues, church members view outsiders as a constant potential source of demonic danger. This is easy to see in the Devil stories discussed above, where the actions of anyone in the community can endanger the salvation of all those in the community. By bringing demons into the community through drinking or other kinds of indulgence—or even through traditional dancing—non–church members are thought by church members to be capable of threatening the life and salvation of those who have already been saved. For this reason, the potential danger of invoking spirits or demons becomes the collective concern of those who know about such things, regardless of the intentions or beliefs of those whose practices are being questioned or opposed.[6]

With visits by the Holy Spirit, however, a curious counter-dynamic is seen. While gifts of faith are seen by church members as signifying the attainment of a certain spiritual communion (with others in the church as well as with God), they are seen by non–church members as being emblematic of the Pentecostal movement as a whole. The term "holy rollers," used in derogatory fashion in Alaska as elsewhere, is a comment on the fact that those who "lie with the Spirit" will sometimes roll around the aisles of the church. No doubt the architectural privacy that accompanies most worship (no windows, limited information on meeting times and places) represents something of an attempt to limit the public face of such practices. As a result, and unlike the native dancing they condemn, the only acceptable audience for church members practicing gifts of faith is the other participants.

But such measures are limited in their effect, and all groups, in the search for new members, must open their doors to those whose reaction will be uncertain. For this reason the practices of Pentecostals are well known in the community. In villages where tensions between church members and a culture movement have moved into the open, culture-group members will challenge the idea that their own practices involve dangerous spirit possession. They point to the practices associated with gifts of faith, asking how church members know that they are not being fooled into possession by demons. Such accusations have caused churches and prayer groups that practice gifts of faith—especially those in villages where tensions have flared—to close themselves off further from those around them.

Apart from the immediate, often physical distance that comments by both sides have created, the accusations and counter-accusations point to a critical dynamic in relations between church members and culture-group members over how this division will be understood. Culture-group members point out that dancing allows them the same sort of communion with fellow participants and the spirits of past ancestors that church members claim for their own gifts of faith. In so doing, they invoke a language of cultural equivalence that is very familiar to anthropologists—known since the early part of the twentieth century as the idea of cultural relativism. In rejecting these claims, church members reject not just the "relative" conclusions, but the entire possibility of comparison and equivalence. They will state quite plainly that the differences are based entirely on the fact that they are possessed by the Holy Spirit, that there is only *one* Holy Spirit, and no equivalent. Likewise, Jesus is, for church members, not a symbol of God, similar in ways to other symbols; rather, Jesus *is* God. This dispute, then—containing as it does both an implicit assumption about the preeminence of symbolic representation on the one side and an absolute denial of this on the other—is critical, for it shows that the dispute between culture-group members and church members is not simply over the theological standing of native culture. Rather, what is at stake in this dispute is the place of Culture in general. We take up this point more thoroughly in the next chapter; but it is worth exploring further here, for it shows up in testimony and, for church members, completes the understanding of the phrase "Jesus loves you." This point (of being against Culture in the anthropological sense of recognizing symbolic form rather than content as preeminent) is complicated, but evidence of ideas about Culture (and not just native culture) is available in church testimonies. Much of this comes through in statements about what it means to be native in a Christian church.

Martha's Testimony

In chapter 4 we noted that what it means to be native within a community was frequently uncertain and the focus of much political manipulation. Some of these issues show up in testimonies and other church-based expressions as well, though here in very different form. In testimony, "native" generally signifies something quite different from the meaning discussed in part 1. By way of example:

Martha is native and an active member of one of the more radical churches in the region. She doesn't usually vote in village elections, she says, and has little to do with most of the village meetings, for her soul is "Christ's," she says. She grew up in the village and worked in Juneau for a few years. She had also at another time tried working in Anchorage in a hotel, but found the work repetitive and returned to the village to be with her family. Her father and mother were both native, but of "mixed blood," and she says that she has "some Filipino and some white in [her]."

Martha first started going to church when she was little. Her mother worked during the summer, and Jean D. took care of her and her brother. And she would take them to church during the summer for Bible school and to other services like the Wednesday service. Jean D. was white, and the preacher at the church was white. That was before the church got popular. After she came back to the village, they had this guy come through who was a native preacher, and who came to speak at a revival. He had worked down south [meaning in Washington State] in an airplane factory and had become involved in the ministry down there. He gave good sermons and told people about how Jesus was coming and it didn't make a difference if you were ready or not, and that he was going to come and save the good, "his people," and punish the others. Most of the people who went weren't sure whether they were going to be saved, Martha said, because not many of them had had much to do with church or "with Jesus as their personal savior." But for most of the people there, she said, because they were the kind of people who hadn't done a whole lot that "counted against themselves," they thought that they could be saved by being born again. None of the real bigwigs in the village were there, though, she said, and for her it was obvious why. They couldn't be saved unless they were willing to give up what they had in this world, and for them that was a lot more than for some others. She said that she thought that people thought more about it when there was native preaching because they knew that he knew about their lives, and that he knew that most of the people there needed to be saved. When she had heard white preachers talk about these things in the past, she said, it had always been "like a speech." But she felt that the native preacher really wanted to save souls.

It is significant that the native preacher had worked down south in an industrial job, a prospect that is common to many of those in the village without strong family patronage ties to the ANCSA corporation or village bureaucracy—those made marginal by these structures who are, simultaneously, the most likely prospects for Pentecostal participation. The implied point is that this minister would, as a result, know about people's souls and want to save them in a way that a white minister could not.

Such a notion stands in marked contrast to the way "native" is understood or made useful to the culture movement, the BIA, or ANCSA corporate boards, for the commonalities it draws upon invoke both the wider political-economic context and the lines of differentiation within that political economy. Note here also that it is unclear whether the native preacher was Tlingit or not, as Martha would identify herself to be. In fact, as mentioned above, the preacher was a Makah native from Washington State (also mentioned in Tom's testimony above). Yet for Martha, he was "native" in the same way that she was, subjectively, in the sense of what he was subject to.

This is a common theme in testimonials, and it is a critical point in the testimony narrative. Most people's lives, before receiving Christ, are disappointing, painful, and depressing. After being born again, however, these same lives—and everything in them, including what most natives would think of as what it meant to them to "be native"—can be viewed as lessons on the path to salvation. Once viewed in this way, growing up "native" does not define the present life of the speaker. Rather, it simply becomes one among many elements left behind by salvation, something that has significance as it is lived *against*. It is a marker that shows where people have come from, but it says little about where they are going.

This is the essence of the "you" in "Jesus loves you." It is a "you" that is absolutely individual and solitary. It is not "Jesus loves everyone," or "Jesus loves the poor," or "Jesus loves Indians"—all of which, church members would say, are quite true but not theologically important. Jesus loves "you," church members say, apart from, in spite of, regardless of, whether you are poor or Indian or both of these things.

This is significant for the point raised above. It posits a self apart from any social category, membership, stigma, or past. It says, in a point we shall return to in the next chapter, that people have a self that exists regardless of the signs attached to them by birth or life. This argument runs directly counter to the logic of identity politics, which often states that what a person is depends on the person's ability to discover and understand the signs attached by one's birth and subsequent life—whether that identity is based on race, ethnicity, gender, or sexual preference.

Beyond this, several other issues emerge from the testimonies presented here. From them it is clear that while the narrative form of most people's testimony is drawn from beyond the community, the actual path to salvation for most church members lies in resignifying their own lives in the language of church membership and church practice. In so doing, this language also allows people a means to resignify what they consider the pressing problems in their communities—alcohol abuse, physical and sexual abuse, and suicide—in a way that invokes different sorts of collective responsibility and accountability than do the normal discourses of psychology, economy, identity, or social work.

In so doing, church members find themselves recognizing and giving voice to powerful anticultural feelings—feelings that express many people's disappointment at failing to achieve meaning in conventional, local cultural ways. Much of the criticism aimed at the culture movement stems from the knowledge gained in church that these failures are a failure of culture, not a failure of the people themselves.

That such anticultural sentiments find expression in a language of spiritual beliefs—which seem to anthropologists, as they do to culture-group members, to be so thoroughly cultural—should not surprise us, though it often does.

7

Indianness and Conversion

The man I will call "Billy" stopped by while Joe and I were working on fish in the yard. He had heard we had some king salmon, and he was also hoping for a ride to Craig, if we were going. Billy was a little drunk, though it was only about ten o'clock in the morning. It was the first time I had met Billy, though I had seen him around town, and he was very friendly—which is not always the case for me here. Joe asked him if he had been working. He said he had not, not for a few weeks, but that he was going back now, and that was the reason he was going to town, to see if there was any work around. Joe seemed to think he'd have no trouble finding work and said so, more as a simple fact than as a compliment. Billy didn't respond. Joe gave him some fish and said that we would come get him if we were going to town.

After he left I asked Joe about the work. Billy is a choker setter with one or another Alaska logging outfit. After a tree has been taken down, he climbs up the side of the mountain, over the other felled trees, with a twenty-five-to thirty-foot-long, three-quarter-

inch-thick steel cable that he puts around the tree and cinches up tight by passing the cable through a metal nooselike fitting on one end—called a "choker." The cable is then attached to a hook from a tower crane, and the tree is hoisted up and maneuvered to the road. Here it's put on a truck and taken down the mountain to a sort yard and eventually sent to Korea or Japan.

Choker setters occupy the lowest rung on the logging production hierarchy. The work is physically grueling, and few stay at it past their late twenties. The cable weighs about forty pounds, and the ground the choker setters move over is a recently logged contesseration of felled trees up to six feet in diameter and over a hundred feet long, interspersed with the limbs of previously felled trees and bushes and small trees not worth cutting. The real ground is often ten or more feet below the surface on which people work, and the cracks and holes between the logs are just as deep, made more dangerous with the constant rain which make the logs slick. Choker setting is done almost entirely by Indians, and it is often the only job Indians hold in Alaskan logging outfits.

"You have to be part animal to do that job," Joe said. I spent a lot of time thinking about what he meant by this—I'm still not sure I know, or how much of what I now think about the job he had in mind when he said it. Joe has worked in logging off and on for fifteen years as well, and though now unemployed, he was at one time one of the few native heavy-equipment drivers in the sort yard. His understanding is likely to be far more complex than my own, his intentions far less clear. My own thoughts are these:

Being "part animal to do the job" may mean . . .

First, and the easiest, that you are considered by the society in which you live a little less than human to be made to do a job that difficult, for as little pay and with no reward beyond pay. That is, you had to be an animal already in the eyes of those around you, and fit for animal work—a denial of humanity common to many forms of appropriation and one carried out in many social arenas outside of work. This sort of explanation points to social injustice and so appeals to my Marxist ideals, but it is probably too simple to ever be entirely true, even in logging.

Second, more optimistically, but in the end equally innocent,

"part animal" may mean that you must be, in your heart, somehow divorced from your own humanity—your own susceptibility to suffering, your desire for a future that you can live in and still live to see—to be able to do the job at all. That you have to be "part animal" in your own eyes, immune from, if temporarily, any humanity you might feel in or toward yourself. This is not always negative, and in places where animals often have been accorded supernatural abilities it might be supposed to involve a belief in special "animal" skills, like the ability to move over logs better than others or being at home in the woods. At best it can involve blurring the line between nonhuman and superhuman in an optimism that, though brief, can be liberating and even uplifting. This sort of explanation appeals to me as an anthropologist, mainly because it tells me that the often unbelievable things we anthropologists seem willing to believe about people are, in fact, true. Yet like the first, this explanation is probably partial at best. Beliefs in such a supernatural humanness are doomed to run up against the very human limits of endurance and age, which, in their own way, bring everyone back down to earth.

Local church members would have a very different interpretation, though they would very likely agree with the assessment that logging requires people to act like, and be treated like, animals. Billy's drunken condition that day would be another sure sign of this interpretation. He is a prime prospect for Pentecostal evangelizing, and I wonder if it is this same issue—of being "part animal"—that church members will seek to "save" him from.

Gifts of Faith

The distinguishing feature of Pentecostal church practice, for most church members as well as for outsiders, is the practice of gifts of faith. These acts lie at the center of church members' ideas about their religion because they are understood to be a manifestation of possession by the Holy Spirit. For many church members, this contact is at the heart of their religious ideas and practices, though this is not because they value experience above religious ideas, such as faith. Possession by the Holy Spirit actually performs several functions beyond experience. Foremost, it is a sign of acknowledgment from God, a confirmation that a person's willingness to be saved is accepted and assured—hence the term "gift." For reasons discussed below, it is critical to Evangelical practice that such practices are given, not achieved or learned. For non–church members, gifts of faith also serve to define church members, for they are at once the most identifiable and least understandable part of "holy roller" religious practice.

The scriptural basis for speaking in tongues comes from the second chapter of the Acts of the Apostles. In the story, the apostles are in Jerusalem during the feast of Pentecost when they are visited by the Holy Spirit:

> And suddenly there came a sound from heaven as of a rushing mighty wind, and it filled all the house where they were sitting. And there appeared unto them cloven tongues like as of fire, and it sat upon each of them. And they were all filled with the Holy Ghost, and began to speak with other tongues, as the Spirit gave them utterance. (Acts 2:2–4)

When church members speak in tongues today they replay this biblical event. Pentecostalism throughout the United States and now the world has grown out of the "Holy Ghost" or "Holiness" movement of Appalachia, where such behaviors were first practiced on an organized basis. Contemporary Pentecostal practice is the result of the spread of the Holiness movement into working-class Los Angeles in the early twentieth century, and from there out into working-class communities in most parts of the United States. Shorn of its rural roots and meeting-house format, Pentecostalism has taken on more standard church form, though many contemporary practices might surprise more conventional suburban Protestant congregations.

The Bible story of the Pentecost visit continues with a discussion of the reaction of those around the apostles when the speaking in tongues began:

> And there were dwelling at Jerusalem Jews, devout men, out of every nation under Heaven. Now when this was noised abroad, the multitude came together, and were confounded, because that every man heard them speak in his own language. And they were all amazed and marveled, saying one to another, Behold, are not all these which speak Galileans? And how hear we every man in our own tongue, wherein we were born? Parthians, and Medes, and Elamites, and dwellers in Mesopotamia, and in Judea, and Cappadocia, in Pontus, and Asia, Phyrgia and Pamphylia, in Egypt, and in the parts of Libya about Cyrene, and strangers of Rome, Jews and proselytes, Cretes and Arabians, we do hear them speak in our tongues the wonderful works of God. And they were all amazed, and were in doubt, saying one to another, What meaneth this? (Acts 2:5–12)

The confrontation with nonbelievers is replayed today as well. Critics, especially non-Pentecostal Fundamentalist Christians, often point to this portion of the story when condemning the practice of speaking in tongues. They point out that if today's church members were really possessed of the Holy Spirit they would speak in actual languages, rather than the nonsensical utterances performed by most Pentecostals. Some Pentecostal church members respond by saying that they do, in fact, speak in actual languages, though today these "extinct biblical" languages are no longer understood or easily recognized. Others simply say that they begin to "babble" uncontrollably when they "feel" the Holy Spirit enter their body. Also, they add, the Bible passage does not say that the apostles spoke only recognized languages, just that some of what they said was recognized as such.

Yet for most church members, challenges to Pentecostal practice come not from other Fundamentalists, but from non-Fundamentalist Christians within their communities. The Pentecost story continues with the challenges put forward by "unbelievers" in the audience of the apostles as well:

> Others mocking said, These men are full of new wine. But Peter, standing up with the eleven, lifted up his voice, and said unto them, Ye men of Judea, and all *ye* that dwell at Jerusalem, be this known unto you, and hearken to my words: For these are not drunken, as ye suppose, seeing it is *but* the third hour of the day. But this is that which was spoken by the prophet Joel; And it shall come to pass in the last days, saith God, I will pour out my Spirit upon all flesh; and your sons and your daughters shall prophesy, and your young men shall see visions, and your old men shall dream dreams: And on my servants and on my handmaidens I will pour out in those days of my Spirit; and they shall prophesy: And I will show wonders in heaven above, and signs in the earth beneath; blood, and fire, and vapor of smoke: The sun shall be turned to darkness, and the moon into blood, before that great and notable day of the Lord come: And it shall come to pass, *that* whosoever shall call on the name of the Lord shall be saved. (Acts 2:13–21)

This passage includes both a list of other acts performed by some Pentecostals—including prophecy and the reading of signs in nature—and a description of challenges that parallels many contemporary Pentecostal church members' relationship with those around them. The first is easily seen during some revivals, though prophecy and reading of signs in nature remain much more rare than speaking in tongues. However, the latter—the relationship between church members and those around them who do not share their beliefs—is equally important and far more difficult to understand.

For Pentecostals in Alaska, like those in Acts, gifts of faith take place within a context of viable, popular, and reasonably well founded alternatives; the skeptics in Peter's audience were, after all, "devout men," people of faith who do not share the same faith as Pentecostal church members. And the first charge of these "devout men" involves alcohol—a subject familiar to many church members who were frequently, at some point in their past life, drunk in "the third hour of the day," like Billy the choker setter on the day he and I met. As it turns out, the issue of alcohol is important not only for understanding the doubts of non–church members, but for understanding church members' own views of their practices.

Alcohol

As chapter 6 showed, many—in fact, virtually all—church members have had immediate, firsthand experience with alcohol, and many root their own church experience in an escape from alcohol addiction. Alcohol also played a role in the divisions within the community that came to the surface in the Flo Ellers incident discussed in the introduction. In the year prior to the Flo Ellers revival a less obvious but equally revealing conflict had split the same village along similar lines. This conflict centered on a radical drug and alcohol treatment program that had been held in the village, whose methods were thought to be very dangerous by the more radical Christians. Run by the Alkalai Lake organization, the treatment involved a program of spiritual reflection and rebirth and incorporated several very general "spiritual" practices modeled after traditional sorts of Native American ceremonies. Pentecostals, with their ideas about spirits, thought these practices were dangerously close to demonism.

At first, however, the program was enthusiastically received. The perceived need for some dramatic intervention was rooted in an earlier set of problems within the same village, for in the year prior to the intervention the village had had the highest suicide rate in the United States and among the highest accidental death rates as well. The accidental deaths very often bordered on passive suicide—as in the case of deaths due to exposure or accident when the deceased was heavily intoxicated. Beyond this, most of the deaths or suicides had also involved alcohol abuse.

Though it is difficult to say why the suicides happened in such large numbers, and so suddenly, changes in the local economy discussed in part I had done much to alter the patterns of alcohol use and abuse, here and elsewhere in Southeast Alaska. Alcohol problems had been widespread in this village since the early 1960s. Yet in some ways, past drinking, though fairly widespread and at times heavy, was not so different here from similar problems in other working-class villages. And as in those villages, drinking problems were kept in check by these same forces that created them—individuals who drank to drown the drudgery of a life of difficult work and minimal rewards could not stay drunk for too long, and had to sober up and go to work to keep their jobs. Fishing communities in particular seem subject to these sorts of patterns, prompted by a work schedule where boats and their crews fish for several days, pay out the shares owed the crew in one lump sum, and then tie up at the dock for several days, until the next quota opening or until the boat can be refitted and the crew made ready for new sorts of fishing. With money and time, drinking among boat crews is common, and some remain drunk for days, many right up until the boat is about to leave the dock. Yet once they are at work, alcohol is forbidden on almost all fishing boats, and many of the most severe drinkers are among the best and most valuable workers.

The above pattern does not apply to everyone who fishes, of course, although it is common enough to be well known to those around fishing in Alaska and elsewhere. By the 1980s, however, two factors had altered the pattern in Southeast Alaska and created a host of new, larger problems. The first was that the gradual decline of the fishing industry in most Southeast villages meant fewer boats (and hence fewer jobs) and more lengthy layoffs between trips. This had left many village residents with increased financial problems, more time on their hands, and fewer immediate incentives to stop drinking if they started. And while new sources of money lessened the financial side of the problem—welfare and related programs grew steadily as the fishing industry declined, and more recently, Net Operating Loss (NOL) money has helped hide the steady decline of the village fishery—they did little to remedy the impact of the decline of an entire pattern or to force people to stop drinking once they had started.

In the past, drinking and the destruction it caused had been accepted (if not entirely approved of) in part because they remained within certain boundaries—boundaries provided by the pattern of work itself. This is true as well for Billy, introduced above, and for many of the village working poor, for whom alcohol is a regular and predictable part of their lives. Yet the changes in the pattern and boundaries of drinking that arrived in the 1980s were thought by many to be at the heart of the soon-to-follow suicides and deaths. Unchecked drinking was often the cause of drastic and damaging sorts of conflicts or abuse within households. ANCSA (Alaska Native Claims Settlement Act) cash payments had actually exaggerated these effects in several villages.[1] It was shortly after the large NOL payments began to flood the village in which the Flo Ellers incident took place that the suicides and accidental deaths grew to such disproportionate numbers. Teenage suicides at the time compounded the sense of crisis that pervaded the village. Several of these were in homes with chronic alcohol and abuse problems as well. In all eight suicides occurred in a single calendar year—in a village whose population is around seven hundred. This is more than 1 percent of the population, and being primarily young people, it was almost like losing two entire high school grades.

The state reacted by sending counselors and aid workers who targeted young people in the effort to stop what seemed an epidemic. The root causes were left for the time being, for it was assumed that they would require much more local participation. Into this opening stepped the Bahai church, already established in the village but with few active followers. The Bahai organization is a syncretic missionary movement aimed mainly at indigenous peoples in colonized areas of the world, and especially Native Americans. Mission dogma is fluid, an amalgam of spiritual beliefs and practices drawn from many indigenous traditions, including Native American ceremonies. Following the deaths and suicides, the local Bahai church proposed a radical alcohol intervention, run by Native Americans from the continental United States. A dozen people were invited to attend what would have been a two-week program of spiritual and personal revitalization.

From the start, the program aroused suspicions among the Pentecostals within the village. Part of the problem was that the program's participants were not allowed to discuss its nature with those who were not attending. The secrecy heightened fears, and rumors were rampant in the village—though in fact the program quite clearly mirrored similar tactics used by many Pentecostal churches. In addition, there were well-publicized elements of Native American spiritualism that accompanied the program. For many church members this hinted at the invocation of demonic forces. Church members' fears were enhanced by an individual who left the program after only brief participation and who, according to some, told exaggerated stories about the tactics of the intervention and the beliefs of its directors. The result was a rapid groundswell of protest from the Pentecostal members of the community.

Before the end of the program's first week, a village-wide meeting was held and pressure was brought to bear on the tribal government—which had sanctioned and unofficially cosponsored the program—to withdraw its support and force the program leaders and sponsors out of the village. Informal pressure was brought to bear on participants as well, and before the end of the second week the organizers were isolated and most of the participants had withdrawn. Plans for a follow-up program were canceled.

The recriminations that followed were even more exaggerated and unreliable (though also considerably more local) than those that would later follow the Flo Ellers incident. Many at the town meeting actually blamed the new churches for the suicides, for one particularly painful double teenage suicide happened in a home where the parents had recently been "reborn." It was said by culture-group members that the children had been made to feel ashamed of their Indianness and had been taught that their values were wrong. Some felt that the parents of the children had become so convinced of the need for their own salvation that they had lost sight of their children's needs, feelings, or understanding of the situation.

On the other side, church members blamed the tribal government and the culture movement for long ignoring the smoldering alcohol and abuse problems in the village. Rather than addressing and redressing "sin," they noted, the culture movement had invited outsiders and their demons, temptations, and distractions, which pulled people away from what they felt to be the only possible answer to such overwhelming sorrow and pain—salvation.

Most Pentecostals in the villages today remain leery of those in the tribal government who are affiliated with the Bahai intervention, and they often speak with great suspicion of the tribe's sponsoring people to write grants to bring in outsiders or state psychologists. In many ways this confrontation set the stage for the Flo Ellers incident. As it turned out, long before the revival began or Flo Ellers arrived in the village, the lines were clearly drawn between the Pentecostals on one side and the culture movement, tribal government, and ANCSA corporations on the other.

167

After the Flo Ellers incident (while "all hell was breaking loose" in the village, in the words of one culture-group member), the host church and its members tried to maintain a low profile. Realizing that this issue was more likely to draw the ire of people outside the village—though it would perhaps be less divisive within the village than the Bahai intervention—church members closed ranks. The church that hosted the revival continued to be the most well attended of all those in the village, but the congregation's normal inward-looking tendency became even more pronounced, and active evangelizing of new prospects was halted.

That summer, church members stuck together while pursuing subsistence resources, and prayer group meetings were reportedly very low-key. Few were willing to talk about the incident, even though many agreed strongly with what had been done. The church pastor—locally born and himself an Alaska Native—left for a time to pursue work in Seattle, but he returned in the fall as the church season was beginning.

Sermons the following winter tended to focus on the usual issues. Dancing regalia and relations with the culture group were not mentioned, though the long-standing church rule that church members would not remain at social functions where the village dance group was appearing remained in effect. By the following spring, one could attend services and not know that the Flo Ellers incident had even taken place. Things remained the same for nearly three years after the incident, so much so that when I asked church members about the incident I would be told that it was "old news."

In the winter of 1995–96, however, similar issues were raised, this time *within* the church, that split the congregation and, in the end, caused the church's pastor to retire and the congregation to, for the most part, dissolve. The start of the troubles was a sermon given by the pastor about the issue of native culture and congregation members' responsibility to distance themselves from any native cultural activity. While it is difficult to know for certain why the issue was raised anew, the church had begun recruiting new members by this time and it is very likely that the question of relations with the culture group had arisen in that context. Further, it was perhaps the several years of quietude that caused the message to seem so surprising and to be so negatively received; or it may have been the general feeling among Evangelical congregations that no pastor should single out members of the congregation—even new members—for criticism during services.

Either way, the congregation split, with one side remaining with the pastor and the other returning to the local Assembly of God congregation, from which the original independent church had sprung. The financial strain this placed on the church forced the pastor to leave in search of work elsewhere, and while a group of church members (mainly the members of the prayer group) attempted to hold regular services, church attendance and membership gradually declined. By the summer of 1996, the few remaining members opted to affiliate with a national Pentecostal church, with the hope of bringing in an outside pastor and outside support. Forgoing independent status, the church was forced to receive a non-native pastor, and its appeal as an all-native congregation declined instantly.

Many outside the congregation saw this as a fitting end. Culture-group members, while reluctant to appear victorious, noted with some pleasure that the same issues that had originally divided the town had eventually divided and ruined the church. Today, core members of the congregation remain somewhat isolated within the village, partly by choice. The Assembly of God church in the village saw the return of a number of former members. This coincided with the hiring of a new, non-native pastor for the Assembly church who was, because of his distance from the history of the congregations and the village, able to form a single congregation out of those who had left and returned and those who had remained with the Assembly church all along.

The former minister of the church that hosted the Flo Ellers revival—and the individual whom many saw as responsible for the divisions in the village—remains in the village today and is an occasional visitor and guest preacher at the Assembly church. The host church itself has declined from being the most well attended congregation in the village to being among the most marginal. With an Assembly of God church already well established in the same town, it is unlikely that missionary support for this congregation will last very long.

Most of the former members of the host church still refuse to attend events where the dance group will perform. The new missionary minister of the church told me that he felt pressure to do the same, especially given that his few remaining church members had sided with the original pastor in his condemnation of the cultural events and items. Even many of those who left to rejoin the Assembly church remain suspicious of and even openly opposed to the activities of the culture group, though the former Assembly minister did not view this as a necessary conflict. Among the Assembly congregation, issues of culture are seldom mentioned, though past events have shown that this can change very quickly.

Belief and Practice

In discussing the history of the church with me shortly before it broke up, one village resident noted: "It's like a dog with a wound, they just can't leave it [i.e., the issue of native culture] alone." Indeed, this seems true.

At stake in this issue, however, is not a question of theology and its repercussions. As I argued in the introduction, there is much more to these events than simply "wrong" beliefs or misunderstandings across cultural boundaries. Most church members were natives, after all, and most grew up in the same villages as their critics. On the other side, most culture-group members are practicing Christians. Rather, it seems to me that what is at stake in the Flo Ellers incident, and in church members' rejection of native culture, is something much bigger than local disputes or different understandings of the world. It is the relationships among culture, belief, and the collective shaping of people's collective future—that is, politics—that seem inexorably caught up in all of these events. And it is this issue—and its power to touch everyone, regardless of beliefs—that brought to the surface the strong emotional currents one saw in all of these events.

Anthropologist and historian Talal Asad has written about the historical and cultural changes responsible for many contemporary ideas about the relationship between religion and politics (see Asad 1992, 1993), and his discussion can help us understand why issues of religion and politics (of Fundamentalism as it appears in the popular press) seem so important to so many people today—in Alaska and elsewhere. In particular, Asad points out, it is important to understand that there are two distinct sides to the process we have now come to call "secularization." Normally the term is used to describe the process of removing church influence from government bodies in Europe and North America, and later in the colonies of these nations and their neocolonial dependencies. Indeed, in this sense issues of secular government continue to shake countries like Indonesia, Turkey, India, and the United States.

Yet as importantly, Asad points out, secularization involved a transformation of church organizations as well. For Christianity, the expulsion of church influence from national government meant that churches in Europe had to reorient their practice away from what they had been up to that point. Churches before the modern era were founded and organized for a world-transforming mission. For Christianity of the Middle Ages, the Kingdom of God was an earthly goal pursued through conversion and governance—forced conversion and dictatorial governance, if necessary. Extreme measures in both of these cases were justified by the mission they served: the *collective* salvation of humankind according to the teachings of Jesus—a salvation thought to be achievable in the here and now.

In Europe, secularization meant that Christian churches there had to be reorganized around issues of belief and away from practices aimed at bringing salvation to the whole, in the present. Salvation was, in other words, no longer something that churches sought on behalf of humankind collectively and for the earth itself, but rather something churches offered followers on an individual, person-by-person basis—if they, the followers, accepted the beliefs of the church. During secularization, collective salvation was individualized and churches went from governments and institutions of social order to institutions aimed at developing, teaching, and conserving particular theologies. Missionary work became a means for spreading a theology, not governance. Right living was an opportunity offered converts for the purpose of their own salvation, not something intrinsic to the very idea of salvation as a whole, upon which everyone's salvation was dependent.

Pentecostals, like other fundamentalists (whether Christian, Hindu, Islamic, Jewish, Buddhist, or other), reject this sort of secularization and protest easy differentiation between individual and collective salvation. For Pentecostals and many other Christian Fundamentalists, salvation involves Jesus' return to earth and the establishment of a Kingdom of God on earth—notions that hark back to the medieval Christian theology discussed by Asad. And while many Christian Fundamentalists say that human actions can do little to influence the timing of Jesus' return, all agree that the establishment of the Kingdom of God after his arrival will involve and require the triumph of his followers over nonbelievers, and subsequently the forced creation of a Christian politico-theological order over the entire world.

While such ideas would seem familiar to many historians of Christianity, today they seem very foreign to those unaware of this history, even to contemporary non-Fundamentalist Christians. Yet there remain crucial differences as well between the salvationist ideas of today's Fundamentalist churches and the Christian Church of the Middle Ages. Pentecostal church members—like many Protestants—attach little optimism to human attempts at achieving collective salvation. Jesus' Second Coming is often thought to be immanent, but no one I spoke with thought this arrival depended on circumstances being made ready by church members—a concept central to church governance and expansion in the Middle Ages. As a result, there is little institutional focus among Pentecostal churches in Alaska on social or political order, as Carol Greenhouse (1986) points out for many Fundamentalist groups in the southern United States. For the most part, Pentecostal churches in Alaska and elsewhere are organized in much the same way as other Evangelical, theology-oriented mission churches. This is perhaps the source of the apparent passivity of these salvationist churches—about which people have told me, "After they convert, then they are just sitting around waiting for Jesus to arrive at their door."

This mixture—both a notion of collective salvation and the idea that human beings are largely helpless in bringing it about—can help to explain why many non–church members were surprised by both the Flo Ellers incident and church members' resistance to the Bahai intervention. Yet while church members appear to those outside their ranks as politically passive—and it is quite true that many church members shun politics and see it as a distraction from the key social issue of salvation—their insistence on a collective notion of salvation ensures that church members remain hyperaware of issues or events that may have an impact on salvation as a whole. Thus, in the case of the Ellers incident, church members were acting on specific beliefs about the nature of spirits in this world; but as importantly, they were also acting *against* a political situation that they felt jeopardized not just the lives or souls of those involved, but also the lives and souls of everyone around them. In short, while they were acting against the threats of "demons," they were also reacting against a political situation in which resource development and cultural revival took precedent over concerns about the more immanent social and human problems of alcohol addiction, physical or sexual abuse, and suicide.

In the United States, the sort of secularization described by Asad has a peculiar history, linked perhaps to a conflict between the country's colonial history of religious sanctuary and the strong secularist concerns of its bourgeois founders. Separations between church and state played critical roles in the framing of the U.S. Constitution, but so did issues of religious freedom. Courts have been forced to contend with the conflict between these issues since at least the late nineteenth century, when Mormon polygamy prompted the U.S. Supreme Court to distinguish between religious belief and religious practice. In laying out their decision in *Reynolds v. United States* (1879), the Court made it clear that although religious belief was unconditionally, constitutionally protected, religious practice was not. As a result, when state interests came into conflict with religious practice, the decision said that such practices could be outlawed without being in conflict with constitutional protections for religious freedom. *Reynolds* effectively spelled the end of Mormon polygamy, which was officially condemned by the Mormon Church shortly afterward. As case precedent, however, it has continued to influence decisions about religious freedom and the relationship between church and state. Similar logic has played a role in outlawing the sacramental use of marijuana by members of the Rastafarian Church.

In many ways, this split between belief and practice restates the division between collectivist and individual salvation discussed by Asad as central to the process of secularization. Belief is seen by the courts as the appropriate concern of churches. But practices, because they may conflict with other practices of governance, are a domain open to secular state control.

Speaking in tongues, or "receiving gifts of faith," marks an interesting opposition to this division between belief and practice. In the film *Holy Ghost People*, a 1968 documentary of a Holiness church in West Virginia, one of the church members discusses his disappointment with not receiving "the tongues" for the first year of his membership. He states: "But when I did repent, I could feel the quickening power that comes with the Holy Ghost but I didn't have the evidence of speakin' in tongues like I had before. And I prayed to God for might near to a year and seek the Lord, and I thought that He was foolin' with me. And I had never got the power back. And I wondered about the tongues, see, because without the evidence of speakin' in tongues, why, we ain't got it. And that's what I was concerned with."

Here the normal, secularized, and court-sanctioned vision of religion is reversed: belief follows upon practice; practice is demonstration of true belief. To fail to practice is to fail to believe sufficiently or properly. If the man quoted were never to receive "the tongues," as he put it, it would be a sure sign that he would never receive salvation. Many native Pentecostal church members in Southeast Alaska would agree: failure to speak in tongues or be moved by the Holy Spirit is a failure to truly believe, regardless of what you think you believe.

Without much trouble, one can see that the separation between belief and practice completes the transformation begun by secularization. Fundamentalists of all sorts resist this idea, of course, and Pentecostals center their own religious faith on a reversal of its logic. This is precisely what makes radical churches seem so threatening to states. Yet it is also what makes Fundamentalists (again, of all sorts) anti-Cultural (capital "C" indicating not just a particular culture, but the idea of Culture as a defining element of human society as a whole). For at the heart of a notion of Culture, most fundamentalists would say, is the idea that one set of beliefs is just as right, valuable, and true as any other. Such an idea is not simply a negation of particular beliefs that people hold to be absolutely true (though this alone might anger some church members), but rather Culture's denial of the idea that *any* beliefs could be absolutely true. This issue, more than any other, seems to be at the heart of church members' resistance to the social processes in which they are embedded. And it is this idea that provides the incentive for people to overcome their normally hidden propensity for sociopolitical actions.

Drunk in the Holy Spirit

This issue has motivated fundamentalists against the relativizing tendencies of modernity all over the world. It has played a role in nonreligious fundamentalisms—like ethnic nationalism and ethnic cleansing—and been countered by equally diverse secularist forces (usually some combination of military and capitalist economic interests) that seek to enforce the idea that religion and culture are domains of belief, not practice. Yet it does little to explain why people like Billy are such obvious targets for Pentecostal recruiting, and why speaking in tongues and other gifts of faith have become such important practices for those who do join a Pentecostal church. And it does even less to explain why only some parts of native culture have drawn the attention of church members, or why native culture in particular, and not just the notion of Culture in general, has become such a target for church member political action. It is to these more specific questions that we now turn.

The focus on native culture has much to do with issues surrounding alcohol abuse, which was the original impetus for much evangelizing within native villages and the ongoing recruitment of people like Billy, Irene, and Tom. This configuration—of native culture, alcohol abuse, and gifts of faith—is at the center of what it means to be Pentecostal in Alaska, both for church members and for those looking on from the outside—although I am not at all suggesting that there is any actual or essential connection between native cultures or native cultural practices and alcohol.

To examine these issues we must return momentarily to the Bible passages discussed earlier in the chapter. There we noted that part of the context for Pentecostal practice was a skeptical audience of diverse faiths, the multiple ways of seeing the same events. These were the same story characters who claimed that the gifts of faith shown by the apostles were merely evidence of their being drunk on "new wine." Having noted that most church members stand against both these other ways of seeing and the notion that all ways of seeing are somehow equally important, we might have expected Peter to simply cite the prophecy (that he later does), resting his defense on the accepted, absolute authority of a text recognized by his audience (the prophecy of Joel, and for modern-day Pentecostals, the passage cited earlier in the chapter). It is important to note, though, that in the story Peter begins with a very different defense. His own answer is that the events of the Pentecost story are not the result of alcohol, "seeing it is but the third hour of the day."

This point, it seems to me, forces us to reconsider the relationship between specifically Pentecostal practices and the types of relations Pentecostal groups have with those around them. For Peter's explanation seems not to deny the reasonableness of these charges of drunkenness: had the events occurred later in the day, they might very well have been the result of alcohol, he seems to say. This is important, for in a sense Peter acknowledges that the difference between gifts of faith and drunkenness lies not in the actions of those possessed by one or the other, but rather in the fact that these gifts come at the wrong time of day—that they fall outside people's normal routines and expectations, and as such appear alongside, rather than opposed to, the alternatives the audience proposes. To risk a further gloss on this brief passage, what Peter seems to be saying is that gifts of faith are unique and special because they can do many of the things that alcohol can, but in a very different way, one that connects with the rest of people's lives (the rest of their day, as it were) very differently.

My intention is not to engage in overly risky biblical interpretation, but to draw our attention to a series of parallels and hence consequent differences between alcohol use and Pentecostal practice today. For while people on the outside continue to see church practice as suspiciously similar to the types of delusions that alcohol dependency produces—people go from "drunk on liquor to drunk on the Holy Spirit," as one woman church member explained her family's understanding of her own church membership—church members do not necessarily disagree. The woman who told me this seemed moderately content with this characterization. After saying it she laughed, seemingly acknowledging and even enjoying some notion of similarity between the two states. When I raised this issue to church members, several laughed, particularly those who had been "off the bottle" for a long time. For them, the parallels seemed interesting on an abstract level and were not perceived as threatening or upsetting.

This contrasts strongly with people's reactions to other sorts of comparisons. In chapter 6 I pointed out that many culture-group members see Pentecostal practices—in particular, speaking in tongues—as precisely the sorts of behavior that Pentecostals condemn in native dancing. That is, many non–church members see similarities between possession by the Holy Spirit and the sorts of spirit possession that Pentecostals so vehemently condemn in native dancing. This parallel, however—unlike the one between alcohol use and these same gifts of faith—is not readily accepted by church members. Suggestions of this sort were invariably met with serious denials and rejection, and frequently anger. One church member told me that if I thought that, I missed the whole point of "going to church."

The reason for this difference in people's reactions is perhaps the most important element in understanding the popularity of Pentecostal churches and the place of Pentecostalism in the political and economic changes discussed in part 1 of this book. The answer lies, initially, in the suggestion put forth above—that the uniqueness of gifts of faith comes not from what they do or say to church members, but from their very different place in people's ordinary lives. For people like Billy—who are, quite ordinarily, drunk by the third hour of the day—the power of such a notion is enormous.

Many church members explain to me that they first turned to alcohol to drown out the daily events of their lives. As with Tom in chapter 6, the pains they sought to avoid came not from momentary tragic events—like the loss of a parent or even both parents, as was the case in his testimony—but from the impact such events continued to have on a life already made marginal by much larger political and economic processes. It is from the ongoing difficulty of Billy's life as a choker setter that he seeks refuge, not the daily aches and pains; he drinks to hide the increasing transparency of his own tattered body and a job that includes fewer and fewer opportunities for escape.

The parallels between alcohol use and Pentecostal practice first became apparent to me when I was more concerned with understanding the former (drinking) than the latter (church practice). When traveling in Alaska, I once saw a bumper sticker that read, "Jesus can fill that empty place in your life." Many church members agreed, and noted that this was the crucial difference between their experience with church and their experience with alcohol. While alcohol could temporarily take away the pain of daily living, it could not do so for very long—leaving people with a greater awareness, they say, that something was missing. Church practice—becoming drunk on the Holy Spirit, as some say—filled a void that people had first tried to fill with alcohol. In the light of this, there is little wonder that Pentecostal practice appeals so immediately to former alcohol users and abusers. What is more, church members explained, by going to church rather than drinking, their lives no longer fell further apart, as had occurred with alcohol. Rather, their lives began to "get back to normal," even if what they meant by "normal" had never actually been part of their lives. The high they get from the Holy Spirit, one person explained, not only lasts for eternity, but as importantly, it comes with no hangover.

In this way, and as important as the actual feelings of divine grace involved in church practice, Pentecostalism promises people like Billy something more than a relief from daily life. Instead, beyond simple feelings of relief, church membership offers the possibility of an ordinary life—a life whose everyday difficulties suddenly leave room for hope, the promise of a future. Indeed, what strikes one immediately upon meeting new church members is the extent to which they suddenly embrace the elements of ordinary living—sobriety, domesticity, passivity, community. It is, I remember remarking to myself, as though church converts join more than the church; it is as though they convert to the American middle class!

They do not, of course. Most remain in very difficult economic circumstances, in marginal villages and marginal jobs. Many are further alienated from the only source of political power they once possessed, village families, most of which will reject those who become church members. Likewise, most church members reject vehemently what they consider contemporary American middle-class values (as do Fundamentalists all over the United States). But the personal and interpersonal transformations are dramatic. People who had lived lives so thoroughly marginal (economically, socially, and politically) seem after conversion to embrace an entirely new set of understandings. They stop being "Indians," in the sense raised in the introduction and in chapter 4. And what remains most amazing about these changes is that the ordinariness people achieve seems to be not just a product of their conversion, but the goal.

In reality, the actual changes in people's lives are not quite so dramatic. Many remain in the same sorts of jobs they had before, living in the same houses in the very same towns. The changes offered by church membership are not rooted in dramatic changes in the content of people's daily lives. Rather, the change seems to be in their ability to "live with" their lives—to find in these lives more than the very high cost of being rural, marginal, and Indian in America. Put another way, the normalcy promised by church membership is tied not to a different life, but to a different way of living—different, that is, from that which people lived before converting. And among the most notable characteristic of this new way of living is its insistence on its own ordinariness, even in villages and among people whose actual ordinary lives remain necessarily very different.

This same issue, it seems to me, is what causes church members to view the celebration of native culture with such suspicion. It is difficult to imagine two more different sorts of social trends than the ordinariness promised by church membership and the differentness celebrated by culture groups and native dancing. It is the difference between a plaid shirt and button blanket—of speaking English and speaking Tlingit or Haida. For all of the rhetoric and theology of dangerous spirits that accompany church members' condemnations of native dancing and the culture movement as a whole, it is, I believe, the differentness that is so intrinsic to a notion of "Indianness" that most church members reject. In this way, church members can accept the parallels between alcohol use and church practice, for in their own experience the latter does what the former could not. People turn to one and then the other for many of the same reasons. On the other hand, very few are willing to accept any notion of similarity between church practice and native dancing, for any apparent similarity is overwhelmed—in the minds of church members—by the radically different goals toward which these two projects are aimed. If alcohol abuse is a cry for help, church practice and native dancing are two very different, perhaps even opposite, answers. The success of the former lies in its appeal to ordinariness, the latter in its appeal to difference.

The two currents within Pentecostal practice discussed in this chapter— its resistance to any separation between belief and practice, and its promise of ordinary hopefulness—help make sense of the apparent suddenness of church members' political agency, as well as the targets of this agency (in particular, village dance groups and native cultural projects). And both of these (the basis for new political agency and its anticultural focus) seem to account for the success church evangelists have had among Southeast Alaska's more marginal individuals and households. The link between practice and belief appeals to many marginal people through its insistence on the collective nature of salvation, what we might call the sociality of hope. And the promise of ordinary hopefulness has used people's own responses to their marginality (particularly alcohol) as a way to introduce church practices and to insinuate a sort of sacredness to the ordinariness it promises.

Legacies of alcohol use and abuse in most villages have played into this process, simultaneously setting the groundwork for a rejection of native cultural practices. Some of this rejection is based on church cosmology—one that sees alcohol abuse as a demonstration of demonic possession which, once introduced to a village, becomes a threat to all residents, unsaved and saved. But even more important than church theology, it is the way Pentecostalism sees itself as an answer to the questions raised by alcohol abuse—and the desperation it implies. In response to these questions, church membership offers a new hopefulness to people whose lives prompted the turn to alcohol in the past. Yet so do native culture, identity politics, and the ideology of the culture group, though notably, this answer is based on creating difference. This, I have argued, is a critical part of what church members reject—and so it remains a crucial issue in their condemnation of village dance groups and identity projects.

Conclusion

CULTURE IN HISTORY

Pentecostal church membership is a relatively new phenomenon in Southeast Alaska, but one with parallels in many areas of the neocolonial world. Everywhere, it has found special appeal among those made marginal by the history of colonial expansion and by the continuing ebb and flow of capital penetration. It has also, and perhaps at first surprisingly, inspired in many of its converts distinct anticultural feelings—feelings that, in Alaska, have encouraged some people to look with great suspicion on the native cultural practices engaged in by their neighbors and kin. They are not alone. I am told that other churches have had similar success by preaching an anticultural message elsewhere in the developing world. In Highland New Guinea, Seventh-Day Adventist churches have proved popular despite the fact that (or, if the parallel with Alaska is true, because) they have forbidden their members to have contact with pigs—this in an area where pigs have always provided the main means for participation in funerals, weddings, politics, and virtually all cultural events that form the basis of specifically local inequalities.

I have argued here that the anticultural activities of church members in Alaska are more than simply the result of theological intolerance. Rather, the roots of Pentecostalism's appeal grow in the increasing internal differentiation that has accompanied the most recent wave of colonial expansion in the region—ANCSA. The Alaska Native Claims Settlement Act of 1971 has laid the foundation for new forms of local economic and political stratification in every village. And it has done so by invoking and enhancing claims of cultural distinctiveness of natives in the region, often at the expense of other sorts of identifications (e.g., working status, gender, age, or class). Some in Alaska have advocated the use of this politically reinforced cultural distinctiveness to overturn ANCSA. Others, specifically church members, have rejected strategies of cultural distinctiveness altogether. On the surface, this puts the more radical culture advocates and church members on opposite sides. Yet it should be clear by now that the two sides share many of the same goals.

Central among these goals is the rejection of the ANCSA-inspired changes, particularly those that have led to a decline in community (regardless of whether that community is thought of as native or as Christian). As shown in the part 2, church membership often provides members with new means for expressing their dissatisfaction. It also creates and maintains a set of social relations largely outside the political economy in which most of their other relations are embedded (relations of tribe, family, shareholder status, or even subsistence work). These new relations can and frequently do serve as an alternative to those caught up with ANCSA or family or other, more clearly political relationships.

Yet it is equally easy to see how these same feelings — desires for a set of relations outside those that are so clearly destructive of community — might push some people to embrace native culture, which is also, potentially, a set of social practices capable of creating distinctive groups and social dynamics. In many ways the two endeavors are very similar. One critical difference — one that makes the situation something more than simply a set of symmetrical alternatives — is church members' rejection of this very equivalency. Without exception, church members deny that there is any sort of equivalence between the two strategies. In important ways, this rejection seems almost incomprehensible to those in the culture group, who are much more willing to accept the idea that there are multiple ways of pursuing the same goals and that there should be some room for all of them. This is likely the reason why many are so willing to attribute Pentecostal resistance to theological intransigence.

Yet by rejecting the idea of alternative political or social strategies, church members do more than simply advocate a particular theological stand or their own moral superiority. They advocate a strategy of collectivity over one rooted in difference. They advocate collective practice over individual belief in a way that insists upon the mutual interdependency of collective representations, that is, all collective representations. This idea places church members not just against native culture, but against some of the foundational ideas of Culture itself—which contains, implicitly and explicitly, the assumption that all cultural representations are inherently arbitrary and rooted in tradition, not truth (or Truth).

Conclusion

In coming to see themselves, via church membership, as against culture, native church members are aided in two ways. The first, as I argued in the introduction, is rooted in the fact that all people find themselves, at certain times and in certain ways, necessarily against a culture that they simultaneously consider very much their own (i.e., against a set of locally defined and locally valued meanings and the practices associated with their explanation and reproduction). Those from whom cultural reproduction exacts a particularly high price—those whose participation is the most tenuous, and so who are forced to absorb the greatest emotional, economic, or political risk in participating in culture—are apt to be the ones most frequently confronted by their own anticultural feelings. It is no coincidence, then, that radical churches have had their greatest successes among marginal groups, whether in large cities or the rural third world. Alaska Natives, having borne the brunt of hundreds of years of colonial extraction, have been placed at the margins of the Western world and have borne a particularly heavy portion of the burden of reproducing Western culture. Marginal members of these communities continue to bear the burden of the cultural resistance that these communities have created to engage and counter this domination.

In a second way, though, Native Americans are forced into an even more ambiguous relationship to their culture than marginal people elsewhere. For Native Americans are forced to view their culture in particularly narrow terms, mainly by laws (like ANCSA and the Indian Reorganization Act) that have linked their participation *as natives* (i.e., as people with a historical claim to special status and participation based on past and present ownership of disputed resources) to their ability to maintain an acceptable level of cultural distinctiveness. In the introduction I linked this fact to the recognition that there are no Indian subcultures. Native culture, unlike many other kinds of culture, is an all-or-nothing endeavor for its members, according to the laws of the society in which Indians are embedded. As a result, ordinary (in the sense of universal) tensions between people and the culture they claim as their own are especially exaggerated among Native Americans, who are never entirely free to make of their culture what they otherwise might. These two factors provide much of the answer to the question of why Pentecostal church practice has proven so popular here and elsewhere.

183

Such an approach may strike some as an overly politicized view of culture, one that places an undue emphasis on culture's place in ideology and power at the expense of questions of meaning. Admittedly, this has not been an ethnography in the conventional sense of that term. Most ethnography is concerned with descriptions of a people's culture, that is, with questions of meaning per se. In the introduction I questioned the usefulness of the notion of culture when used in this way. There are critical problems that stem from thinking that "a people" can have "a culture." Important social divisions exist within every group—divisions of class, age, gender, or ethnicity—and these divisions make culture or "local meaning" an issue for struggle, not something unconsciously accepted among those in a particular locality. Though sometimes these lines are less obvious in a native village in Alaska than in other places, a sense of these divisions and the struggles they create is critical for understanding how people's everyday lives shape and are shaped by themselves and those around them.

In the past, many ethnologists were able to justify a notion of shared culture by ignoring these divisions and choosing instead to look at how aspects of meaning are linked to cosmologies, social organization, traditional beliefs, and so on. The connections they found are interesting and often quite complex. Yet most ethnology stops here, taking these connections to be characteristic of culture in some general sense, rather then viewing them as the outcome of an ongoing set of social processes, processes that are located very specifically in a particular time and place. Absent this realization, culture always seems fixed in the past, arriving on the scene preformed, predetermined, or a priori—as though all cultures were created at the dawn of time, as anthropologist Gerald Sider notes critically (1987). Culture, in this view, is something that can be lost, but seldom is it considered something that might be, or must be, made and remade if it is to exist at all. And perhaps more importantly, when such questions are asked, most anthropologists forgo asking whether such making and remaking is done at the expense of some more than of others.

On the other hand, looking at culture for its place in ongoing processes of social differentiation is not to eliminate questions of meaning from questions of history or to reduce meaning to political expedience. Putting aside the notion of culture as a fixed way of looking at the world—a view normally associated with the term "a culture"—means only that we begin to think of "culturing" instead. In such a view, what seems most important is how people of a particular geographic and historical locale are able to make meaningful the world around them, or, less innocently, how people are made to accept some meanings they would prefer not to. Either way, the focus would be on how they do one or the other (and most often both) in ongoing fashion, over and over again, in ever-changing contexts amid ever-changing desires, hopes, and worries, and with different access to the resources need to do these things, amidst others trying to do similar things, for different reasons, with different access to these same resources (see, e.g., Roseberry 1989).

To view culture in this way we must begin by going beyond questions about what is "shared" by people who are said to possess the same culture, and to ask: does the stuff of culture—the rituals, symbols, meanings, customs, and social and cognitive structures—tell us about culture as a thing in itself, or can it be used to understand the specific sorts of historical processes through which the worlds and lives of particular people come to be, and how these worlds are seen by themselves and others as particularly meaningful or particularly meaningless, and in either case, as something worth struggling for or over? Too few ethnographers have gone to the field with the intention of asking such questions, particularly among Native American societies. Nor are the answers to these questions either simple or widely agreed upon. But for reasons we shall come to below, it seems increasingly important that they be asked.

Part of the problem with even asking these sorts of questions is that to do so, one must confront particularly political uses of the term "culture," introduced in chapter 4. In Alaska and elsewhere, culture is part of several political projects, often *the* central part. To understand why this is so—and thus to understand why new ways of looking at culture are often seen with great suspicion by people whose culture is being discussed—one must look back over the relatively brief history of the term, a history very much caught up with the emergence of political modernism in the world.

"Culture" (as it has been used by anthropologists and is now used by many people) is complex and problematic, to the point that many social scientists have begun to avoid the term altogether. There are good reasons for *not* doing so, however, and much of this book can be read as an argument about why I feel this to be so. Some of these reasons are historical. Others are quite contemporary, such as Owen's use of the term to describe important parts of his life—and not others: for example, few Alaska Natives would say it is an element of their culture that some are forced by economic necessity to hunt in the winter while others are not, despite the fact that who must hunt in the winter and who need not is often determined by very local issues (see chapter 4).

To understand why culture has come to mean so many very different things to so many different people, it is necessary to step back in time—though not very far back—and examine two distinct historical and political situations that played a critical role in forming current ideas about "culture" and the even more difficult term "cultures." As many anthropologists are now beginning to acknowledge, the notion of "a culture" has its roots in two quite distinct social situations, both of which occurred at the end of the nineteenth century.

Some readers might be surprised to learn that contemporary ideas about culture are little more than one hundred years old. Yet as anthropologists Eric Wolf and Ernest Gellner both show, "culture"—as a term for a way of life and interwoven system of meanings that is shared by a small, face-to-face community—has its roots in the budding nationalist movements of central Europe of the late 1800s (Wolf 1999; Gellner 1983, 1998). As Gellner points out, after the collapse of the Ottoman Empire, the Habsburg Empire—the Ottoman Empire's Christian/European foe and the self-appointed guardian of the Counter-Reformation—faced a political crisis. The Habsburg Empire had originally been assembled through the addition of willing parts as much as it was won by conquest. And with the threat of Turkish invasion no longer imminent, many of the smaller satellite territories began to assert the desire for more local control. In these outer regions, as local elites sought a means to mobilize popular sentiment against Habsburg control, there evolved an idea that Gellner calls the "organic vision" of "community" (1998:5).

At the ideological center of this vision was the notion of culture as shared meaning. Previously, culture had stood for courtly life—for those individual and collective signs that separated the nobility from the rustic residents of their own regions (think of "high culture"). Through careful manipulation, this same term gradually came to mean the sorts of things that separated people along regional lines—language, costume, custom, religion. Differences between political and economic classes *within* regions were downplayed, while differences across other sorts of boundaries were emphasized. Language played a crucial role in defining the new dividing lines, but it was not the only factor. In places where local elites sought greater control at the expense of both the empire and the elites of neighboring regions, smaller divisions could be asserted that cut across linguistic zones.

Gellner writes: "It was with the rise of nationalism that the deep confrontation . . . really came into its own within the Danubian Empire. The opposition between individualism and communalism, between the appeal of *Gesellschaft* ('Society') and of *Gemeinschaft* ('Community'), a tension which pervades and torments most societies disrupted by modernisation, became closely linked to the hurly burly of daily political life and pervaded the sensibility of everyone" (1998:12).[1]

More recently, we have come to call this "balkanization"—the process whereby a constructed sense of community is used politically and economically to differentiate societies and nations. But today's version is of a far more limited territorial scale than that which sprang from the nationalisms of the late nineteenth century. And as Gellner makes clear, it was the birth of nationalism that married the concept of local ways of life to anti-imperialist, nationalist projects.

Much of this discourse of culture survives today. For those who continue to live under one form of external domination or another, the language of culture that emerged from early central European nationalist movements is ideally suited for contemporary nationalist and subnationalist movements. Such feelings are common among Alaska Natives, and Owen's and others' use of the term "culture" must be understood partly as a result of those feelings. In short, "culture" has become important in Alaska in large part because the notion of culture was created during similar times, to work on similar feelings.

A second discourse, the anthropological use of the term "culture," is related to the first historically but contains elements of another sort of political battle—this one over the emergence of the modern social science disciplines in the early decades of the twentieth century.

Several of cultural anthropology's founders were immersed in or influenced by the Habsburgian dilemma—as were many of the turn-of-the-century intellectuals of Europe. Gellner discusses Malinowski's work in this context and sees it as both influenced by and simultaneously seeking to escape this same organic vision of community. Franz Boas, too, was deeply influenced by Adolf Bastian's arguments for a similar notion of culture arising from the field of *Völkerpsychologie*.[2] Yet it is too simple to say that anthropology merely adopted nationalist definitions of culture—or even those of Malinowski or Boas.

Anthropological definitions of culture were also greatly influenced by the conditions under which the discipline of anthropology emerged as an independent academic pursuit. In *Marxism and Literature* (1977), Raymond Williams pointed out that much of what we think of as culture arises outside the Habsburgian dilemma, beginning instead with the birth of sociology, psychology, political science, and economics. For as these fields emerged as organized disciplines from their original place in moral philosophy, they quickly sought out and defined novel objects of study that helped justify their independent existence. Sociology redefined (and largely invented) "society"—which had also, up to that time, been used along class lines as a synonym for "fellowship" (again think of the term "high society"). Sociology defined society in general, abstract terms, much as nationalists had done with culture. Thus we now think that everyone is a member of "a society." In this view, socializing went from meaning something that people did at parties to something that people did as an adjunct to the formation of an organic whole: "society."

The success of sociology along these lines had a profound impact on the founders of anthropology, and the sociologists were not alone. Late in the previous century, economics had done much the same with economy, changing its definition from a characteristic of certain behaviors ("economizing") to an object-like entity—"the economy"—which in turn required study by a specialized field. Psychology followed suit, and emerged in its modern form largely at the same time as sociology by inventing and then centering its attention on another thought-to-be object-like entity: "personality." Like society and economy, personality was treated as a thing in itself, rather than a term to be applied to particular aspects of human behavior. Thus while we still use the term "personality" to describe people's idiosyncrasies, we also now believe that everyone has "a personality" that is akin to an organic whole, and that a "personality disorder" reflects a mechanical problem, akin to the misassembly of a person's internal life, rather than simply a category of unaccepted behavior.[3]

Importantly, Williams makes clear that "culture" emerged from these fields not as an object of study in its own right, but as a catchall used by sociologists, psychologists, and economists for individual and collective human behaviors that did not fit neatly into either "society," "economy," or "personality." Rather than being a "thing" that might be studied (like "a society" or "a personality"), culture was a waste bin for those areas of individual and collective life that did not fit into any of these categories—things that did not conform neatly to the implicit explanations that formed the basis of the new fields of economics, sociology, and psychology.

In this way, culture represented a problem: it was by definition composed of things that did not make sense. And in this way, it was a problem that cried out for an answer. Anthropologists rushed to give this answer, but so did future generations of sociologists, economists, and psychologists (and later, literary critics, linguists, and philosophers). Another problem with culture stemmed from the fact that culture had no objective or object-like reality of its own—it was not a thing, as society, personality, and economy were thought to be by their respective disciplines. As a result, those things labeled "culture" included both behaviors and psychic phenomena. And while some elements of culture clearly pertained only to individuals, others were equally clearly collective. Sometimes it seemed as though culture consisted mainly of irrational ideas (e.g., nonmaximizing behaviors in economics), while at other times it was thought to be composed entirely of the customs of a place. Altogether, culture was a hodgepodge of leftover behaviors unaddressed directly by other emerging disciplines, a collection that said much more about the formation of academic disciplines than it did about the "stuff" that wound up included under the heading.

Anthropology rushed to fill this void, at first simply by adding "culture" to its list of concerns.[4] Yet it was the students of Boas and Malinowski who sought to more thoroughly colonize the ground left vacant (if only briefly) by other social sciences, and in so doing to establish a special field, a special object of study, that would define anthropology as an independent discipline. In so doing, anthropology inherited the traditional ethnologists' subject—non-Western, small-scale communities. But anthropology's "object" became those elements of human behavior and belief that did not make sense according to sociologists, economists, or psychologists. Cultural anthropology was born with the invention of "culture," fueled by the integrative passions of Mead, Benedict, Evans-Pritchard, and others.

Still, the process involved more than simply taking up the piecemeal study of what had been left behind by these older fields. For while anthropology inherited many of its concerns from those largely ignored or dismissed by other disciplines, those same disciplines continued to look upon these topics as the edges of their own scientific understanding. And, as sociology, economics, and psychology matured as disciplines, they turned again to those issues that had been put aside in their early days. Anthropologists, having inherited these leftovers, were thus under great competitive pressure to define their object in holistic terms—to define culture as a singular, object-like thing, as sociology had for "society," economics had for "economy," and psychology had for "personality," and on a par with these same object-like entities. If they did not, it seemed likely that those things cast off to anthropology as "culture" would eventually be taken back in piecemeal fashion by the other social sciences. Thus while Boas never felt compelled to see any "culture" as a single, unified entity, equally present in all of its particular manifestations, all of his students did (though differing among themselves over just what sort of thing it was). In the end, anthropology assumed its current form largely in response to the efforts of other fields to encroach on this newly chosen ground.

The effort by structuralists—whether French, British, or American (in the form of culture and personality studies)—to secure for anthropology a unique object of investigation occupied the emerging discipline until the late 1960s. The result of these efforts is a notion of culture as a closed system of concepts whose internal logic is capable of absorbing any sort of worldly event on its own terms. Yet this effort had several unintended consequences that, having emerged since, have caused anthropologists much anguish, especially where notions of culture as closed and fixed have been wedded to the sorts of nationalist imaginings discussed by Gellner and Wolf.

It is by now no longer surprising to many anthropologists that anthropology's notion of culture—culture as a "way of life" of a particular, small-scale community which is both ecologically and personally sensible; which underwrites both social structure and normative personality; and finally, which is functionally interrelated, such that each of these parts supports all of the others—continues to help justify the extreme social conservatism of nationalist ideologues everywhere. Indeed, contemporary versions of the ethnic nationalisms discussed by Gellner now seem to work directly with notions of culture taken as much from anthropology as from other nationalist literature, for anthropology's object-like notion of culture has made culture something that may (and thus must) be defended in its entirety. It is something that not only might be lost, but something so fragile that the loss of any single part spells the end of the whole. Ruth Benedict's fragile "clay cup" has become the talisman of ethnic nationalism the world over.

These same nationalisms have become the most potent form of political change in the late twentieth century. In most parts of the world, violent ethnic nationalism has replaced the "peasant wars" of the first half of the century, exceeding them in brutality and duration. Calls for land reform have given way to ethnic cleansing in the politics of the present, with anthropology's own contribution to the discourse—culture in its most objectified form—featured prominently.

Marxist theorists such as Williams and Wolf have long lamented anthropology's efforts to tidy up the social science muddle through its efforts at objectifying culture (i.e., treating it as though it were an object). By asserting coherence in a collection of things initially ignored by other fields, anthropology has, they feel, justified the false academic divisions it inherited. Instead, the impossibility of reconciling the elements of culture—either with themselves or with the concerns of the fields that cast them off—represents for Williams (1977) and Wolf (1982) the chance to undo the easy disciplinary division of the social sciences. In place of this fractured picture, each of these theorists has in his own way argued for a total theory of human collective life, without regard to the conventional objective divisions of society, personality, economy, and culture.

Beyond Wolf and Williams, many in anthropology have also begun to reject outright the notion of cultural wholeness and uniformity, turning instead to notions like "hybridity" and "creolization" to talk about how meaning is constructed. Many others have rejected "culture" altogether, disappointed by its complex history and compromised position in contemporary politics. Yet at the same time, quite a few anthropologists are now confronted—as I was—with the past ethnography of the region in which they are doing field research. These ethnographies are now held up as authoritative sources, standards by which the current performance and coherence (of both the subjects of research and the ethnographer) can be judged.

As such, while culture seems on its way out of anthropology (even, ironically, cultural anthropology), its importance seems to be growing in non-academic circles. Indeed, one reason why anthropologists must continue to deal with culture is precisely because today's nationalist movements (and subnationalist resistance movements, like the ethnic politics common to many plural societies) continue to value the term. Indeed, perhaps the most difficult issue facing anthropology today is the fact that many non-anthropologists now find it critically important to imagine or even create the sort of cohesive cultural wholeness anthropology once argued as the hallmark of culture—rooting political necessity in an anthropological fantasy that anthropologists themselves now choose to reject.

Recently, Eric Wolf has pointed out that much of what we call culture has always been used by people to enact larger collective integrations in sociopolitical life (1999).[5] That is, that people frequently use those odds and ends we call culture—the sorts of things that are normally left out of other social science projects and explanations—to organize others by linking the social, cognitive, emotional, and productive parts of their lives. When done well, such integrations fulfill the anthropological fantasy, creating a form of culture whose holism makes it very difficult to separate culture from society, personality, politics, or belief. In these situations, culture suddenly and persuasively seems like a thing in itself, one with which these other things must interact and from which they take their shape.[6]

For Wolf, the central question of culture thus becomes: how do some people's notions of cultural order and wholeness—and thus some historically particular cultural orders or *cultures*—come into being while others do not? He writes: "Immediately, then, we must ask who and what is organized, by what kinds of imperatives, on what level [by culture]. If organization has no central core—no motivating Hegelian spirit, no economy 'in the last instance,' no Mother Nature in the guise of the environment—how are we to understand the manner in which organizing imperatives are orchestrated?" (1999:290).

In an example drawn from the history of the Kwakiutl—a group of West Coast native peoples located several hundred miles south of Alaska[7]—Wolf proposes an answer to this question. He begins by recognizing that much of the "culture" of the Kwakiutl recorded by Boas in the late nineteenth century was that put forward by elites in their struggles to gain and legitimate their own status. Yet, because these elites dominated the means by which Kwakiutl cultural significations were enacted and passed on, these representations did become "Kwakiutl culture," further underwriting and ensuring the "internal ideology of socio-cosmic ontogeny"—the accepted beliefs about the workings of the world and the role of people in it (1999:129). Ceremonial events that tied this ideology into the workings of economy and everyday social life ensured that everyone who depended on the economy had a stake in the "culture" that was developed.

Yet from this it does *not* follow that everyone (even in what Wolf argues to be highly integrated "cultures" like the late-nineteenth-century Kwakiutl) necessarily experienced or felt the same way about the culture in which they lived. This is a critical point I have tried to make clear throughout the previous chapters, and it is a most important step in understanding how it is that ordinary people like those who join churches come to have an antagonistic relationship with a culture that is, for the most part, very much their own.[8]

Wolf's description of the Kwakiutl of classical ethnography makes clear that those things we call culture (the rituals, cosmologies, ideas, relations, traditions, and compacts of cosmo-political organization) continue to be important to global historical processes, especially when attempting to consider what people—most especially those who ostensibly "share" the same culture—can and will do to one another. Such a view has been very much a part of this monograph.

Yet there is another side to this same process that is less discussed by Wolf, and one that has concerned us here as well. This begins at the opposite end of the scale of social inequality from the sorts of elite manipulation discussed by Wolf, starting instead with the sorts of understandings and resistances that ordinary people mount against the integrating imperatives of those around them. This process—more egalitarian perhaps, than those discussed by Wolf—has also come to invoke the language of culture, and thus the same possibilities of emotional, relational, and cognitive connectedness.

Critical to this argument has been the idea that, quite often, culture does more than simply order the world "as given" to those on the margins of power. For many people, what we have come to call culture makes possible life and even hope in a world that—given the "reasonableness" or presumed rationality of sociology, political science, economics, or psychology—no "normal" person might choose to live. I think here of Owen and others like him who fish and hunt in weather they know might kill them, for less money than they would make behind a fast-food counter, at longer hours and greater personal and emotional strife. When Raymond Williams noted that "culture" was those things that did not make sense to early theorists, this is the sort of situation he had in mind.

Yet as such, the term "culture" is used by ordinary Alaska Natives to no less an extent than by those ideologists discussed by Wolf. This point is critical. To the extent that culture allows people to live a meaningful life in a situation that sometimes—or even, often—seeks to take their lives through risk and toil, it becomes a form of self-assertion that they must, at some level, embrace as well as reject. This also is the basis of the fundamentally antagonistic yet necessarily ambiguous relationship that ordinary people must have with and to the sources of meaning in their lives, and most especially, with and to those cultural meanings they often call "their own." Put another way, if culture allows ordinary people to live with a world they otherwise might not, it still does little to change that world—little to end the elements of daily life that make it so close to being unlivable. And by making a difficult world livable but no less difficult, culture becomes something less than an absolute savior. I began this book with the idea that no one (singly or collectively) can live easily with *his or her own* culture—his or her own partly successful ways of making meaning and hope in exceedingly, increasingly difficult circumstances—and this is simply an expansion of that point.

Yet here "culture" no longer refers to the sorts of ideological plans put forward by those with power over the means of cultural production, though indeed it may contain some of the same elements. Rather, "culture" here refers specifically to the ongoing "culturing" that ordinary people enact on the world, despite (and frequently against) the demands and integrations of others around them. This, it seems to me, is very much what is at stake for those who join Pentecostal churches—and who in the process lose their place in "family," "identity," and "native culture." The results they seek, though quite ordinary by middle-class American standards, are extraordinary given the lives they lived before becoming church members. Ironically, it is those who find themselves "against culture" who find they must culture the world on their own, often "against" the only lives and "cultures" they have ever known or are likely to know.

The importance of this culturing was made apparent to me by a recently converted church member named Mary, who, like many of those in the past chapters, had come to church after several years of alcohol abuse. As we stood on the edge of the boardwalk, near the center of town, surrounded by the older downtown houses and shops, with the bay in front of us and the mountains beyond that, she said, "I'm trying to live where all of this can make sense." As she spoke, her hand swept out in front of her, motioning toward all of what was before us. Her thoughts were at once theological and deeply personal—for it was plain that success in this effort, and thus her success in staying "off the bottle," was, in her eyes, by no means assured. Nor was it quite clear how much of what came within the sweep of her hand had to be included for her efforts to be a success—just how much of what she saw or what happened around her had to make sense for her to be able to stay in the new life she was living. But her effort to see a world in which she might live a meaningful life seemed at the heart of what she sought in church, and simultaneously what she sought from those around her, for it was clear that the sweep of her hand was intended to take in the houses in the village. In this way it seems equally clear that any success she might have depends in part on what those around her are willing (or unwilling) to have her imagine.

The philosopher Charles Peirce once noted that most of what we think of as "the real" is simply habits of the mind. Equally important for Peirce was that "the mind" that held these habits referred not to the thoughts of a single individual. Mind, for Peirce (and anthropologists like Gregory Bateson [1972] and others), was a collective endeavor, and reality was a habit necessarily collectively held. Church members often seek to impress upon those around them the importance of this collective imagining, but so do, sometimes, those they oppose. For both church members and their opponents, the stakes of this collective imagining seem very high indeed. Drawn from the ranks of those made marginal by the reality around them, church members seek a new sort of world that includes some of the more basic elements of human life: hope and dignity among the most important, but also basic needs like safety, subsistence, and sobriety. For their opponents, many of these same issues are also at stake, though the context of their hope and worry is perhaps far more closely linked to the larger processes of political economy and identity in the late twentieth century.

For those in between, then, the consequences are immense. Owen, the subsistence hunter from chapter 4, is one of those in between. Owen's wife is a member of the Hoonah prayer group, and most of her family is "saved." Owen is a member as well, though he does not attend quite so regularly as she does. Nor is he quite so ready to be "against culture" as are some other members of the group. "I still got to feed my family," he explains. And so he continues to hunt seals in the winter at great personal risk, and to dance in the dance group when he can. Owen is a "like a real old-time Indian," I was often told. For this same reason, he is very much a prospect for local church recruiting.

Series Editors' Afterword

Each of the books in the Fourth World Rising series will have, in addition to a brief series introduction, an editorial afterword in which the series editors raise for consideration some of the issues at stake, that is, how we think the particular book bears upon, expands, confronts, and alters our understanding of issues germane to the series as a whole. There are several reasons for doing so—a preeminent one is to lend the series a level of coherence and comparability generally absent in other ethnology series. Yet the main purpose of the afterwords, and of the Fourth World Rising series as a whole, is to introduce a range of significant case studies to an even broader range of interpretations and strategic discussions. The afterwords are intended to mark out a new range of theoretical issues that, again, we (the editors) see in each book in the series. This notion is underwritten by the understanding that doing something new is more a process than a fact, and this series in its multiplicity is designed to encourage that process and a discussion of its results. The purpose of these afterwords is, then, to generate and even, when necessary, provoke discussion without overshadowing the author's intentions or overwhelming the nonspecialist reader who is the primary audience for the work (hence their place at the end of each book).

Against Culture lends itself to such a discussion, for it raises from the beginning the problematic disjuncture between the image of Alaska Natives that is encouraged and even required by the federal government and tourist trades and the one emerging from the actions of newly converted Pentecostal and Evangelical church members. Such issues, though perhaps not entirely new in any Alaska village, are generally unexpected in such dramatic form and are, when so suddenly thrust on village public life, deeply problematic for those involved. Indeed, the split between church members and village cultural advocates shocked other village residents and focused the attention of non-natives throughout Alaska and beyond on what many felt was a private, village affair that had somehow escaped its normal confines. The struggles that ensued, over very different meanings and consequently different futures for natives *as natives*, mark the issue of religious division in the village as one with important practical and political stakes.

Here, the series focus on internal differentiation is taken by the author to include divisions over the definition of what it means to be native and over the significance of the signs and symbols of nativeness. Importantly, as the author's introduction makes clear, this division derives its political significance from its real-world importance to village residents. *Against Culture* seeks to show how such general and seemingly abstract divisions can relate to—can help produce and make problematic—a broad range of specific differences such as those between wealthier and poorer natives, between genders, and especially in this case, between those who are significantly dependent upon subsistence resources and those whose primary dependence is on a cash income, particularly from timber production.

Yet, as *Against Culture* shows, each of these specific divisions is, in turn, problematic as well. Everyone in the village now depends upon some cash income, usually in increasing amounts, and dependence upon subsistence resources is far more complex than the producer's direct need for food. A deeper sense of the issues and tensions involved, as we have seen, comes from looking not just at subsistence, and at the ways timber production limits the possibilities for getting subsistence goods, but also from looking at the increasing differentiation between shareholders in the village-based native corporations and nonshareholders.

In so doing, the author makes two crucial points particularly clear: first, that the nativeness associated with subsistence production (and the social relations that go into and come out of subsistence production) is simultaneously being made both more important and less possible; and second, that all such divisions within the community—subsistence producers and wage earners, shareholders and nonshareholders—are neither entirely separable nor fully overlapping. Together this produces a complex and ever-changing field of vulnerabilities, and equally complex and changing ways of coping with these vulnerabilities.

Differences over the meanings of native cultural items are caught up with differences in the vulnerability of individual villagers and households to the whims of the larger political economy, with native-white relations, and with state and federal Indian policies. Political differences in particular—mainly over the place of development in village and regional economies — find their way into divisions between church congregations, and vice versa. And throughout, differences between the roles of men and women come to reflect, and sometimes to reverse, differences in job opportunities spawned by radical changes in the global economy. And in each of these cases, different, often opposed visions of what it means to be native in Alaska emerge from each side, forcing everyone to ask just what such a notion means and can mean. The answer to this question seems to be inescapably complex and caught up with the particular circumstances of the case.

Yet while such a conclusion may seem to argue for an extreme relativist view, there are other ways of looking at the situation in Southeast Alaska as well. In particular, the complex contingency of what it means to be native, in Alaska and very likely in a great many other places, derives its complexity from the politics and history involved, and not from some supposed, intrinsic, or primordial "localness" (see, e.g., Geertz 1983). Thus rather than ask whether native-led Pentecostal churches, with virtually all-native congregations, are in fact elements of native culture, or whether a native corporation is somehow different from one whose shareholders and directors are not native, it seems more important to ask why nativeness is suddenly so critical to so many different projects. The current book does not address this issue directly, though it does point out in the introduction that the conditions under which people assert their indigenism or native identity are perhaps different for Native Americans than they are for other, non-indigenous groups.

This claim warrants more discussion here. Indigenism has recently become increasingly significant politically, and has become, therefore, an increasingly popular topic among academics, advocates, and others. As a result it has been the subject both of much celebration and of considerable scrutiny. Several voices — political, academic, and native — have weighed in on the subject (see Dombrowski 2000; Lee 2000; Li 2000; Niezen 2000; Friedman 1998, 1999; Warren 1998; Beckett 1996; Perry 1996; Neitschmann 1994; Sider 1987), many, though by no means most, in celebratory if cautious tones. Of these, the United Nations' decision to proclaim 1993 the International Year of the World's Indigenous People was perhaps the most politically influential.

In facing its own questions about what constituted indigenism, the UN was guided by the so-called Cobo definition, named for the director of the original UN indigenous project. The Cobo definition laid out five criteria for being considered an indigenous people. Indigenous communities are peoples who:

1. have "historical continuity with pre-invasion and pre-colonial societies that developed on their territories";

2. "consider themselves distinct from other sectors" of these societies;

3. "form at present a nondominant sector of society";

4. "are determined to preserve, develop and transmit to future generation their ancestral territories and their ethnic identity"; and

5. seek to do so "according to their own cultural patterns, social institutions and legal systems." (Cobo 1987:48; this division into five criteria follows Lee 2000)

The Cobo definition has proved widely influential, helping to put indigenism in its current form on many political agendas and making it a specter on the horizon for many contemporary nation-states. Yet, as becomes clear from the material discussed in *Against Culture*, it is not just the generality of these five criteria that ensures their wide appeal — as though the members of the UN committee had somehow hit upon a common denominator of ready-made indigenous peoples. Rather, what marks these criteria and the concept of indigenism they enshrine as something with real-world political appeal is their ability to bring into focus a host of incipient relationships between potentially indigenous groups, surrounding non-indigenous peoples, and an overarching state. That is, it is the possibility that this definition held out to both those who might claim it (i.e., the indigenous), *and* those who will decide on their claims (the state), *and* those who will be affected by it (the non-indigenous public) that ensures its importance. It is this last contingency that we usually forget.

When looked at in this way, notions of indigenism — and the associated rights and claims — are not seen as something emerging entirely from those communities who would claim it. Rather, indigenism is something of a political middle ground. It is new political territory whose terrain is uncertain and fluid, yet one whose eventual dynamics can greatly affect the societies involved.

And there is much reason to believe that the current dynamics of indigenism *are* largely new, distinct from past relations between states and native peoples. For in the past, states and industries interested in resources claimed by indigenous people have sometimes, perhaps most times, simply taken them—by force, by law, by trickery, and by brutality. Yet less commented on is the fact that recently—in Alaska and elsewhere—states are also willing to recognize and acquiesce to native claims, where doing so provides them opportunities that are otherwise denied. Thus, as *Against Culture* makes clear, changes in the Alaskan logging industry and in environmental laws affecting timber cutting on federal lands have encouraged both government and industry to support the recognition (and even expansion!) of native claims. By awarding land to Alaska Native Claims Settlement Act (ANCSA) corporations, with their partial sovereignty over their own lands, the U.S. government allows land that would otherwise be subject to a host of harvest regulations to be developed without being subject to federal environmental laws. Similar issues regarding Indian lands throughout the United States have allowed the increasing use of reservations for toxic waste dumping, high-stakes gambling, and, as with the notorious Black Mesa projects, strip mining and electricity generation. All of these are destructive and harmful forms of industrial exploitation, both to natives and to their neighbors, yet each offers recognition of a sort to the indigenous claims involved. Together, situations like these encourage us to look further into the meaning of indigenism, for it would seem that the current stakes of nativeness, in the United States and beyond, are very high.

Of the five characteristics of the Cobo definition, all are of interest to states and their corporate allies. First, according to criterion 1, indigenous groups are those with claims to what Dombrowski (2000) calls special status political-economic participation based on a priori claims to important resources. That is, what marks potentially indigenous ethnic minorities as distinct from other ethnic minorities (in the eyes of surrounding states and often in their own eyes) are claims to significant resources other than their own labor, resources that they still, in some measure, possess. Importantly, these claims are often quite different from the way that property is normally recognized, as reflected in Cobo criteria 4 and 5, where we note that these claims are supported neither by force nor on obvious legal grounds, but rather through claims to continuity based on cultural tradition. This idea that indigenousness is intrinsically related to resources held insecurely (but held or claimed nonetheless) is perhaps the main reason why so many groups and surrounding states found much to like, as well as to protest, in the definition.

Beyond this, we note that according to criteria 2 and 3, indigenous groups are defined as not holding state power, nor yet are they simply one among the other ordinary subjects denied access to state power. To be indigenous, that is, one must be neither; yet for anyone to be indigenous, the others must exist. This last part is deeply ironic, for it points out that, in contemporary global politics, for any group to be indigenous there must exist not only a state, whose interests are different from those of the indigenous group, but also others who are both excluded from power and considered both by the state and by the indigenous themselves to be non-indigenous. For natives in Southeast Alaska, this includes both the non-native population of the region and, perhaps more importantly, the larger American middle class. The latter, at least recently, has altered the terrain upon which the claims of Southeast Alaska Natives are made by seeking to limit the power of the government and logging industry to clear-cut national forests as they have in the past. In so doing, they have greatly affected the way long-standing native claims to land and rights are now heard by federal, state, and industry officials, to the extent that the federal and state government are more fully engaged in a dialogue over these claims than they have been in the past—even though these claims have been argued since the early 1900s and ostensibly closed by Congress since the early 1970s.

This new dialogue, which is at bottom a way of using native land ownership to allow industrial clear-cutting of old-growth forests—a very profitable and very destructive practice, no longer as possible to do in national forests as it once was—represents a shift in the realpolitik of nativeness, but it makes use of a host of older images of nativism in its public representation. Native peoples emerge, originally, in advertising and in popular imagery, as peoples with a special tie to nature. In the nineteenth century this special connection was used to argue, by representatives of the dominant society, that native peoples both must and should give way before the "progress" of "civilization." In the twentieth century, many of the same corporations, such as Disney, that so loudly proclaim a stereotype of native peoples' ties to nature, quickly and profoundly take advantage of native peoples' political and economic vulnerability to encourage the clear-cutting of native-owned forests or to spread toxic wastes. The simultaneous public production of the children's movie *Pocahontas* and the purchase of Net Operating Loss moneys is, to put it mildly, deeply ironic.

Yet the tie to nature has lingering effects on what may and may not be done by states to, and on behalf of, native peoples. Indeed, one of the key features of native political sovereignty, as it has been defined and limited by the U.S. courts, is that native political entities, insofar as they are recognized by the federal government, are considered to be governed by the U.S. criminal code, but to be exempt from the U.S. civil code, in recognition of (what is regarded by the dominant society as) the remaining or "residual" sovereignty of native peoples. This recognition of that sovereignty allows native peoples to partially govern their own affairs, and also to have high-stakes gambling casinos, to store nuclear wastes, and to clear-cut their own forests, all things that suppose a somewhat mystical relationship to particular pieces of land, a relationship that does not, however, include outright ownership or full national sovereignty as defined by the state for itself. The task of the dominant society is, in the emerging politics of indigenism, to "recognize" and produce new and lingering images of native sovereignty in ways that harness native groups' existing sovereignty to corporate and state interests, as did ANCSA. Note, for example, how far the U.S. federal government went, under ANCSA, to avoid past notions of sovereignty and to define new sorts of specifically "corporate" Indian country in Alaska.

Thus, as *Against Culture* shows, while it is certainly true that the first set of Cobo characteristics (an indigenous group's largely unenforceable claims to significant resources) has meant that these groups have often found themselves buffeted by the combination of state power and national populations, this is not invariably the case, in Alaska or elsewhere. In fact, it seems that both strategies—thought of, perhaps, as domination on the one hand and recognition on the other—are used together by states toward identical ends: domination to so thoroughly marginalize native peoples that many are later willing to accept recognition on very narrow terms.

Native peoples must, to the contrary, use their own understandings of their sovereignty, and their own social relations and legal and political resources, to shatter or slip out of this yoke. Yet when native groups resist such manipulation—and the short- and long-term, ecologically devastating results it promises—as Alaska Natives have, the federal government has been quick to pass legislation to significantly sweeten the short-term financial pot, in this case encouraging other Southeast Natives living as far away as Seattle, Anchorage, or San Francisco to override the votes of those most affected by the logging: the village residents themselves. The result is that virtually all native-owned land in Southeast Alaska, somewhere on the order of 625,000 acres, has been clear-cut, most in the last fifteen years.

In cases like these, indigenism or nativism must be seen for the political dynamics it contains. Likewise, responses to indigenism or nativism—like those of the Pentecostal church members that are the focus of *Against Culture*—must be understood in this broader political context as well. The challenge for those working in native studies, including the editors and authors of the current series, is to recognize these politics. Put another way, the underlying lesson of *Against Culture*—and to some extent, of the Fourth World Rising series as a whole—as it addresses contemporary anthropologists working in and with indigenous communities is that we would be of the most service to our native hosts when we go beyond the effort to authenticate their claims (whether to longevity, property, continuity, or authenticity) and rather help clarify how issues beyond these are likely to play a role in how their claims are heard, and used, by those in power.

Native peoples have, we argue, long known this in some capacity, and have, in the midst of their struggles against the imposed reshaping of their lives, continually developed ways of putting the issues that truly matter to them beyond the reach of power. This has often meant that the continuity of native existence both within and beyond domination and exploitation entails continual, and often fundamental, cultural transformations. Pentecostalism, in this perspective, is part of (but not reducible to) the continuity of native culture.

Thus we must do more than understand Pentecostalism as part of the continually changing process of "being Indian." We must also come to live with, and struggle through, the partiality of our understandings: partial in the sense of limited, and partial in the sense of taking sides. As the unfolding nightmare of anthropological "science's" involvement with the Yanomami reveals, "objectivity" turns out to contain, in very basic ways, betrayals not only of the people we study but also of ourselves. To the extent that so many indigenous people have gone so far in breaking out of the old, homogeneous, and bipolar paradigms of indigenism, native studies—and native advocacy—must do no less.

Gerald M. Sider   Kirk Dombrowski

Series Editors' Afterword

REFERENCES

Beckett, Jeremy. 1996. "Contested Images: Perspectives on the Indigenous Terrain in the Late Twentieth Century." *Identities* 3:1–13.

Cobo, José R. Martinez. 1987. "Study of the Problem of Discrimination against Indigenous Populations." Vol. 5. UN document E/CN.4/Sub.2/1986/7/Add.4.

Dombrowski, Kirk. 2000. "Discussion of Richard Lee's 'Indigenism and Its Discontents.'" American Ethnological Society Annual Meetings, Tampa, Florida, March 25, 2000.

Friedman, Jonathan. 1998. "Class Formation, Hybridity, and Ethnification in Declining Global Hegemonies." In *Globalization and the Asia Pacific*, ed. K. Olds, P. Dickin, P. Kelly, L. Long, and H. Yeung, 183–210. New York: Routledge.

————. 1999. "Indigenous Struggles and the Discrete Charm of the Bourgeoisie." *Australian Journal of Anthropology* 10:1–14.

Geertz, Clifford. 1983. "Local Knowledge: Fact and Law in Comparative Perspective." In *Local Knowledge: Further Essays in Interpretive Anthropology*, 167–234. New York: Basic Books.

Lee, Richard. 2000. "Indigenism and Its Discontents: Anthropology and the Small Peoples at the Millennium." Paper presented as the 2000 Keynote Address, American Ethnological Society Annual Meetings, Tampa, Florida, March 25, 2000.

Li, Tania Murray. 2000. "Articulating Indigenous Identity in Indonesia: Resource Politics and the Tribal Slot." *Comparative Studies of Society and History* 42(1): 149–79.

Neitschmann, Bernard. 1994. "The Fourth World: Nations versus States." In *Reordering the World: Geopolitical Perspectives on the Twenty-first Century*, ed. G. Demko and W. Wood. Boulder: Westview.

Niezen, Ronald. 2000. "Recognizing Indigenism: Canadian Unity and the International Movement of Indigenous Peoples." *Comparative Studies in Society and History* 42(1): 119–48.

Perry, Richard. 1996. *From Time Immemorial: Indigenous Peoples and State Systems*. Austin: University of Texas Press.

Sider, Gerald. 1987. "When Parrots Learn to Talk and Why They Can't: Domination, Deception, and Self-Deception in Indian-White Relations." *Comparative Studies in Society and History* 29(1): 3–23.

Warren, Kay. 1998. *Indigenous Movements and Their Critics: Pan-Mayan Activism in Guatemala*. Princeton: Princeton University Press.

Notes

1. Unlike church members, who self-identify as such, few village residents are likely to refer to themselves as members of a culture movement. People in the dance group do identify themselves as dance group members, and when village residents were asked who the key members of the village culture movement or culture group were, no one misunderstood the question. Any movement referred to in the text should be understood, however, as an informal group or collection of groups. The agreement among the members of these groups, both on the issues at stake and the sides of the disputes, justifies their formalization in the text.

2. There is some variation in the definitions of the terms "Evangelical," "Fundamentalist," and "Pentecostal," especially among church members. As used here (and as is generally the case), Fundamentalist Christian churches are those that insist on a literal reading of the Bible, usually the King James Version (which many consider an inspired translation with a standing equivalent to that of the original texts). Evangelical churches are those that consider the spreading of Christianity a religious obligation. As I discuss in chapter 7, notions of collective salvation are very important in many Fundamentalist and Pentecostal churches as well. Evangelical church members consider witnessing (discussed in chapter 5) a sacrament of sorts, one that is necessary for the full development of one's faith and understanding. Pentecostal churches are those that practice "gifts of faith," minimally including speaking in tongues—termed "glossolalia" by academic observers—but also possession by the Holy Spirit, the casting out of demons, prophecy, and other practices that are considered divinely inspired. Most Pentecostal churches are Evangelical and Fundamentalist, and most Evangelical churches are Fundamentalist as well, but in each case the name is meant to denote an

emphasis the others are thought to lack. Likewise, many Fundamentalist church members disapprove of Pentecostal practices,
despite the fact that many Pentecostals consider themselves Fundamentalists.

1. POLITICS ON THE OTHER SIDE OF THE MOUNTAIN

1. "Where was the old, the real Lahore? In order to get to it, on
   the far side of these badly laid out and already decrepit suburbs,
   I still had to go through two miles of bazaar, where, with the
   help of mechanical saws, cheap jewelry was being manufactured
   out of gold the thickness of tin-plate, and where there were stalls
   displaying cosmetics, medicines and imported plastic objects. I
   wondered if I was at last discovering the real Lahore in dark little
   streets, where I had to flatten myself against the wall to make
   way for flocks of sheep with blue-and-pink dyed fleece, and for
   buffaloes—each as big as three cows—which barged into one in
   friendly fashion, and, still more often, for lorries. Was it when
   I was gazing at crumbling woodwork, eaten away with age? I
   might have got some idea of its delicate fretting and carving had
   the approach to it not been made impossible by the ramshackle
   electrical supply system, which spread its festoons of wire from
   wall to wall, like a spider's web all through the old town. . . .
   "Then, insidiously, the illusion began to lay its snares. I wished I
   had lived in the days of real journeys, when it was still possible to
   see the full splendor of a spectacle that had not yet been blighted,
   polluted and spoilt; I wished I had not trodden that ground as
   myself, but as Bernier, Tavernier or Manucci did" (Lévi-Strauss
   1978:42–43, emphasis in source).
2. Gold strikes—including strikes at the head of the Stikine River
   (located in the Southeast Alaska region), the Klondike (which
   could be reached over the Chilkoot Pass, the northern boundary of
   the coastal Tlingit), and finally the large strike at Juneau, located
   within the region itself—confirmed for the federal government
   that Alaska was better off without the sort of support that would
   make permanent settlement possible. Miners received little incentive to remain in the region, and only laws that facilitated the
   actual harvest of the region's mineral wealth were reliably enforced
   or maintained.

3. In addition, the rapid development of fur farms in the region and the gradual end of the sea otter pelt trade made winter trapping economically unfeasible.

4. In his report, the auditor noted: "It is difficult to understand why approximately forty percent of the funds appropriated by Congress for the financing of Indians is confined to four communities with a total estimated resident population of 1,445 persons when there are approximately 500,000 Indians in the United States" (LaVerdure 1961:5).

5. See Lantis and Fuller (1948) for early indicators of this trend.

6. This was perhaps legally necessary as well, for the ANB at the time had greatly expanded its associate membership and had many more non-native members than native members.

7. The Indian Self-Determination and Education Assistance Act of 1975 (P.L. 93-638) instructed the BIA to turn over the administration of some Indian programs to tribes themselves. The act was not applied to all Indian groups or to all programs administered for these groups by the BIA. In Southeast Alaska, the BIA selected four groups to take over the administration of several programs. These groups were given "638 contracts" (named after the registration number of the law). The contracts worked like block grants to groups for the implementation of specific programs. A tribe could, for example, receive a 638 contract for local general assistance, and then decide for themselves how to spend the portion of those monies allocated for administration (i.e., by hiring a full-time general assistance caseworker or by opening an office within the tribal administration for this purpose, etc.). The four "compacted" tribes in Southeast Alaska are the Tlingit and Haida Central Council and the IRA councils in Kake, Sitka, and Ketchikan.

8. Langdon (1980) points out that this was probably true of fishermen everywhere. The implication, he notes, is that the limited-entry system made it more difficult for fishermen to obtain loans necessary to fish than nonfishermen, preferring those whose accumulated assets were acceptable to creditors.

9. Langdon (1980:59) shows that statewide, rural residents were initially allotted 34 percent of the licenses, but that by 1977 their share had fallen to under 10 percent.

1. For the remainder of this text, I will use the term "household" to refer to the nuclear family/domestic group meaning of "family," and retain the term "family" for the type of political group discussed here.

2. In the mythical nineteenth century this would have meant "mother's brother" and "sister's son," though today few use the terms this specifically—referring instead to bilateral "uncles" and "nephews."

3. Because these examples describe political and personal machinations that participants would find embarrassing, some effort has been made to disguise their actual identities. Thus the names have been changed, even in abbreviation, and the villages in which these families live have not been identified.

4. All figures for 1990 were taken from the 1990 U.S. Census.

3. THE ALASKA NATIVE CLAIMS SETTLEMENT ACT

1. Dr. Walter Soboleff, Chairman, Board of Trustees, Sealaska Heritage Foundation, from *Celebration '96 Official Program*, p. 1.

2. The most important contribution of the "invention of tradition" literature has been its uncovering of how contemporary identities have emerged within, and not simply against, modernity (Hobsbawm and Ranger 1983; also Dombrowski 1998).

3. Gerald Sider makes this point clear in critical ways for Native Americans in his article "When Parrots Learn to Talk, and Why They Can't" (1987).

4. Since the 1970s, ANCSA and its consequences have been subject to much criticism from non-native observers and from native advocates themselves. Yet, though few have pointed this out, ANCSA works differently and has markedly different consequences throughout the state, from region to region and even from village to village. This is particularly true for Southeast Alaska, where a past federal court settlement caused the near exclusion of the region from the provisions of the act. Though the region was eventually included, it was under special provisions, and as such Southeast Alaska has experienced a distinct political reorganization quite unlike those of other regions.

5. The potential for disparities in developable resources was apparent

from the beginning. As a partial remedy, the act included a profit-sharing provision among the regions. Seventy percent of the net profits from the regional corporations were to be distributed to the other twelve regional corporations—with the idea that resource-rich areas such as the Arctic Slope and the Southeast would help support those regions less endowed with oil or timber. This, like several of the act's other provisions, marks these corporations as special sorts of corporate entities that, despite their official for-profit status, were expected to take over the welfare responsibilities of the state and federal government. Since that time, provisions like this one have been the source of an endless stream of lawsuits among the various corporate entities, further draining the corporations of operating monies.

6. The original ANCSA legislation, most especially the provisions that placed ownership of tribal territories in the hands of privately held ANCSA corporations, had been designed specifically to avoid creating Indian territory in Alaska. "Indian territory" is a legal term with a long history. Originating in the earliest years of the United States, the possession of "Indian territory" is the basis for many native groups' claims to alterior status—including the right to operate gambling facilities and sales-tax-exempt stores. Yet it is, at best, a category that is difficult to define precisely, and since the turn of the century Congress has tried many times to eliminate Indian territory through privatization. All of these attempts have failed (eventually), often because of resistance on the part of natives. Yet part of the resistance has come from others in the federal government as well, and from some natives or native advocates whose motives were less pristine. In particular, the ambiguousness of "Indian territory" as a legal term and form of property has been the basis of its recurrent usefulness to tribes, to government agencies, and to non-native individuals and businesses that have found means to take advantage of the ulterior conditions that Indian territory creates—including, for the moment, exemption from some state and federal laws. Such an exemption is the reason why many native claims and the native identity movement are now finding support and offers of alliance from organized gaming interests throughout the United States.

7. The Southeast Alaska regional corporation Sealaska actually cut some of its own timber (which it sold at depressed but still break-even prices) and used the NOL monies generated from the sale of those "paper losses" to purchase village corporation standing timber holdings. Since the early 1990s, in fact, the majority of Sealaska's timber harvests have taken place on village corporation lands, cutting timber purchased on the stump during the NOL heydays of the early and mid-1990s.

8. The only village corporation that I know to have issued shares to new natives is Angoon. Most have yet to deal with the problem in any serious way. Yet by not voting one way or another, this is also, in effect, a vote of exclusion.

4. SUBSISTENCE AND THE COST OF CULTURE

1. Neither of these uses is actually new or limited to Southeast Alaska.

2. *Tlingit and Haida Indians v. United States*, 177 F.Supp. 452 (Court of Claims, 1959) and 389 F.2d 788 (Court of Claims, 1968).

3. Indeed, so important was the political place of subsistence to village residents that overwhelming popular resentment arose when the native leadership involved in the lawsuit decided to accept a cash settlement in place of the return of land or a guarantee of continued use rights. The Alaska Native Brotherhood—a long-standing association of Southeast Natives—went as far as suing the leadership involved in the case, stating that the Central Council was not empowered to reach that kind of settlement. Regardless, the success of the Central Council suit did much to allow other Alaska Natives to extract the largest settlement (in terms of both cash and territory) in the history of U.S.-native relations and to place subsistence issues at the center of struggle between local and larger interests.

4. See Berger 1985:59–70. For a full discussion on the issues at stake in meeting the federal requirements of ANILCA, see Alaska Department of Fish and Game (Division of Subsistence) 1995. ANILCA is officially the Alaska National Interest Land Conservation Act of December 2, 1980 (94 Stat. 2371).

5. The term "subsistence"—which is used by virtually all natives in the region—derives, ironically, from the rules and laws governing

the harvest of resources in Alaska. Subsistence is both an administrative division within the state enforcement bureaucracy and a legislated form of use, defined as such by the Alaska legislature, the U.S. Congress, and the Alaska Department of Fish and Game. For this reason, some advocates now prefer the term "traditional use," which points to a different origin for current practices and these advocates' unwillingness to presume the very administrative categories they wish to challenge. Yet for most ordinary Alaska Natives, the origins of the term "subsistence" have not diminished its central symbolic role in their own assertions about native culture.

6. Throughout his text, Berger points out that his use of the term "subsistence" is meant to indicate more than simply a means for basic survival. He writes: "The word 'subsistence' reminds most Americans of dirt-poor farmers, scratching a hard living from marginal land. In Alaska, however, subsistence means hunting, fishing, and gathering. More than that, it means a way of life that—far from being marginal—fulfills spiritual as well as economic needs" (1985:5). In the remainder of his text, Berger continues to refer to this as the "subsistence way of life," reinforcing the distinction between the hunting and gathering practices of Alaska Natives and some presumably more marginal food search that also contains these elements. For the critical issue of livelihood, see Gavin Smith's discussion of subsistence and resistance (Smith 1989).

7. For a discussion of ongoing uses of moieties or sides among some Southeast Alaska communities, and for the importance of traditional foods to mortuary practices, see Kan 1989.

8. In past presentations of this material, questions have been raised over whether partners are ever or often kin. They can be, though this is not nearly as regular an occurrence as one might assume. One reason is that because subsistence is pursued most actively by the village's poorest residents, these also tend to be individuals whose kin networks are the most disrupted by work outside the village and extended periods of residence away from their natal household. As pointed out in chapter 2, larger and steadier groups of kin tend to be those most well off in any village. Subsistence users are those whose village relations tend to be subject to the

most change. In this way, partnership contains a flexibility that kin often cannot.

9. A series of studies has been conducted on the traditional-use and subsistence harvests by the Alaska Department of Fish and Game, Division of Subsistence. These are available in the Technical Papers series published by the Alaska Department of Fish and Game, Division of Subsistence, Juneau.

10. Note that those who work for the schools have the summer for subsistence work while still holding a job that carries benefits. For this reason, these are often seen as good jobs despite relatively low pay.

11. The state and federal commercial management schemes are also unpredictable, and little advance notice is given for the various openings. As a result, most crews and boats have to be ready to go at any time, making complementary full-time work difficult to plan or achieve.

12. *Ketchikan Daily News*, Sunday edition, September 3–4, 1994, p. A-3.

13. *Ketchikan Daily News*, September 2, 1994, p. A-3.

14. *Ketchikan Daily News*, September 2, 1994, p. A-3.

6. "JESUS LOVES YOU"

1. During this time fishing was on the decline regionwide, and the cannery, like the several other native-owned canneries in the region, was in a constant state of flux. Year-to-year operation depended mostly on the ability of the Juneau Area Office to secure BIA loans to cover operating costs. Eventually all of the BIA-financed canneries failed, but this was gradual, with one cannery in one village closing first and the boats from that village being sent to fish for one of the other BIA-financed canneries that remained open. By the mid-1960s, though, all had ceased to operate regularly and the four cannery-owning tribal councils had accumulated several million dollars in debt.

2. It is important to note here that it is possible to look at Pentecostalism entirely in this light, as a means of moral purity or behavioral reform with functional consequences that contribute to its popularity and survival. My analysis goes in a different direction, but one consequence of this is that I do not address the morals question in any thorough way. A more full analy-

sis of Pentecostalism would require addressing this element as well.

3. It should be noted that many Pentecostals resist (whether through theological instruction I do not know) the Manichean idea that there is an equivalence in these two sets of entities. The power of the Holy Spirit or of Jesus, people will say, far outweighs that of the Devil and his helpers, who rely on human frailty and invocation (whether conscious or not) for their efficacy.

4. By way of explanation, the blades in timber-processing mills are large, bandsaw-like blades: a long hoop of thin steel with teeth along one edge. The saw blade passes over pulleys on the top and bottom — usually located on the floor above and the floor below the room where the logs are cut — which turn at thousands of rotations per minute. A metal spike — sometimes used in rafting, at other times as industrial sabotage by ecologists — that is left in a log will, when struck by the blade, break the teeth from the blade, and quite often the entire blade, sending razor-sharp metal shards flying around the room.

5. The way such stories have been used to account for, and indeed compensate for, these incidents has led some to charge Pentecostals elsewhere with political passivity. Where work and community relations are seen to be shaped by spiritual forces, and thus relatively uninfluenced by individual activity, people are less likely to take matters into their own hands or seek solutions to their problems (see Greenhouse 1986). There is some truth to such charges, of course, and subordinating worldly events to a struggle between demons and angels may be the cause of some working-class quiescence, as Marx himself sometimes charged. Yet these claims often ignore the fact that the relevance of these sorts of examples is often limited to specifically religious circumstances. This story was told to a large group at a church dinner. Later, outside this context, the same individual noted that he quit that job immediately after, saying that there was no sense staying in a job where you could get killed that easily, no matter how much they are paying you. As with testimonies, much of the power of these narratives (and thus any quiescence that might result) seems dependent on particular audiences and circumstances.

6. The insistence on community responsibility is an insistence on

215

community in an older sense: the common lot of those who live together. Differences in the community are, as such, spiritually suspect, and mutual accountability is held as a high priority. This is apparent within church groups, but it also extends to those in the community who would not consider themselves saved. This is a crucial point for the following chapter, for it lies at the heart of the eventual conflict between church members and the culture groups.

7. INDIANNESS AND CONVERSION

1. This was not entirely a surprise, and when cash dividends were first proposed, many people in the villages noted with uncharacteristic bluntness that if the corporation began giving out cash in large amounts some people were going to "drink themselves to death." Protest along these lines was unheeded, and the dividends were paid. Several deaths followed.

CONCLUSION

1. Gellner expands this point later in the same work: "It was widely believed by many of the early commentators of the social transformation, both Liberals and Marxists, that there would be a kind of direct transition from the traditional closed worlds to a kind of universal human society. In other words—and this, notoriously, was their greatest and deepest mistake—they failed to foresee nationalism. What did in fact take place was a transition from the old world of endless cultural diversity and nuance, not directly linked to the political order, to a new world of mass, anonymous, but not universal, societies. And it is these internally mobile, but externally closed, societies which discovered and made a cult of *Gemeinschaft*, of the closed society, and claimed (quite falsely) to be implementing and exemplifying it. In forging new state-linked 'high' (educationally transmitted, codified) cultures, they used folk themes and invoked the *Gemeinschaft* of the village green: but they were neither establishing a village green, nor did they greatly appeal to those who were still in the village. They were creating a new kind of society based on shared educationally instilled culture, and their clientele were the new entrants into that society. Nationalism is born of the needs of *Gesellschaft*, but it speaks *Gemeinschaft*. . . .

"It is not entirely clear why this has happened, why the old

216

man-tied-to-his-niche should have been replaced, not, as the Enlightenment taught and hoped, by Universal Man committed to a corresponding universal brotherhood, but by an ethnically specific man, detached from rigid links to the old niches, but mobile only within the limits of a now formally codified and state-protected culture, i.e. within the bounds of a nation-state. That it has happened is one of the most significant facts of the last two centuries" (1998:22–23).

2. For the novelty of Bastian's notion of *Völkerpsychologie*, and the differences between his own notions and those of Wundt or the early German philological psychology, see Whitman 1984. On Bastian's influence upon Boas and its effects on his own ethnological pursuits, see Stocking 1968, especially "From Physics to Ethnology," pp. 133–60.

3. The leading critic of this sort of thinking in the United States has been Thomas Szasz. See his *The Myth of Mental Illness* (1984) for an introduction to his work and a far more critical assessment of psychology and psychiatry than that offered here.

4. Earlier anthropology had actually paid little attention to the things sociologists and psychologists wanted to call culture. At the time anthropology was primarily concerned (in America) with human biological form and race. The related fields of British anthropology and American ethnology originally had more overlap with the emerging field of psychology, or with politics and law. Boas's use of the term "culture" gave it currency in America, but his definition remained tied to a particular vision of language and collective genius derived from the philological traditions of nineteenth-century German thought.

5. Wolf argues in *Envisioning Power* (1999) that some people are more prone to work on cultural integration, and—more importantly—some are more empowered to work on cultural integration and to put their integrations in place. The validity of the first part of this argument is difficult to gauge. I tend to agree more with Sider when he says that all people think about the future, rather than just some (see Sider 1986:1). Still, saying that such integration is something that all people engage in does not take anything away from Wolf's point that some people's integrations tend to influence history more than others'.

6. The larger integrative role of culture in organizing people emotionally, cognitively, and socially is perhaps behind the consistent difficulty anthropologists and now people more generally have had distinguishing culture from religion (see Morris 1987).

7. Called Kwakiutl by Franz Boas and subsequently by all anthropologists, the current descendants prefer to be called Kwakwaka'wakw (see Galois 1994).

8. In the case of the Kwakiutl, diverse opportunities and the "individualizing" of cultural privileges resulted in the decline of those people or groups made powerful by cultural means, and simultaneously allowed the fissures in the cultural edifice that had been created by Kwakiutl elites to become more and more apparent. Wolf concludes: "This decline was occasioned by changes that altered the social and cultural contexts under which power related to ideas" (1999:129–30). Eventually the elites fell, and the cosmology they had created, inherited, manifested, and exaggerated resumed its piecemeal nature—only later to be resurrected in the identity politics of the late twentieth century (Wolf 1999:130–31).

Notes on Sources

Virtually all of the topics raised in the introduction are revisited in more detail in later sections of the book. Notions of going "against culture" as a topic for anthropological investigation are first raised by members of the Culture and Personality school, in particular by Sapir (see 1949). Surprisingly little work was done on the topic, however. Part of the problem is that being against culture is also a critical discourse of modernity (see, e.g., Rabinow 1996), and anthropologists, being in many ways antimodern, expressed this in being proculture. This book aims not at advancing the project of modernity (of which, in the guise of development, it is very critical), but rather at uncovering some of what was lost when the idea of being against culture was put aside.

Along these lines, a reexamination of the Mashpees' situation is very telling (see Clifford 1988 and Campisi 1993). As discussed in the introduction, the special qualities of Native American ethnicity become readily apparent there. My own understanding of this situation was gained largely from reading and studying with Gerald Sider, whose work on these topics (1986, 1993, 1997) deals in a far more sophisticated fashion with this topic.

The term "subculture" has been domesticated to the point where it no longer implies the sort of automatic resistance that it once did. Work in this area has come mainly from outside anthropology, very likely for reasons that have everything to do with the discipline's procultural stance. For a review of work in cultural studies in the United States see Aronowitz (1993). Critical sources from the original cultural studies include Raymond Williams's *Marxism and Literature* (1977; see also 1980), Paul Willis's *Learning to Labor* (1981), and Dick Hebdige's *Subculture: The Meaning of Style* (1979).

On the issue of divisions within native societies, I have always appreciated two older works: Preston Holder's *The Hoe and the Horse on the*

Plains (1970) and Fred O. Gearing's *Priests and Warriors: Social Structures for Cherokee Politics in the Eighteenth Century* (1962). Although both deal with far more distant historical periods, they encouraged me to wonder about how lines of cleavage within native groups dictated these groups' relations with those outside. Studies of class formation among native societies has tended to focus on how natives were made working class. This is a fairly narrow view of the topic, though on the whole it is true that very few natives have avoided the general impoverishment that capitalism brings to the periphery. The continuous resurgence of native societies as native societies, however, argues against such a simple view. Sources on class formation among native societies in Alaska (or the general lack thereof) are discussed in the next section.

PART I: LANDSCAPES

1. *Politics on the Other Side of the Mountain*

For the early history of American Alaska generally and for the way it involved native people in the region, see Hinckley (1972, 1996); Nichols (1924) provides a description of the early neglect of the region. For the position of the frontier in the place of American industrialism (Alaska still proclaims itself the "last frontier"), see Slotkin (1973, 1985).

Anthropological work on the northern Northwest Coast is as old as American anthropology, yet the majority of the ethnography produced reflects little of the political or economic context of the work itself. Philip Drucker's work is one exception within anthropology (see Drucker 1957, 1958), though most of his historical work outside of his monograph on the native brotherhoods aims at the period prior to his own work on the coast (see, e.g., Drucker 1965). Rolf Knight (1978) produced a masterful labor history of the coast that is still underappreciated by ethnographers. There have been several recent dissertations with a more contemporary slant as well (Vaughan 1985; Langdon 1977; also see Wyatt 1985 and 1987 for more recent historical concerns), but only Langdon takes a specifically presentist approach. In his important and recent Heiltsuk monograph (1998; see also 1997), Michael Harkin takes history and the present (the latter in particularly subtle fashion) as his topic and advocates replacing the romance of pristine with notions of hybrid contact. The virtue of this approach is that tradition is liberated from some of its historical anchors and can appear, as it must, as an element of political discourse that has emerged at many times, and for many reasons. The idea that all of these emergent views of tradition ought, in some way, to be consistent is equivalent to asking that history itself cease.

Of course, Joyce Wike's early dissertation (1947) led the way in studies of contact, followed by a regionwide (indeed continent-wide) contextualization by Wolf (1982). Studies like Wolf's, Wike's, and Harkin's help us rethink the context of earlier work in more productive ways, and they provide a context for early ethnography.

Yet little recent ethnography has been undertaken outside of a focus on what of the past can be recovered (Kan 1987, 1989; Blackman 1982; Dauenhauer and Dauenhauer 1994). While enlightening past ethnography, these works simultaneously darken their own.

The cannery history of the coast is yet to be written, though portions of its accompanying political dynamics have been explored by non-anthropologists (e.g., Price 1990; Case 1984). The documentation on canneries abounds (Cobb 1930; DeLoach 1939; Gregory and Barnes 1939). My own preliminary work in just one town is available in Dombrowski 1995. Some work on this era has been done by Ted Hinckley (1972, 1996), and on the earlier Russian attempts at Sitka, Sergei Kan has provided much invaluable translation and interpretation (1985, 1991); Richard Dauenhauer (1982) provides an interesting addition and interpretation.

Bureau of Indian Affairs (BIA) reports, hired out to anthropologists, contain an elaborate picture of the social conditions in Alaska during the period in which anthropology was fully ensconced in debates about Northwest Coast culture. I think here especially of BIA 1938–41 (MS), and reports by Goldschmidt and Haas (1946), Lantis and Fuller (1948), Camarot and Wentworth (1958), and LaVerdure (1961). This was also the period of intensive political activity on the part of Southeast Natives, a startling picture of which is available in the Curry-Weissbrodt Papers—the archives of the successive representatives of the Tlingit and Haida Central Council in its suit for land compensation. The Hydaburg Reserve is documented in Curry Weissbrodt MS CI-II.I and in the paperwork surrounding the "Folta Decision" (1952).

The changing economics of the region, as a prelude to limited entry, are interestingly documented in two different ways by Rogers (1960) and Rogers, Listowski, and Brakel (1974) on the one hand and by Cooley (1963) and Crutchfield and Pontecorvo (1969) on the other.

Langdon (1980) remains the best source on the initial rationale and early impact of the limited-entry system (also Adasiak 1977), and his later work (1989) provides a criticism of the program based on a longer historical view. Morehouse and Rogers (1980) provide immense statistical evidence that documents the transformations caused by recent management regimes. Dinneford and Cohen (1989) show that there has been little reversal of the initial trends fifteen years after their implementation. Guimary's (1983) report on the condition of historic canneries offers compelling visual testimony of the death of the industry. On the global status of fisheries see work by James McGoodwin (1990), Acheson (1981), Durrenberger and Palsson (1988), and McCay (1981), as well as "Warning: How to Lose a Family" (1988).

Historical work on West Coast unions and labor patterns has been largely ignored by anthropologists. Masson and Guimary (1981) give an interesting thumbnail of what remains the untold side of American colonialism in the Pacific, namely, the vast movement of labor across the region in the period prior to the beginnings of World War I. I rely here for statistics and overview on an unpublished master's thesis in the Business School of Columbia University (Arbogast 1947).

2. The Ins and Outs of Village Social Organization

I first began to formulate the idea of "family" when I read Claudia Lewis's *Indian Families of the Northwest Coast* (1970), though this is not because Lewis uses the term in the sense it is used here. Lewis's "community study" approach to the "Camas" Indians, as she calls them, focuses mainly on the "disorganization that often accompanies the impact of modern life on Indian groups in America" (1970:3), which comes later in the work to mean a lack of the values normally associated (often wrongly) with white nuclear families. For the most part, Lewis sees the family as what is left when other forms of social organization are stripped away through a history of colonialism (though she does not quite use these terms either) and an anachronistic retention of "native" values. As is clear in the chapter, I view the family as an entirely contemporary phenomenon, without relation to past forms of social organization or the values associated with these forms.

The continuation of clan organization is a second issue. Some, such as Kan (1991, 1989; see also Dauenhauer and Dauenhauer 1987), have argued that clans continue to operate, especially in the context of potlatch ceremonies. This would seem true to an extent in Sitka, judging by Kan's data, and perhaps in Angoon, though in neither of these towns do clans have any corporate existence outside of ceremonial contexts. In other areas the moiety division between Ravens and Eagles is enjoined for some ceremonial purposes, such as the sort of funeral services Kan discusses, though here it is worth questioning the use of the term "moiety," for the groups are seldom exogamous. Vaughan (1985) makes a similar point. The classic works on northern Northwest Coast social organization include Emmons (1991), Garfield (1939), Jones (1914), Krause (1956), Laguna (1952, 1972), Murdock (1934), Niblack (1888), Oberg (1973), and Swanton (1905, 1908). For a comparison with the southern Northwest Coast see Rosman and Rubel (1971, 1986), and, alternatively, Boxberger (1988), Bracken (1997), and Knight (1978).

Perhaps more interesting for issues of current social organization in Southeast Alaska is a report to the BIA by two anthropologists, Lantis and Fuller (1948, MS; the report was never accepted and exists only in manuscript form). The report gives a town-by-town breakdown of household expenditures and incomes, local business accounting (including the income of particular seiners), and, for some towns, information on parentage and place of birth. Importantly, Lantis and Fuller refer throughout to "families," even for groups of more than one household and more than ten people, perhaps indicating that the term was used even then as it is today. Just as often in the report, however, "family" is used to refer to households, as it is by people today as well, as the authors indicate (1948:15). In one case they indicate that "family" may also mean clan, though it is unclear whether this means clan in the restrictive unilineal sense of the past (1948:13).

Clear throughout the report, though, is that while families at the time continue to move around for work and subsistence (especially during the summer), it is households and groups of bilateral kin that move—husbands and sons and their families on boats, a woman and her children and perhaps a parent to the canneries. Nor, as with the Goldschmidt and Haas (1946) report, is there any indication of clans retaining control over subsistence resources. By 1948 areas tend to be considered to belong to towns, though often in 1948 past clan jurisdiction was still remembered.

When discussing incomes, Lantis and Fuller note that additional-income earners greatly affect the overall well-being of the household.

But when enumerating the types of additional workers they included wives, sons, and daughters. Extended kin ties (however conceived) seem to play an important role in household economics. When they do, the emphasis is on bilateral linkages and the parents of grown children. They conclude: "Such a family is known technically as an 'extended family.' Important to this study is the fact that it is almost invariably also an 'economic family'" (1948:16). Finally, Lantis and Fuller note that many of the services once shared by clan members (used in the corporate, nineteenth-century sense) have been replaced by cash transactions: "Children are paid for running errands and tending neighbors' babies. Men are paid for any boat construction work on other than the parental or possibly a brother's craft. Women are paid for clerking in a relative's store" (1948:56).

3. The Alaska Native Claims Settlement Act

Much has been written on the Alaska Native Claims Settlement Act (AN-CSA) (Public Law 92-203, 1971). For a review of the legal and economic conditions that preceded the act see University of Alaska (1967); the Federal Field Committee's report (1968); and Robert Arnold's *Alaska Native Land Claims* (1978). Thomas Berger's *Village Journey* (1985) shows clearly the dissatisfaction with the act present in villages throughout Alaska even after the beginning of the oil and timber booms. For the North Slope perspective see Chance (1990). For the role of the Alaska pipeline and the discoveries at Prudhoe Bay see Berry (1975).

Recent evaluations of Southeast Alaska corporations are available in Schiller (1984), Colt (1991), and especially Knapp (1992). Advice for corporations from the original ANCSA lobbying group, the Alaska Federation of Natives, reveals the anticipated impact of the 1991 amendments; see Alaska Federation of Natives (1988). Two three-part series in the *Anchorage Daily News* by Hal Bernton are critical for understanding the context of corporate harvest in the mid-1980s (1985a, b, c) and the importance of the Net Operating Loss issue (1987a, b, c). I have also had the chance to see annual reports from the late 1980s from Kake Tribal Corporation (1988–89), Huna Totem Corporation (1988), and Goldbelt Inc. (1989) (the urban corporation for Juneau-area natives). See also Ortega (1988) for a description of late-1980s corporate successes.

On issues of federal law and Native Americans, valuable guides are Deloria and Lytle (1984), Taylor (1980), and Washburn (1984). Felix

Cohen's famous *Handbook of Federal Indian Law* (1942; revised in 1982) remains invaluable, and David Case's *Alaska Natives and American Laws* (1984) undertakes a similar task for Alaska specifically. An interesting alternative raised by Berger but yet to become a critical factor in Alaska is a strategy of pursuing status international law; see National Lawyers Guild (1982) and Barsh (1984).

The situation of the landless is discussed in Gorsuch et al. (1994), and the 1994 Senate bill proposed by Senator Murkowski (1994, S. 2539) is discussed by Sanders (1995) and Southeast Alaska Conservation Council (1995).

For the role of tribes and native groups in resource-producing industries see Jorgensen et al. (1978, 1984); Faiman-Silva (1997) provides an overview of the Choctaw Nation's role in timber production in Oklahoma.

4. Subsistence and the Cost of Culture

For a relatively recent view of the State Fish and Game Department's understanding of subsistence laws and their history, see Alaska Department of Fish and Game, "Report on Implementation of 1992 Subsistence Law" (1995). Here the history of Alaska's 1978, 1986, and 1992 subsistence laws are discussed, as are the case histories by which they were all overturned (e.g., *McDowell v. State of Alaska*; the "Madison Decision"; the "Katy John" case; and *State of Alaska v. Secretary of the Interior Babbitt*).

For information on local subsistence practices and harvest levels in Southeast Alaska, see a series of studies published by the State Fish and Game Department, including Ellana and Sherrod (1987), Leghorn and Kookesh (1987), George and Bosworth (1988), Cohen (1989), Firman and Bosworth (1990), and Schroeder and Kookesh (1990). The amount of material on current use in these volumes is impressive, and all seem relatively accurate given my own research in the area—with one exception. It seems, given what I have seen and been told by some users, that the harvest levels for those most actively involved in subsistence use are consistently underreported to Fish and Game, and hence are underrepresented in their reports. For example, it is perhaps no coincidence that no household reports harvesting more than twelve deer annually, given that this is the legal maximum per household. However, quite a few households take as many as twenty deer annually, and some twice this many.

There is one further problem as well. In all of these studies the majority of the interpretations continue to be based on aggregate numbers and village-wide averages. In one brief exception, Schroeder and Kookesh (1990:114–16) provide charts on deer harvests by household. Here, half of the households in the village report harvesting no deer, while the highest users are again said to have harvested twelve. And while the 1985 average for Hoonah is 2.09 deer per household, twenty-one households took twice this number or more, and thirty-four households harvested none (1990:115). Reasons for—and the impact of—these differences are not explored.

Historic use within the region is documented in Goldschmidt and Haas (1946), Lantis and Fuller (1948), and Langdon (1977). Oberg's classic 1938 monograph (see Oberg 1973) and Emmons (1991) provide accounts of earlier use. Dauenhauer and Dauenhauer (1987) have collected a number of stories that speak to the importance of subsistence practices within past village communities.

Leacock and Lee's edited volume on band politics (1982) is critical in two aspects. It raises the issue of hunters and gatherers in state societies (see essays by Lee and Hurlich, Feit, and Vachon) and the idea of differentiation with apparently egalitarian groups (see essays by Briggs and Lee).

On the topic of subsistence production within larger systems of production, expropriation, and domination I have counted on Gavin Smith's *Livelihood and Resistance*, especially chapter 5, where he notes that experience might "occur behind the backs of people in a way which actually contributes to their subjectivity" (1989:223). Also on the logic of subsistence production see Sider (1989) and his critique of Meillassoux and Chayanov. Sider remains one of the few anthropologists to raise the issue of internal inequalities as they come to effect local/larger disputes, which is crucial to the current argument and largely missing from most anthropological discussions of subsistence production. Wilmsen (1989) is a second example of this.

On the issue of native courts and issues of local-level differentiation, an excellent treatment is available in Miller (2001). The argument made here draws on work by Laura Nadar (1990), who is also concerned with the ideological functions of small-scale court proceedings. In some accounts with similar emphases, it is difficult to see why people might continue to invest importance in culture when it seems so easily manipulated (e.g., Brakel 1979), which has prompted something of a rejection of these issues by some Native American/First Nations peoples (see Denis 1997).

PART 2: CHURCHES

Influential theoretical work on religious conversion can be found in Schneider and Lindenbaum (1987) and Asad (1993). I have also found suggestions in theories of performance (where these have been directed toward anthropological situations; see Turner 1987 and Schechner 1993). Particularly interesting, though I received it only after completing the manuscript, is Cynthia Keppley Mahmood's *Fighting for Faith and Nation: Dialogues with Sikh Militants* (1996).

Contemporary approaches to Baptists, Pentecostals, and other born-again sects include works by Greenhouse (1986), contributors to the volume by Hall and Stack (1982; especially Grindal 1982), the collection of case studies in Garrard-Burnett and Stoll (1993), and the recent ethnography by Chesnut, *Born Again in Brazil* (1997). Histories of the Pentecostal movement in North and South America include those by Anderson (1979) and Burdick (1993).

Jean and John Comaroff's discussion of Reformed churches in southern Africa propose a model that questions the colonization of consciousness and the consciousness of colonization (Comaroff 1985; Comaroff and Comaroff 1991). Though I find their work sympathetic to what I try to do here, there are critical differences in the way culture and representation are thought to proceed, and hence a somewhat different approach to some similar social processes.

Religious conversion was an early topic in Native American studies, and I still find James Mooney's Ghost Dance monograph (1896, 1965) to be critical. The collection of essays by "Natives and Christians" assembled by Treat (1996) attempts to address why the issue of religion and religious conversion has often been seen as outside native concerns about culture, and to remedy the situation.

In Alaska the majority of the work on conversion has centered on the nineteenth and early twentieth centuries (Drucker 1958; Kan 1985, 1989; Oleska 1987), even when people themselves have raised the importance of church in their ongoing lives (see Blackman 1982; Eastman and Edwards 1991), a point Kan (1991) addresses as well. The relation of current church movements to previous practices on the coast have been

227

dealt with only briefly by Kan (1991). Links to shamanism are doubtful, however, in any current context (though see Hugh-Jones 1996 for an interesting counterexample from South America). More interesting might be the connection between current church movements and the Indian Shaker churches further south, or the prophet movements of the late nineteenth century that occurred along much of the Northwest Coast. Indian Shakerism (sometimes lumped with Western Shakerism) was and is mainly centered in Washington State, western Oregon, northern California, and southern British Columbia (see Ruby and Brown 1996, and early work in Collins 1950, M. W. Smith 1954, Barnett 1957, and Suttles 1957). Shakerism and the prophet movement are interesting not because the practices are similar, though they may be (confusion made worse when Pentecostals are compared to shamanic sorts of possession simply because people describe what they are feeling in similar terms), but rather because they occur in a similar period of dramatic change and prove widely popular. Shamanism was never a popular movement, meaning that it was not practiced by a large number of people, though many may have employed shamans and thought their work effective.

Issues of testimony have been dealt with only briefly by several of those above who have researched Pentecostal, Evangelical, or Baptist practice more generally. Greenhouse (1986) discusses witnessing (which includes testimony and efforts aimed at recruiting non–church members to the congregation) but relates no direct testimony and discusses it only briefly. The importance of church service is discussed by the contributors to the Garrard-Burnett and Stoll (1993) volume, but the language and role of any sort of expression of faith is not dealt with directly by any of the authors in the collection. Chesnut (1997:79) gives examples of several testimonies (as does Burdick 1993), which, though familiar, remain quite distinct from those discussed here. Interestingly, Chesnut also provides an interesting description of exorcism practices that parallel somewhat the event discussed in chapter 5.

CONCLUSION

Beyond the sources discussed directly in the chapter—Williams (1977), Wolf (1999), and Gellner (1998)—the collective work of Gerald Sider (especially 1993, 1987) is critical.

On writing ethnography, I have been influenced by Clifford and

228

Marcus's edited volume (1986) and by Marcus and Fischer's notion of "anthropological critique" (1986). Clifford's "Partial Truths" and Rabinow's "Representations Are Social Facts," both from the former volume, are particularly relevant. On the whole, however, my own response has been motivated equally by a distrust of positivist language learned from Rorty (1989); from Wittgenstein (see Bloor 1996); and most of all from Peirce (1955).

Peirce's notion of reality and representation is critical in two ways. It is the center of the analysis of what may be accomplished in Pentecostal practice and what might be accomplished in writing ethnography. Both depend, I argue, on a vision of the wider world (theology on the one hand, anthropology on the other), but neither is comprehensible simply as an aspect of such a larger order. Both ethnography and religious practice or representation must be understood in terms of what they might do. This is the debt to Peirce that runs throughout this work.

References

LAWS AND COURT CASES

(1879) *Reynolds v. United States*, 98 U.S. 146.

(1902) Proclamation no. 37, 33 Stat. 2025, creating the Alexander Archipelago National Forest in Southeast Alaska.

(1944) "Hanna Opinion": Report of the Presiding Chairman, Richard A. Hanna. Hearings on Claims of Natives, of the Towns of Hydaburg, Klawock, and Kake, Alaska, Pursuant to the Provisions of Section 201.21b of the Regulations for Protection of the Commercial Fisheries of Alaska.

(1952) "Folta Decision": *United States of America v. Libby, McNeil & Libby*, District Court for the Territory of Alaska (no. 6445-A).

(1968) *Tlingit and Haida Indians v. United States*, 177 F.Supp. 452 (Court of Claims, 1959) and 389 F.2d 788 (Court of Claims, 1968).

(1971) *Alaska Native Claims Settlement Act*, Public Law 93-203. 85 Stat. 689; 43 USCA 1601 et seq.

(1975) *Indian Self-Determination and Education Assistance Act*, 25 USC 450 et seq.

(1980) *Alaska National Interest Land Conservation Act of December 2, 1980, 94 Stat. 2371.*

(1987) *Alaska Native Claims Settlement Act Amendments of 1987*, Public Law 100-241. 101 Stat. 1788.

(1990) *Tongass Timber Reform Act*, Public Law 101-626—November 28, 1990.

(1994) *Alaska Wilderness Recreation and Tourism Association; Organized Village of Kake; Southeast Alaska Conservation Council; Natural Resources Defense Council; and the Wilderness Society v. U.S. Forest Service.* No. J94-033-CV (JWS), U.S. District Court for the District of Alaska.

ADDITIONAL REFERENCES

Acheson, James M. 1981. "Anthropology of Fishing." *Annual Review of Anthropology* 10:275–316.

Adasiak, Alan. 1977. "Limited Entry in Alaska." In *Pacific Salmon Management for People*, ed. D. V. Ellis. Western Geographic Series, vol. 13. Victoria BC: University of Victoria Press.

Alaska Department of Fish and Game (Division of Subsistence). 1995. "Report on Implementation of 1992 Subsistence Law." Juncau: Alaska Department of Fish and Game.

Alaska Federation of Natives. 1988. "1991—Making It Work: A Guide to Public Law 100-241, 1987 Amendments to the Alaska Native Claims Settlement Act." Anchorage: Alaska Federation of Natives.

Anderson, Robert. 1979. *Vision of the Disinherited.* New York: Oxford University Press.

Arbogast, Dean. 1947. "Labor in the Alaskan Salmon Industry." Master's thesis, Faculty of Business, Columbia University.

Arnold, Robert D. 1978. *Alaska Native Land Claims.* Anchorage: Alaska Native Foundation.

Aronowitz, Stanley. 1993. *Roll Over Beethoven: The Return of Cultural Strife.* Boston: Wesleyan University Press.

Asad, Talal. 1992. "Religion and Politics: An Introduction." *Social Research* 59(1): 3–16.

———. 1993. *Genealogies of Religion: Discipline and Reasons of Power in Christianity and Islam.* Baltimore: Johns Hopkins University Press.

Barnett, Homer G. 1957. *Indian Shakers.* Carbondale: Southern Illinois University Press.

Barsh, Russel L. 1984. "The International Legal Status of Native Alaska." *Alaska Native News,* July 1984.

Bateson, Gregory. 1972. *Steps to an Ecology of Mind.* New York: Ballantine Books.

Berger, Thomas R. 1985. *Village Journey: The Report of the Alaska Native Review Commission.* New York: Hill and Wang.

Bernton, Hal. 1985a. "Logging Hard against Debt." *Anchorage Daily News,* August 11.

———. 1985b. "Hope Fuels Expanded Cut." *Anchorage Daily News,* August 12.

———. 1985c. "Ecology Impact Debated." *Anchorage Daily News,* August 13.

———. 1987a. "Tax Amendment Proves Boon for Native Logging." *Anchorage Daily News,* June 21.

———. 1987b. "Logging Takes Toll on Habitat in Southeast." *Anchorage Daily News,* August 23.

———. 1987c. "Native Groups Turn Losses into Assets." *Anchorage Daily News,* December 20.

References

Berry, Mary C. 1975. *The Alaska Pipeline: The Politics of Oil and Native Land Claims.* Bloomington: Indiana University Press.

Bidney, David. 1973. "Phenomenological Method and the Anthropological Science of Cultural Live-World." In *Phenomenology and the Social Sciences*, vol. 1, ed. M. Natanson, 109–40. Evanston: Northwestern University Press.

Blackman, Margaret B. 1982. *During My Time: Florence Edenshaw Davidson, a Haida Woman.* Seattle: University of Washington Press.

Bloor, David. 1996. "The Question of Linguistic Idealism Revisited." In *The Cambridge Companion to Wittgenstein*, ed. Hans Sluga and David Stern, 354–82. New York: Cambridge University Press.

Boxberger, Daniel L. 1988. "In and Out of the Labor Force: The Lummi Indians and the Development of the Commercial Salmon Fishery of North Puget Sound, 1880–1900." *Ethnohistory* 35(2): 161–90.

Bracken, Christopher. 1997. *The Potlatch Papers: A Colonial Case History.* Chicago: University of Chicago Press.

Brakel, Samuel J. 1979. *American Indian Tribal Courts: The Cost of Separate Justice.* Chicago: American Bar Association.

Brown, Beverly A. 1995. *In Timber Country; Working People's Stories of Environmental Conflict and Urban Flight.* Philadelphia: Temple University Press.

Brusco, Elizabeth. 1993. "The Reformation of Machismo: Asceticism and Masculinity among Colombian Evangelicals." In *Rethinking Protestantism in Latin America*, ed. V. Garrard-Burnett and D. Stoll, 143–58. Philadelphia: Temple University Press.

Burdick, John. 1993. *Looking for God in Brazil.* Berkeley: University of California Press.

Bureau of Indian Affairs. 1938–41. (MS) "Economic Survey." Photocopied manuscript in possession of Alaska Historical Library, Juneau.

Camarot, Henry, and Marjory Wentworth. 1958. "A Report and Recommendations on the Study of the Problems in the Fishing Industry." Compiled for the Alaska Legislative Council.

Campisi, Jack. 1993. *Mashpee Indians: Tribe on Trial.* Syracuse: Syracuse University Press.

Case, David S. 1984. *Alaska Natives and American Laws.* Anchorage: University of Alaska Press.

Central Council of the Tlingit and Haida Indian Tribes of Alaska (CCTH). 1992. Historical Profile of the Central Council, Tlingit and Haida Indian Tribes of Alaska. Juneau: CCTH.

233

References

Chance, Norman A. 1990. *The Inupiat and Arctic Development*. Chicago: Holt, Rinehart and Winston.

Chesnut, R. Andrew. 1997. *Born Again in Brazil: The Pentecostal Boom and the Pathogens of Poverty*. New Brunswick: Rutgers University Press.

Clifford, James. 1986. "Introduction: Partial Truths." In *Writing Culture*, ed. J. Clifford and G. Marcus, 1–26. Berkeley: University of California Press.

———. 1988. *The Predicament of Culture: Twentieth-Century Ethnography, Literature, and Art*. Boston: Harvard University Press.

Clifford, James, and George Marcus, eds. 1986. *Writing Culture*. Berkeley: University of California Press.

Cobb, John N. 1930. "Pacific Salmon Fisheries." Bureau of Fisheries Document no. 1092. Washington DC: Government Printing Office.

Cohen, Felix S. 1982 (orig. 1942). *Handbook of Federal Indian Law*. Charlottesville VA: Michie, Bobbs-Merrill.

Cohen, Kathryn A. 1989. "Wrangell Harvest Study." Technical Paper no. 165. Juneau: Alaska Department of Fish and Game.

Collins, June McC. 1950. "The Indian Shaker Church: A Study of Continuity and Change in Religion." *Southwestern Journal of Anthropology* 6:399–411.

Colt, Steve. 1991. "Financial Performance of Native Regional Corporations." *Alaska Review of Social and Economic Conditions* 28, no. 2.

Comaroff, Jean. 1985. *Body of Power Spirit of Resistance*. Chicago: University of Chicago Press.

Comaroff, Jean, and John Comaroff. 1991. *Of Revelation and Revolution*. Chicago: University of Chicago Press.

Cooley, Richard A. 1963. *Politics and Conservation: The Decline of the Alaska Salmon*. New York: Harper and Row.

Crutchfield, James A., and Guilio Pontecorvo. 1969. *The Pacific Salmon Fisheries: A Study in Irrational Conservation*. Baltimore: Johns Hopkins University Press.

Curry-Weissbrodt Papers. (MS) Correspondence and collected documents of the lawyers representing the Central Council of the Tlingit and Haida. Microfilm. Juneau: Alaska State Historical Library.

Dauenhauer, Nora M., and Richard Dauenhauer. 1987. *Haa Shuká, Our Ancestors: Tlingit Oral Narratives*. Seattle: University of Washington Press.

———. 1994. *Haa Kusteeyí, Our Culture: Tlingit Life Stories*. Seattle: University of Washington Press.

Dauenhauer, Richard. 1982. "Two Missions to Alaska." *Pacific Historian* 26:29–41.

References

DeLoach, Daniel B. 1939. *The Salmon Canning Industry*. Corvallis: Oregon State College.

Deloria, Vine, Jr., and Clifford Lytle. 1984. *The Nations Within*. New York: Pantheon Books.

Denis, Claude. 1997. *We Are Not You: First Nations and Canadian Modernity*. Peterborough, Ontario: Broadview Press.

Dinneford, E., and K. Cohen. 1989. "Changes in the Distribution of Permit Ownership in Alaska's Limited Fisheries: 1976–1988." Commercial Fisheries Entry Commission, Report no. 89-3.

Dombrowski, Kirk. 1995. "Totem Poles and Tricycle Races: The Certainties and Uncertainties of Native Village Life, Coastal Alaska, 1878–1930." *Journal of Historical Sociology* 8(2): 136–57.

———. 1998. Review of *Quaqtaq: Modernity and Identity in an Inuit Community* by Louis-Jacques Dorais. *American Anthropologist* 100(4): 1056–57.

Drucker, Philip. (MS) Field notes from Southeast Alaska dated 1957; interviews with William Paul and others on the Alaska Native Brotherhood and its early formation. Juneau: Alaska State Historical Library.

———. 1958. *The Native Brotherhoods: Modern Intertribal Organizations of the Northwest Coast*. Bureau of American Ethnology Bulletin 168. Washington DC: Bureau of American Ethnology.

———. 1965. *Cultures of the North Pacific Coast*. San Francisco: Chandler.

Durrenberger, E. Paul, and Gisli Palsson. 1988. "Anthropology and Fisheries Management." *American Ethnologist* 15:530–34.

Eastman, Carol M., and Elizabeth A. Edwards. 1991. *Gyaehlingaay: Traditions, Tales, and Images of the Kaigani Haida (Traditional stories told by Lillian Pettviel and other Haida elders)*. Seattle: Burke Museum.

Ellana, Linda J., and George K. Sherrod. 1987. "Timber Management and Fish and Wildlife Use in Selected Southeastern Alaska Communities: Klawock, Prince of Wales Island, Alaska." Technical Paper no. 126. Juneau: Alaska Department of Fish and Game.

Emmons, George Thorton. 1991. *The Tlingit Indians*. Seattle: University of Washington Press.

Faiman-Silva, Sandra. 1997. *Choctaws at the Crossroads: The Political Economy of Class and Culture in the Oklahoma Timber Region*. Lincoln: University of Nebraska Press.

Federal Field Committee of Development Planning in Alaska. 1968. "Alaska Natives and the Land." Washington DC: Government Printing Office.

235

References

Ferguson, James. 1996. *The Anti-Politics Machine: "Development," Depoliticization, and Bureaucratic Power in Lesotho*. Minneapolis: University of Minnesota Press.

Firman, Anne S., and Robert G. Bosworth. 1990. "Harvest and Use of Fish and Wildlife by Residents of Kake, Alaska." Technical Paper no. 145. Juneau: Alaska Department of Fish and Game.

Galois, Robert. 1994. *Kwakwaka'Wakw Settlements, 1775–1920: A Geographical Analysis and Gazetteer*. Seattle: University of Washington Press.

Garfield, Viola. 1939. *Tsimshian Clan and Society*. University of Washington Publications in Anthropology, vol. 7. Seattle: University of Washington Press.

Garrard-Burnett, Virginia, and David Stoll, eds. 1993. *Rethinking Protestantism in Latin America*. Philadelphia: Temple University Press.

Gearing, Fred O. 1962. *Priests and Warriors: Social Structures for Cherokee Politics in the Eighteenth Century*. American Anthropological Association, Memoir 93. Washington DC: American Anthropological Association.

Gellner, Ernest. 1983. *Nations and Nationalism*. Ithaca: Cornell University Press.

———. 1998. *Language and Solitude: Wittgenstein, Malinowski, and the Habsburg Dilemma*. New York: Cambridge University Press.

George, Gabriel D., and Robert G. Bosworth. 1988. "Use of Fish and Wildlife by Residents of Angoon, Admiralty Island, Alaska." Technical Paper no. 159. Juneau: Alaska Department of Fish and Game.

Goldbelt Inc. 1989. "1989 Annual Report." Juneau: Goldbelt Inc.

Goldschmidt, Walter R., and Theodore H. Haas. 1946. "Possessory Rights of the Natives of Southeast Alaska: A Report to the Commissioner of Indian Affairs." Washington DC: U.S. Bureau of Indian Affairs.

———. 1998. *Haa Aaní, Our Land: Tlingit and Haida Land Rights and Use*. Edited with an introduction by Thomas F. Thornton. Juneau: Sealaska Heritage Foundation.

Gorsuch, Lee, Steve Colt, Charles Smythe, and Bart K. Garber. 1994. "A Study of Five Southeast Alaska Communities." Washington DC: U.S. Department of Agriculture, U.S. Forest Service, U.S. Department of the Interior (Bureau of Land Management and Bureau of Indian Affairs).

Greenhouse, Carol J. 1986. *Praying for Justice*. Ithaca: Cornell University Press.

Gregory, Homer E., and Kathleen Barnes. 1939. *North Pacific Fisheries with*

Special Reference to Alaska Salmon. New York: American Council, Institute of Pacific Relations.

Grindal, Bruce T. 1982. "The Religious Interpretation of Experience in a Rural Black Community." In *Holding on to the Land and the Lord*, ed. Robert L. Hall and Carol Stack. Athens: University of Georgia Press.

Guimary, Donald L. 1983. "Salmon Canneries in Southeast Alaska: A Documentation of Selected Historic Salmon Canneries and Cannery Sites." Anchorage: Office of Historical Archeology, Alaska Division of Parks.

Hall, Robert L., and Carol Stack, eds. 1982. *Holding on to the Land and the Lord.* Athens: University of Georgia Press.

Harding, Susan F. 1987. "Convicted by the Holy Spirit: The Rhetoric of Fundamentalist Baptist Conversion." *American Ethnologist* 14(1): 167–81.

Harkin, Michael E. 1997. "A Tradition of Invention: Modern Ceremonialism on the Northwest Coast." In *Past Is Present*, ed. Marie Mause, 97–112. Lanham MD: University Press of America.

———. 1998. *The Heiltsuks: Dialogues of Culture and History on the Northwest Coast.* Lincoln: University of Nebraska Press.

Hebdige, Dick. 1979. *Subculture, The Meaning of Style.* Routledge.

Hinckley, Ted C. 1972. *The Americanization of Alaska.* Palo Alto: Pacific Books.

———. 1996. *The Canoe Rocks: Alaska's Tlingit and the Euramerican Frontier, 1800–1912.* Lanham MD: University Press of America.

Hobsbawm, Eric, and Terence Ranger, eds. 1983. *The Invention of Tradition.* New York: Cambridge University Press.

Holder, Preston. 1970. *The Hoe and the Horse on the Plains.* Lincoln: University of Nebraska Press.

Holy Ghost People. 1968 (reissued 1984). Directed by Peter Adair and produced by Blair Boyd for Thistle Films.

Hugh-Jones, Stephen. 1996. "Shamans, Prophets, Priests, and Pastors." In *Shamanism, History, and the State*, ed. N. Thomas and C. Humphrey, 32–75. Ann Arbor: University of Michigan Press.

Huna Totem Corporation. 1988. "Huna Totem Corporation and Subsidiaries, Consolidated Financial Statements and Schedules for January 1, 1987 and 1988." Hoonah AK: Huna Totem Corporation.

Jones, Livingston F. 1914. *A Study of the Thlingets of Alaska.* New York: Fleming H. Revell.

Jorgensen, Joseph, et al. 1978. *Native Americans and Energy Development.* Cambridge MA: Anthropology Resource Center.

————. 1984. *Native Americans and Energy Development II*. Cambridge MA: Anthropology Resource Center.

Kake Tribal Corporation. 1988–89. "Kake Tribal Corporation and Subsidiaries Consolidated Financial Statements and Supplementary Information for Years Ended December 31, 1988 and 1989." Kake AK: Kake Tribal Corporation.

Kamenskii, Anatolii. 1985. *Tlingit Indians of Alaska*. Trans. Sergei Kan. Fairbanks: University of Alaska.

Kan, Sergei. 1985. "Russian Orthodox Brotherhoods among the Tlingit: Missionary Goals and Native Response." *Ethnohistory* 32:196–223.

————. 1986. "The Nineteenth-Century Tlingit Potlatch: A New Perspective." *American Ethnologist* 13(2): 191–212.

————. 1987. "Memory Eternal: Orthodox Christianity and the Tlingit Mortuary Complex." *Arctic Anthropology* 24(1): 32–55.

————. 1989. *Symbolic Immortality: The Tlingit Potlatch of the Nineteenth Century*. Washington DC: Smithsonian Institution Press.

————. 1991. "Shamanism and Christianity: Modern-Day Tlingit Elders Look at the Past." *Ethnohistory* 38(4): 363–87.

Knapp, Gunnar. 1992. "Native Timber Harvests in Southeast Alaska." U.S. Forest Service/Pacific Northwest Research Station General Technical Report PNW-GTR-284.

Knapp, G., P. Peyton, and C. Weiss. 1993. "The Japanese Salmon Market: An Introduction for Alaskans." Juneau: Alaska Department of Commerce and Economic Development, Division of Economic Development.

Knight, Rolf. 1978. *Indians at Work: An Informal History of Native Indian Labour in British Columbia, 1858–1930*. Vancouver: New Star Books.

Krause, Aurel. 1956 (1885). *The Tlingit Indians: Results of a Trip to the Northwest Coast of America and the Bering Straits*. Trans. Erna Gunther. Seattle: University of Washington Press.

Laguna, Frederica de. 1952. "Some Dynamic Forces in Tlingit Society." *Southwestern Journal of Anthropology* 8(1): 1–12.

————. 1972. *Under Mount Saint Elias*. Washington DC: Smithsonian Institution Press.

Langdon, Stephen. 1977. "Technology, Ecology, Economy: Fishing Systems in Southeast Alaska." Ph.D. diss., Stanford University, Palo Alto.

————. 1980. "Transfer Patterns in Alaskan Limited Entry Fisheries;

Final Report for the Limited Entry Study Group of the Alaska State Legislature." From tables 6, 8, and 9, pp. 20–29.

———. 1989. "From Communal Property to Common Property to Limited Entry: Historical Ironies in the Management of Southeast Alaska Salmon." In *Cultural Survival Report 26: A Sea of Small Boats*, ed. John Cordell, 304–32. Cambridge MA: Cultural Survival.

Lantis, Margaret, and Varden Fuller. 1948. (MS) "Economic Needs of Natives of Southeastern Alaska." Draft report to the U.S. Bureau of Indian Affairs. Juneau: Alaska State Historical Library.

LaVerdure, George A. 1961. (MS) "A Study: Alaska Native Cannery Operations and Allied Activity." Juneau: Alaska State Historical Library.

Leacock, Eleanor, and Richard Lee, eds. 1982. *Politics and History in Band Societies*. New York: Cambridge University Press.

Leghorn, Ken, and Matt Kookesh. 1987. "Timber Management and Fish and Wildlife Utilization in Selected Southeast Alaska Communities: Tenakee Springs, Alaska." Technical Paper no. 138. Juneau: Alaska Department of Fish and Game.

Lévi-Strauss, Claude. 1978. *Tristes Tropiques*. New York: Atheneum.

Lewis, Claudia. 1970. *Indian Families of the Northwest Coast: The Impact of Change*. Chicago: University of Chicago Press.

Mahmood, Cynthia Keppley. 1996. *Fighting for Faith and Nation: Dialogues with Sikh Militants*. Philadelphia: University of Pennsylvania Press.

Marcus, George E., and Michael M. Fisher. 1986. *Anthropology as Cultural Critique*. Chicago: University of Chicago Press.

Masson, J., and D. Guimary. 1981. "Pilipinos and Unionization of the Alaskan Canned Salmon Industry." *Amerasia* 8(2): 1–30.

McCay, Bonnie. 1981. "Optimal Foragers or Political Actors? Ecological Analyses of a New Jersey Fishery." *American Ethnologist* 8:356–82.

McGoodwin, James R. 1990. *Crisis in the World's Fisheries*. Stanford: Stanford University Press.

Miller, Bruce. 2001. *The Problem of Justice: Tradition and Law in the Coast Salish World*. Lincoln: University of Nebraska Press.

Mooney, James. 1896. "The Ghost Dance Religion and the Sioux Outbreak of 1890." In *Fourteenth Annual Report of the Bureau of Ethnology, 1892–93*, Part 2. Washington DC: Government Printing Office.

———. 1965. *The Ghost Dance Religion and the Sioux Outbreak of 1890*. Ed. A. Wallace. Chicago: University of Chicago Press.

References

Morehouse, Thomas A., and George W. Rogers. 1980. "Limited Entry in the Alaska and British Columbia Salmon Fisheries." Anchorage: Institute of Social and Economic Research, University of Alaska.

Morris, Brian. 1987. *Anthropological Studies of Religion*. New York: Cambridge University Press.

Murdock, George Peter. 1934. "Kinship and Social Behavior among the Haida." *American Anthropologist* 36:355–85.

Nadar, Laura. 1990. *Harmony Ideology: Justice and Control in a Zapotec Mountain Village*. Stanford: Stanford University Press.

National Lawyers Guild. 1982. "Rethinking Indian Law." Committee on Native American Struggles.

Niblack, Albert P. 1888. *The Coast Indians of Southern Alaska and Northern British Columbia*. U.S. National Museum Annual Report, pp. 225–386. Washington DC: U.S. National Museum.

Nichols, Jeannette P. 1924. *Alaska*. Cleveland: Arthur H. Clark Company.

Oberg, Kalvervo. 1973. *The Social Economy of the Tlingit Indians*. Vancouver: J. J. Douglas.

Oleska, Michael, ed. 1987. *Alaskan Missionary Spirituality*. New York: Paulist Press.

Ortega, Bob. 1988. "Sealaska Posts Record Income." *Anchorage Times*, September 11.

Paolino, Ernest N. 1973. *The Foundations of the American Empire: William Henry Seward and U.S. Foreign Policy*. Ithaca: Cornell University Press.

Paul, William L., Sr. Papers. Microfilm. Juneau: Alaska State Historical Library.

Peirce, Charles. 1955. *Philosophical Writings of Peirce*. Ed. J. Buchler. New York: Dover.

Price, Robert E. 1990. *The Great Father in Alaska: The Case of the Tlingit and Haida Salmon Fishery*. Douglas AK: First Street Press.

Purdon, Ruper L. 1925. "World Trade in Canned Salmon." Washington DC: Department of Commerce, Government Printing Office.

Rabinow, Paul. 1996. *Essays on the Anthropology of Reason*. Princeton: Princeton University Press.

Rogers, George W. 1960. *Alaska in Transition: The Southeast Region*. Baltimore: Johns Hopkins University Press.

Rogers, George W., Richard F. Listowski, and Judith Brakel. 1974. "Final Report: A Study of the Socio-economic Impact of Changes in the Harvesting Labor Force in the Alaska Salmon Fishery."

Rorty, Richard. 1989. *Contingency, Irony, Solidarity.* New York: Cambridge University Press.

Roseberry, William. 1989. *Anthropologies and Histories.* New Brunswick: Rutgers University Press.

Rosman, Abraham, and Paula Rubel. 1971. *Feasting with Mine Enemy: Rank and Exchange among Northwest Coast Societies.* Prospect Heights IL: Waveland Books.

————. 1986. "The Evolution of Central Northwest Coast Societies." *Journal of Anthropological Research* 42(4): 557–72.

Ruby, Robert H., and John A. Brown. 1996. *John Slocum and the Indian Shaker Church.* Norman: University of Oklahoma Press.

Sanders, Vance A. 1995. "Murkowski's Landless Bill." *Ravens Bones Journal* 3(1): 3–5.

Sapir, Edward. 1949. *Selected Writings of Edward Sapir.* Ed. D. G. Mandelbaum. Berkeley: University of California Press.

Schechner, Richard. 1993. *The Future of Ritual: Writings on Culture and Performance.* New York: Routledge.

Schiller, Robert. 1984. "Overview of the Timber Industry in Southeast Alaska." Department of Commerce and Economic Development, State of Alaska, Research Monograph no. 84-013. Juneau: State of Alaska.

Schneider, Jane. 1990. "Spirits and the Spirit of Capitalism." In *Religious Orthodoxy and Popular Faith in European Society,* ed. E. Badone, 24–53. Princeton: Princeton University Press.

Schneider, Jane, and Shirley Lindenbaum, eds. 1987. "Special Issue: Frontiers of Christian Evangelism." *American Ethnologist* 14(1).

Schroeder, Robert F., and Mathew Kookesh. 1990. "Subsistence Harvest and Use of Fish and Wildlife Resources and the Effects of Forest Management in Hoonah, Alaska." Technical Paper no. 142. Juneau: Alaska Department of Fish and Game.

Shkilnyk, Anastasia M. 1985. *A Poison Stronger Than Love: The Destruction of an Ojibwa Community.* New Haven: Yale University Press.

Sider, Gerald. 1986. *Culture and Class in Anthropology and History: A Newfoundland Illustration.* New York: Cambridge University Press.

————. 1987. "When Parrots Learn to Talk, and Why They Can't: Domination, Deception, and Self-Deception in Indian-White Relations." *Comparative Studies in Society and History* 29(1): 3–23.

————. 1989. "A Delicate People and Their Dogs: The Cultural Economy

of Subsistence Production—A Critique of Chayanov and Meillassoux."
Journal of Historical Sociology 2(1): 14–40.

———. 1993. *Lumbee Indian Histories.* New York: Cambridge University
Press.

———. 1997. "Against Experience: The Struggles for History, Tradition,
and Hope among a Native American People." In *Between History and
Histories,* ed. G. Sider and G. Smith, 62–79. Toronto: University of
Toronto Press.

Sider, Gerald, and Gavin Smith. 1997. "Introduction." In *Between History
and Histories,* ed. G. Sider and G. Smith, 3–30. Toronto: University of
Toronto Press.

Slotkin, Richard. 1973. *Regeneration through Violence: The Mythology of the
American Frontier, 1600–1860.* Middleton CT: Wesleyan University Press.

———. 1985. *The Fatal Environment: The Myth of the Frontier in the Age of
Industrialization.* New York: Atheneum.

Smith, Gavin. 1989. *Livelihood and Resistance: Peasants and the Politics of Land
in Peru.* Berkeley: University of California Press.

Smith, Marian W. 1954. "Shamanism in the Shaker Religion of Northwest
America." *Man* 54:119–22.

Southeast Alaska Conservation Council. 1995. "Senator Murkowski's
New Native Claims Bill: A Destructive Raid on Public Lands." Juneau:
Southeast Alaska Conservation Council.

Stocking, George W., Jr. 1968. *Race, Culture, and Evolution: Essays in the History
of Anthropology.* Chicago: University of Chicago Press.

Suttles, Wayne. 1957. "The Plateau Prophet Dance among the Coast
Salish." *Southwestern Journal of Anthropology* 13:352–93.

———. 1960. "Affinal Ties, Subsistence, and Prestige among the Coast
Salish." *American Anthropologist* 62:296–305.

Swanton, John R. 1905. "Social Organization of the Haida." In *Proceedings
of the International Congress of Americanists, Thirteenth Session, New York,*
327–34. Easton PA: Eschenbach Printing Co.

———. 1908. *Social Condition, Beliefs, and Linguistic Relationship of the Tlingit
Indians.* House Document 1528, 60th Cong., 2nd sess.

Szasz, Thomas. 1984. *The Myth of Mental Illness: Foundations of a Theory of
Personal Conduct.* Rev. ed. New York: Harper Collins.

Taylor, Graham D. 1980. *The New Deal and American Indian Tribalism.* Lincoln:
University of Nebraska Press.

Thornton, Thomas F., ed. 1998. "Introduction: Who Owned Southeast

Alaska? Answers in Goldschmidt and Haas." In *Haa Aani, Our Land: Tlingit and Haida Land Rights and Use,* by Walter R. Goldschmidt and Theodore H. Haas, xiii–xxii. Juneau: Sealaska Heritage Foundation.

Treat, James, ed. 1996. *Native and Christian: Indigenous Voices on Religious Identity in the United States and Canada.* New York: Routledge.

Turner, Victor. 1987. *The Anthropology of Performance.* New York: PAJ Publications.

U.S. Department of the Interior, Bureau of Education. 1907–15. (MS) Village reports to the U.S. Commissioner of the Bureau of Education. Microfilm. Juneau: Alaska State Historical Library.

U.S. Forest Service. 1989. "Timber Supply and Demand, 1988 Report." ANILCA, section 706(a), Report no. 8, R10-MB-78. Juneau: U.S. Department of Agriculture.

———. 1990. "Timber Supply and Demand, 1989 Report." ANILCA, section 706(a), Report no. 9, R10-MB-113. Juneau: U.S. Department of Agriculture.

University of Alaska. 1967. "Native Land Claims." *Review of Business and Economic Conditions* 4(6).

Vaughan, James Daniel. 1985. "Toward a New and Better Life: Two Hundred Years of Alaskan Haida Culture Change." Ph.D. diss., University of Washington.

"Warning: How to Lose a Family." 1988. *National Fisherman,* September 7.

Washburn, Wilcomb. 1984. *A Fifty-Year Perspective on the Indian Reorganization Act.* American Anthropological Association Monographs, no. 86. Washington DC: American Anthropological Association.

Whitman, James. 1984. "From Philology to Anthropology in Mid-Nineteenth-Century Germany." In *Functionalism Historicized,* ed. G. Stocking, 214–30. History of Anthropology Series, vol. 2. Madison: University of Wisconsin Press.

Wike, Joyce. 1947. "The Effects of the Maritime Fur Trade on Northwest Coast Indian Society." Ph.D. diss., Columbia University.

Williams, Raymond. 1977. *Marxism and Literature* London: Oxford University Press.

———. 1980. *Keywords: A Vocabulary of Culture and Society.* London: Oxford University Press.

Willis, Paul. 1981. *Learning to Labor: How Working-Class Kids Get Working-Class Jobs.* New York: Columbia University Press.

References

Wilmsen, Edwin N. 1989. *Land Filled with Flies: A Political Economy of the Kalahari.* Chicago: University of Chicago Press.

Wolf, Eric. 1982. *Europe and the People without History.* Los Angeles: University of California.

————. 1999. *Envisioning Power: Ideologies of Dominance and Crisis.* Los Angeles: University of California.

Wyatt, Victoria. 1985. "Ethnic Identity and Active Choice: Foundations of Indian Strength in Southeast Alaska, 1867–1912." Ph.D. diss., Yale University.

————. 1987. "Alaskan Indian Wage Earners in the Nineteenth Century." *Pacific Northwest Quarterly* 78(1–2): 43–55.

Index

245